CRIMINAL MOCK TRIALS

CRIMINAL MOCK TRIALS

TERRY ADAMSON

Distinguished Jurist in Residence
Trial Advocacy Team Coach
Pepperdine University School of Law
Malibu Superior Court Commissioner (retired)

H. MITCHELL CALDWELL

Professor of Law
Head Trial Advocacy Team Coach
Pepperdine University School of Law

VANDEPLAS PUBLISHING, LLC
UNITED STATES OF AMERICA

Criminal Mock Trials
First Edition 2012

Adamson, Terry and Caldwell, H. Mitchell

Published by:

Vandeplas Publishing, LLC – February 2012

801 International Parkway, 5th Floor
Lake Mary, FL. 32746
USA

www.vandeplaspublishing.com

ISBN 978-1-60042-153-2

Dedications

To my loving mom, Eleanor, who instilled in me a love for creative writing.

- Terry Adamson

To my wonderful loving wife who is always there for me.

- H. Mitchell Caldwell

Acknowledgments

The authors gratefully acknowledge the generous support they have received from Pepperdine University School of Law in the preparation of this book and to the talented, dedicated students who worked enthusiastically as research assistants. The authors are deeply indebted to the faculty support staff and, in particular, to Candace Warren for her cheerful and tireless help in preparing this manuscript. They gratefully acknowledge the invaluable research, editing, and graphic arts contributions of the following Pepperdine Law students: Shane Michael, Anthony Greco, Kelly Everett, Brittany Vannoy, Sarah Wild, Elizabeth Sutlian, Richard Rodriguez Campbell, Michael Boyd, Skye Daley, Brittany Henry, Vincent Santos, Rebecca Charlesworth, Rick Loesing, Lukian Kobzeff, and especially RA Editor-In-Chief, Arsineh Martinez Zargarian, RA and Managing Editor, Gor Arevian. They also thank book cover illustrator, Vincent Santos, for his creative and artistic contributions, Grant Adamson for photography, and RA and Copy Editor, Lauren Adamson. Finally, the authors thank their dedicated, talented interns: Megan Adamson, Marie Gribble, Casey Zweig, Harry Glass, and Katherine Skeith.

Table of Contents

CASE FILE No. 1

STATE OF OCEANA

V.

RICHARD BROOKS

(Murder)

SUPERIOR COURT OF THE STATE OF OCEANA

COUNTY OF MALIWOOD

STATE OF OCEANA,		Case No. MW043652
	Plaintiff,	
v.		**FELONY COMPLAINT**
RICHARD BROOKS,		
	Defendant.	

COUNT 1

On or about July 2, CY-1, in the City of Maliwood, Maliwood County, State of Oceana, a felony, in violation of section 187 of the Oceana Penal Code, commonly referred to as MURDER, was committed by the above named defendant, who at the time and place last aforesaid, did willfully and with malice aforethought murder Cheryl Byron.

IT IS SO ORDERED.

Simon Luna

Simon Luna
District Attorney, County of Maliwood

Witness List

Witnesses for the State:

1.   Cameron Hastings**

2.   Jordan Summers**

Witnesses for the Defense:

1.   Richard Brooks*

2.   Jessie Waters**

Each side must call both witnesses listed for their respective party, and both parties stipulate that each party's expert witness would testify consistently with his or her provided statement.

*This witness must be played by a male.

**This witness may be either gender.

Stipulations

1. Federal Rules of Criminal Procedure and Federal Rules of Evidence apply.

2. Each witness who gave an interview reviewed the officer's report of his or her interview and signed the interview verifying it was accurate.

3. All witness statements were given under oath.

4. All witnesses called to testify who have identified Defendant Brooks or any tangible evidence can, if asked, identify the same at trial.

5. All exhibits in the file are authentic and, unless otherwise noted, are the original of that document.

6. Other than what appears in the officer's reports of the interviews, there is nothing exceptional or unusual about the background of any of the witnesses that would bolster or detract from their credibility.

7. All dates are denoted by CY (current year) or CY-*n* (current year minus *n* years).

8. All pretrial motions shall be oral.

9. No party may "invent" witnesses or evidence not specifically mentioned in this problem.

10. "Beyond the record" is not a proper objection. Rather, attorneys shall use cross-examination as a means of challenging a witness whose testimony strays beyond the facts contained in the officer's reports of the interviews.

11. The physical description of a witness shall be tailored to that of the student playing the witness, except for height, weight, and age.

12. The text messages are authenticated under the Federal Rules of Evidence 902(11) and are admissible as certified business records under Federal Rules of Evidence 803(6).

13. The expert witnesses' reports are stipulated to as being an accurate reflection of what each expert would testify to if called as a witness; it is therefore unnecessary to call either expert as a witness.

14. July 1, CY-1 was a Tuesday.

15. The legal limit for operating a vehicle is a Blood Alcohol Content measure of less than .08%.

16. The fingerprints collected from the trunk of Cheryl Byron's vehicle positively matched those of Richard Brooks.

17. Section 187 of the Oceana Penal Code provides: "Murder is the unlawful killing of a human being with malice aforethought."

18. The parties stipulate to the admissibility of the statements of Dr. Shane Chaves and Dr. Toni Cooke, but not to the correctness of their opinions. Their stipulated testimony is subject to the Federal Rules

of Evidence. The parties have agreed to waive hearsay and Confrontation Clause objections for only these witnesses.

19. The prosecution and defense may only call the two witnesses listed on their respective witness list.

20. The Maliwood County Coroner's autopsy report is authentic. The parties have agreed to its admissibility, but not to the accuracy of the coroner's conclusions.

21. The witness Richard Brooks must be a male. The other witnesses may be male or female. The witnesses may be called in any order.

CITY OF MALIWOOD SHERIFF'S DEPARTMENT
INVESTIGATION REPORT

RECORDS & STATISTICS BUREAU'S USE ONLY   DATE: **7/2/CY-1**   PAGE: **1** OF **3**

ACTION	ACTIVE (X) INACTIVE ( ) PENDING ( )	INDEX Yes (X) INFO No ( )	N of Adult Arrests: 1	No of Subject Detentions: 1	URN (File No.) MW043652

CLASSIFICATION
HOMICIDE INVESTIGATION

DATE, TIME OF OCCURRENCE
7/2/CY-1, 01:30 HOURS

LOCATION OF OCCURRENCE	TYPE OF LOCATION	TRACT
MALIWOOD CANYON ROAD, MALIWOOD, OC	CANYON ROAD	

CODE: V - VICTIM, W - WITNESS, I - INFORMANT, R - REPORTING PARTY, P - PARTY

CODE		LAST NAME FIRST MIDDLE	SEX	AGE	RACE
V	NO. 1 OF 1	BYRON, CHERYL	F	29	WHITE

RESIDENCE ADDRESS	RES. PHONE (AREA CODE)
5926 MALIWOOD CANYON ROAD, MALIWOOD, OC	N/A

BUSINESS ADDRESS	RES. PHONE (AREA CODE)

CODE		LAST NAME FIRST MIDDLE	SEX	AGE	RACE
R	NO. 1 OF 1	SUMMERS, JORDAN		26	

RESIDENCE ADDRESS	RES. PHONE (AREA CODE)
833 SUMMERSTONE DRIVE, MALIWOOD, OC	

BUSINESS ADDRESS	RES. PHONE (AREA CODE)

CODE: S - SUSPECT, SJ - SUBJECT, M - PATIENT, S / V - SUSPECT/VICTIM, SJ / V - SUBJECT / VICTIM

CODE		LAST NAME FIRST MIDDLE	DRIVER'S LICENSE (STATE & No)
S	No 1 OF 1	BROOKS, RICHARD	OC X9817388

RESIDENCE ADDRESS	RES. PHONE (AREA CODE)
534 CARILLO CANYON ROAD, MALIWOOD, OC	

BUSINESS ADDRESS	BUS. PHONE (AREA CODE)
1225 ENCINA LANE, SUITE #802, MALIWOOD, OC	

SEX	RACE	HAIR	EYES	HEIGHT	WEIGHT	DOB	AGE	WHERE DETAINED
M	WHITE	BROWN	BLUE	6'0''	180 LBS		54	MALIWOOD

OBSERVABLE PHYSICAL ODDITIES/TATTOOS/SCARS	AKA / NICKNAME	BOOKING No.
N/A	N/A	MW043652

CLOTHING WORN	MAIN
DENIM PANTS, BROWN SWEATER, BROWN LOAFERS	

CHARGE	WEAPON USED
HOMICIDE	CLUB/BLUNT INSTRUMENT

CODE		LAST NAME FIRST MIDDLE	DRIVER'S LICENSE (STATE & No)
	No OF		

RESIDENCE ADDRESS	RES. PHONE (AREA CODE)

BUSINESS ADDRESS	BUS. PHONE (AREA CODE)

SEX	RACE	HAIR	EYES	HEIGHT	WEIGHT	D.O.B.	AGE	WHERE DETAINED OR CITE No.

OBSERVABLE PHYSICAL ODDITIES	AKA / NICKNAME	BOOKING No.

CLOTHING WORN	MAIN

CHARGE	WEAPON USED

VEHICLE USED IN CRIME YES (X) NO ( ) UNKNOWN ( ) STORED ( ) IMPOUNDED (X)	YR 2009	MAKE BMW	BODY TYPE 128i	COLOR RED	BY DEPUTY CHRISTENSEN	BADGE No. 487022
LICENSE (STATE & No.) OC MALIWD	V.I.N./ FRAME No.				DEPUTY HASTINGS	BADGE No. 459003
REGISTERED OWNER CHERYL BYRON				STATION MWD	UNIT / CAR No. 8768	SHIFT
IDENTIFYING CHARACTERISTICS				APPROVED	BADGE No.	TIME
O.H.P. 180 YES ( ) SUBMITTED NO ( )	GARAGE NAME & PHONE			ASSIGNMENT		

Narrative Report – URN MW043652

At approximately 02:00 hours on July 2, CY-1, the Maliwood County Sheriff's Department received a call from Jordan Summers claiming that a friend, named Cheryl Byron, had gone missing. Summers had gone to Byron's residence at 01:45 hours after having received a phone call from Byron approximately 1 hour prior. Byron, Summers reported, was in a drunken and panicked state and claimed that a man was at her door. When Summers arrived, Byron and her car were missing. Summers reported Byron's car as a red CY-2 BMW 128i, but was unable to provide a license plate number. After dispatch received the call, patrol cars were notified of the situation and began patrolling the vicinity of Byron's home, located just off Maliwood Canyon Road.

At approximately 02:37 hours, Deputy Christensen, while in route to Byron's residence, reported seeing faint lights off of Maliwood Canyon Road. Shortly thereafter, the red BMW was discovered midway down the canyon (see attached Exhibit E). Search and Rescue was notified, and at 02:45 hours the team discovered the body of Byron in the car. The coroner was called and the body was sent to the Coroner's Office pending an autopsy to determine time and cause of death (see attached Exhibit A).

Deputy Christensen notified Summers at 02:50 hours. A brief interview was conducted at 03:17 hours, and Summers provided a statement (see attached Statement of Jordan Summers). In the statement, Summers indicated that Richard Brooks was likely the last person to see the victim alive, and believed Brooks may be responsible for Byron's death. Summers had received two text messages from Byron just days prior to the incident and showed them to Deputy Christensen (see attached Exhibit B). The first text message, dated July 1, CY-1, read: "Get this I'm meetn R tonight for dinner at Sunset Shadows. He has gone bizzurk! I told him he better do the right thing by me, n he kinda freaked! I'll call u after w/ details." The second text message, dated June 29, CY-1, read: "Can u believe he had the nerve to send me this?! FWD: 'Just think about it babe. 10K is a lot of money. I need a decision ASAP, we have to get things rolling.'" Summers claimed that Byron had said in a subsequent telephone conversation that the forwarded message had come from Brooks and was regarding the possibility of Brooks paying off Byron

for having an abortion.

Deputy Christensen obtained Brooks's address and reported to his residence at 04:00 hours. At

04:15 hours, Deputy Christensen escorted Brooks to the station for an interview regarding his knowledge

of the victim's last hours (see attached Interrogation of Richard Brooks, 7/2/CY-1).

Signed,

Cameron Hastings

Detective Cameron Hastings

Maliwood County Sheriff's Department
Supplemental Police Report

On July 2, CY-1, at approximately 12:20 hours, I proceeded to Sunset Shadows to speak with witnesses who could place Brooks and Byron at Sunset Shadows on the evening of July 1, prior to Byron's death. When I arrived at Sunset Shadows, the hostess informed me that Jessie Waters had been working the evening of July 1, CY-1. She also told me that Waters had left around 02:30 hours and provided me with Waters's contact information. I contacted Waters, who agreed to meet me at the station at approximately 14:00 hours to provide a statement (see attached, "Statement of Jessie Waters").

At approximately 04:00 hours on the same date, I went to the residence of Richard Brooks. I asked him to come in for an interview at the station and he cooperated. During this initial interview, Brooks confirmed that he had been dating Byron, but he claimed he was unaware of any pregnancy. He also confirmed that they had eaten dinner at Sunset Shadows the night Byron died (see attached, "Interrogation of Richard Brooks, 7/2/CY-1").

At that time, I also asked him for permission to search his vehicle. Brooks consented, so I searched his car pursuant to department procedures. In the trunk, I found a golf bag with eleven golf clubs (see attached Exhibits G & H). However, I noticed that the set of clubs did not include a seven-iron, a club that I would expect any set to have.

On July 3, CY-1, the coroner's autopsy report came in (see attached report, Office of the Maliwood County Coroner). The following findings from the autopsy report were of special note: Byron was seven weeks pregnant; her BAC was .08% (i.e., above the legal limit for a driver); and the cause of death was determined to be blunt force trauma to the head. The coroner believed that this was likely not a result of the accident, but had rather occurred prior to her car leaving the road and falling into the canyon.

On the same day, the DNA and fingerprint results were also returned. The scrapings from beneath Byron's fingernails were positive for skin cells, but the DNA analysis was inconclusive.

Brooks's left hand fingerprints were a positive match for a set of left hand fingerprints found on the trunk of the victim's vehicle (see attached Exhibit F).

Immediately after receiving the coroner's report, I borrowed a seven-iron golf club that was the same brand as the set I found in Brooks's car. I measured the seven-iron and photographed the seven-iron by itself (see attached Exhibits I, J, & K). Its dimensions appear to be consistent with the head wound examined by the coroner. The semi-circular metal striking portion of the seven-iron I borrowed measured four centimeters in diameter and three centimeters in length.

On July 4, CY-1, I met with Brooks at the Maliwood County Jail (see attached transcript of recorded interview, "Supplemental Interrogation of Richard Brooks, 7/4/CY-1"). Following my interview with Brooks, I went to his office in the Maliwood Hills. I was greeted by Ms. Lola Craig, a film director who was working on a horror film with Brooks at the time. Craig informed me that Brooks was not present in the office, but gave me permission to look around. I came across a laptop computer sitting on Brooks's desk. A search of Brooks's laptop revealed an internet search history within the past week which included terms such as "chloroform" and "how to remove blood stains." The dates of these internet searches followed the date Summers claimed Byron had told Brooks about her pregnancy (see attached Exhibit L).

On July 5, CY-1, I impounded Brooks's vehicle, and he was formally charged and arraigned for the murder of Cheryl Byron.

The diagram below accurately depicts the pertinent highway systems, Brooks's office, the crime scene, and the residences of Byron, Brooks, and Summers.

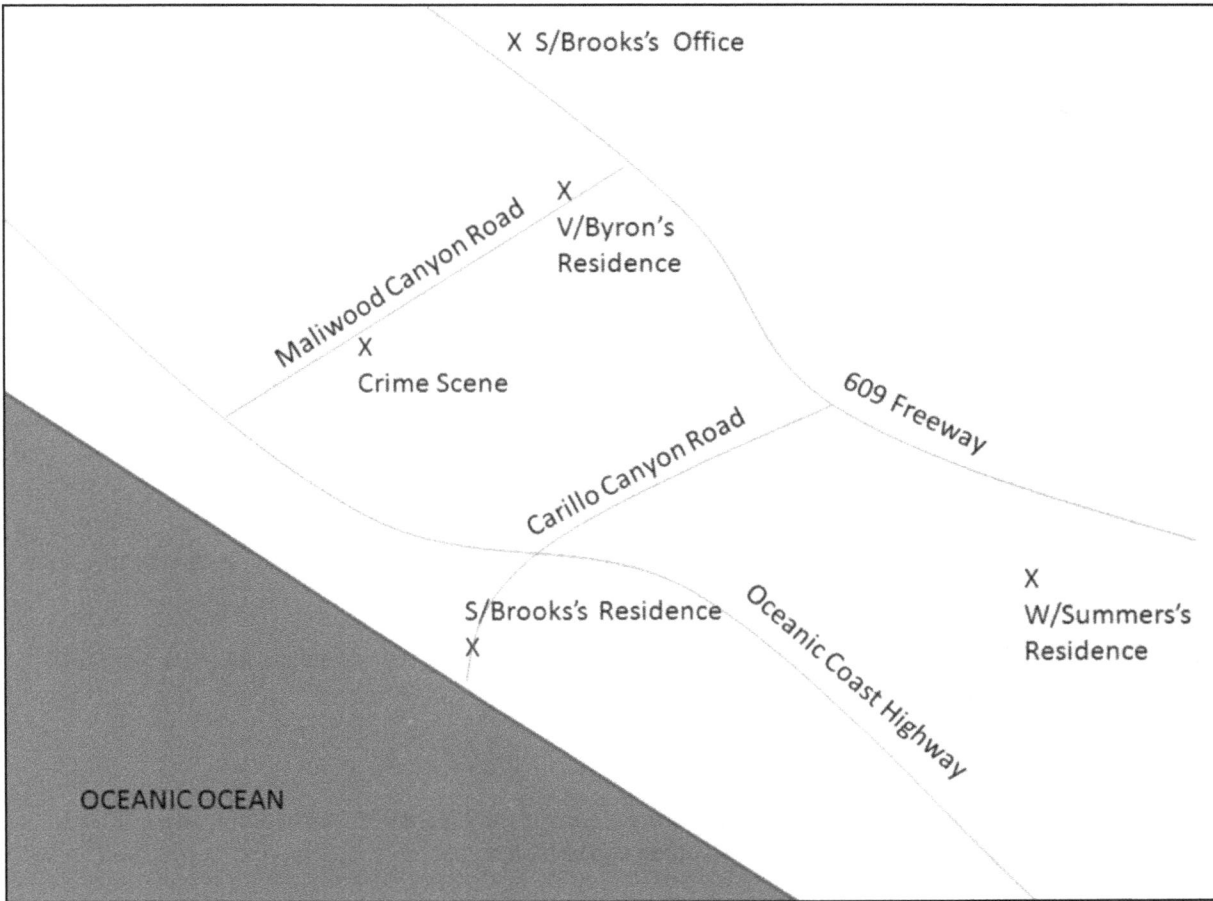

Signed,

Cameron Hastings

Detective Cameron Hastings

Maliwood County Sheriff's Department
Supplemental Police Report

Report Type: Interrogation of Richard Brooks
*Recorded per Maliwood County Sheriff's Department Interrogation Procedures
Interviewer: Deputy Christensen
Date and Time of Interview: July 2, CY-1, 04:00 hours

The first part of the following interview took place at the home of Suspect Richard Brooks at 04:00 hours. The second part of the interview occurred at the Maliwood County Sheriff's Station at 04:30 hours following the transport of Brooks to the station.

Suspect Brooks's Residence (July 2, CY-1, 04:00 hours):

Deputy Christensen (DC): Good morning, Mr. Brooks. I am sorry to disturb you at such an early hour, but I am investigating—

Richard Brooks (RB): I know, I know. You're here about Cheryl Byron. It's terrible what happened! Jordan, that crazy friend of hers, already called and woke me up.

DC: So, you're aware that Cheryl is dead?

RB: Yes. Jordan told me that her body and car were found at the bottom of Maliwood Canyon Road. Can we keep this kind of quiet? My wife is sleeping upstairs.

DC: Mr. Brooks, I am going to have to ask you to come down to the station to answer a few questions.

RB: Right now? It's the middle of the night. Can't we do this tomorrow morning?

DC: I'm afraid not.

RB: Okay. Let me get my shoes.

Maliwood County Sheriff's Station (July 2, CY-1, 04:30 hours):

DC: Mr. Brooks, please state your name and current address for the record.

RB: My name is Richard Brooks. I live at 534 Carillo Canyon Road in Maliwood.

DC: Mr. Brooks, I need to read you your rights, okay?

RB: Sure.

DC: Mr. Brooks, you're into film, you're aware of your *Miranda* rights, aren't you?

RB: What kind of idiot do you think I am? I know I don't have to talk to you and all that stuff.

DC: So you are now agreeing that you understand your rights and are now waiving them? Is that right?

RB: That's right.

DC: I see there are some scratch marks on your wrist. What happened?

RB: Nothing. I haven't had time to get my cat de-clawed, and she scratched me a few days ago.

DC: Yeah, maybe we should get you a bandage for those. They look pretty deep and pretty fresh. Anyway, you have already stated that you are aware of Cheryl Byron's death. What was the nature of your relationship with Ms. Byron?

RB: Do we really have to go into this? I'm a married man and I didn't do anything. I don't know, maybe I need a lawyer.

DC: Well, you are entitled to have a lawyer present if you want to.

RB: Maybe I need my lawyer here, but it's 4:30 in the morning. I don't even know where she is. How long do you think this will take?

DC: Probably just a few minutes. You know, it might take your lawyer a while to get here. I can see if I can wrangle up one of those government lawyers. You know, the ones who are over-worked and don't really have time to think things through.

RB: No, no, no. If I have any lawyer, it will be my own. I'd really like to talk to her before I say anything else.

DC: That's certainly your right. But I gotta tell you, this will only take a few minutes. I just want to get some background information. I just need to know what an older guy like you was doing with a looker like Cheryl Byron. Did you just buy her off?

RB: For your information, she was crazy about me. We've been going strong for more than eighteen months.

DC: So, she was in love with you. And you used her to fulfill your mid-life crisis fantasies?

RB: No! I loved Cheryl very much and I didn't ever want to see anything bad happen to her.

DC: Were you aware that Ms. Byron was pregnant?

RB: Oh man, I had no idea.

DC: Well, according to Jordan Summers, Ms. Byron was pregnant. When was the last time you saw Ms. Byron?

RB: Just last night. We met for dinner.

DC: Where did you meet?

RB: At Sunset Shadows. Look, we weren't there very long. We just had a conversation then Cheryl got upset and left.

DC: What were you talking about that made her upset?

RB: You know, this is getting too heavy. I definitely need my lawyer here.

INTERROGATION TERMINATED.

Maliwood County Sheriff's Department
Supplemental Police Report

Report Type: Supplemental Interrogation of Richard Brooks
*Recorded per Maliwood County Sheriff's Department Interrogation Procedures
Report By: Detective Cameron Hastings
Date and Time of Interview: July 4, CY-1, 13:15 hours

The District Attorney's Office requested that we conduct this interrogation before they would make their filing decision.

Detective Hastings (DH): Good afternoon, Mr. Brooks. This interview is being recorded. Please state your name and address.

Richard Brooks (RB): My name is Richard Brooks. I live at 534 Carillo Canyon Road in Maliwood.

DH: Before I start the interview, I need to read you your rights. You have the right to remain silent. If you waive that right, anything you say will be used against you in a court of law. Mr. Brooks, do you understand this right?

RB: Yes.

DH: You also have a right to an attorney and to have one present with you during this interrogation. Do you understand this right?

RB: Yes, Ms. Ferguson is here as my attorney.

DH: At any time during this questioning, you may choose to exercise these rights or you may elect not to answer any of my questions. Do you understand and do you wish to waive all of these rights?

RB: Yes.

DH: Okay then, we are ready to proceed. Do you wish to speak with me?

RB: Yes.

DH: Mr. Brooks, how old are you?

RB: I am fifty-four years old.

DH: What is your occupation?

RB: I am a producer. I own a company called Five Peaks Productions. We specialize in horror films.

DH: Are you married?

RB: Yes, I have been married to my wife, Ellen, for thirty years. Ellen and I were college sweethearts. We have two beautiful twin daughters, Elsa and Emma. Up until our twins left for college two years ago, Ellen had been a full-time mom.

DH: How did you know Cheryl Byron?

RB: While I am ashamed to admit it, about eighteen months ago, I began an affair with Cheryl. We met through work. She was an aspiring actress who had a small part in a movie my company produced.

DH: And what was the nature of your relationship?

RB: I loved Cheryl, and I never would have done anything to hurt her. But our relationship was temporary, and she knew that. When I first got to know Cheryl, my wife and I were going through a rough transition. When both of our kids left for college, it was depressing to be at home together. Cheryl was a breath of fresh air. She always made me feel full of life. Then our friendship became romantic. Although I cared for Cheryl very much and we had a lot of chemistry together, she knew that I was never going to leave my wife. I told her that from the beginning. We were both simply looking for a diversion. I now realize that I was going through a mid-life crisis. I had never been unfaithful to my wife before and I plan on staying faithful to my wife for the rest of my life.

DH: Okay, let's talk about the night of July 1st. Did you see Cheryl that night?

RB: Yes. Cheryl and I met for dinner and drinks at Sunset Shadows.

DH: What time?

RB: About nine o'clock.

DH: Did you arrive together or did you take two cars?

RB: We took separate cars. I arrived first and waited in the parking lot for a few minutes until Cheryl arrived.

DH: What happened when you got to the restaurant?

RB: As we were walking up to the restaurant, Cheryl said she was cold from the ocean air, so I got her jacket out of the trunk of her car before we went in. The hostess sat us, and the waitress took our drink order.

DH: Do you recall what you two had to drink?

RB: I paid cash for the dinner, so I don't have the receipt. I know that I had no more than two glasses of wine that entire evening. Cheryl had an apple martini before dinner, and we shared a bottle of wine during dinner. Cheryl drank most of the bottle, so I'm guessing she had about three glasses and I had less than two. I know I had less than two glasses because ten years ago I was convicted of a DUI, so I never have more than two glasses of wine over the course of dinner before driving.

DH: What were you and Cheryl discussing during dinner?

RB: Well, it was pretty heavy. Cheryl claimed to be pregnant. We were talking about how we were going to handle the situation.

DH: Wait, didn't you tell Officer Christensen that you knew nothing of Cheryl's pregnancy at the time she died?

RB: Well, I wasn't absolutely sure until my attorney showed me the autopsy report. Cheryl wasn't showing and I thought she might have been bluffing about a pregnancy in order to get me to leave my wife. And she drank so much that night; I didn't think it was possible. So I didn't tell Officer Christensen at the time he originally questioned me.

DH: Okay. So, back to the dinner at Sunset Shadows. You said you were having a serious discussion. Did you discuss aborting the child?

RB: No. I would have left that up to Cheryl.

DH: So you didn't want to abort the child, but you discussed the possibility of abortion?

RB: No. Cheryl and I never discussed abortion. I never would've pressured Cheryl in her decision with the baby. I didn't threaten Cheryl in any way. I've never threatened her. I did remind Cheryl that I told her from the beginning of our affair that I wouldn't leave my wife and that she had told me she wanted a casual relationship. I believe her term was "a fling." At the beginning, Cheryl said her priority was making it as an actress and that she didn't want to have kids. Obviously, our affair was beneficial to her career; I was helping her achieve her goal to be a working actress, but I didn't feel like Cheryl was using me. Even though there was a twenty-five year age difference, it didn't bother me and it didn't seem to bother Cheryl either.

DH: How did Cheryl react to all of this?

RB: As Cheryl drank more wine, she began to get more upset and emotional. Even the waitress seemed to notice that Cheryl was distraught. I suggested that she stop drinking, as the alcohol was adversely affecting her mood and because she claimed to be pregnant, but my suggestion only made her more upset, so I stopped bothering her about it. I'm not sure if Cheryl was emotional that night because of her hormones from the pregnancy, the alcohol, or both. She was distraught when she left Sunset Shadows. She was crying, so I tried to stop her from leaving the restaurant and driving in that condition. I couldn't convince her to let me drive her home or to call her a cab. As I got into my car to drive back to my house, I saw her speed off in her BMW. She left the restaurant around 12:00 a.m. and I went back inside the restaurant to pay the bill.

DH: What happened when you got back inside the restaurant?

RB: The server, Jessie, was staring at me because Cheryl had made a scene by running out of the restaurant. After paying the bill, I got in my car and drove to my house. I only live two miles up the coast from the restaurant, so I arrived home around 12:15 a.m. My wife was already asleep when I got home and obviously I didn't want to wake her up. I had told her previously that I'd be working late that night, supervising the editing of an upcoming movie.

DH: After your dinner, how were you feeling about the whole situation with Cheryl?

RB: I just wanted everything to be okay. Cheryl enhanced my life in so many ways. I never would have wanted any harm to come to her, even if she was pregnant. I had plenty of money to support Cheryl and our child.

DH: Did you try to contact Cheryl later that night or go to her apartment?

RB: Absolutely not! The last time I saw Cheryl was at Sunset Shadows. I woke up to a call from Jordan Summers, Cheryl's best friend, at about 3:00 a.m. on July 2. Jordan told me that Cheryl was dead. I was shocked and devastated to hear this news. According to Jordan, a rescue team found Cheryl's car at the base of Maliwood Canyon Road and presumed that she had driven off a cliff at the top of the road. Jordan was inconsolable and began to blame me for Cheryl's death. I can't recall Jordan's specific statements, but it was implied that I was probably relieved that Cheryl was dead. I was very offended by this and I hung up. Jordan was being irrational. I knew that Jordan never approved of me and has acted cold towards me ever since we first met. Jordan and Cheryl used to do everything together. Jordan resented it when Cheryl began spending a lot of time with me. And Jordan has always held it against me that she didn't land a big part in a movie that my company was producing.

DH: After we searched your car, we found a set of golf clubs in the trunk, but one of the clubs, the seven-club, was missing. What happened to it?

RB: It's been missing for weeks now. I left it at the Riviera Country Club and some other golfer must have picked it up. That happens all the time.

DH: Is there anything else you would like to add?

RB: Just that I miss Cheryl and this whole thing has been devastating. I wish she hadn't driven when she was so drunk and upset.

I have reviewed this transcript. It is a complete and accurate account.

Signed: *Richard Brooks*
                    Richard Brooks

Witnessed: *Cameron Hastings*
                    Detective Cameron Hastings

Statement of Jordan Summers

My name is Jordan Summers and I am twenty-six years old. I met Cheryl in acting class about five years ago and we were close ever since. We were both from small towns, and I think we bonded over adjusting to the fast-paced life in Oceana.

I know Richard Brooks; he was Cheryl's boyfriend. He threw a lot of wild parties at his beach house when his wife was away, and Cheryl and I would go together. I had never seen parties like that before; there were dozens of famous producers, directors, and actresses—and lots of drugs. I kind of got wrapped up in the film industry's party scene, and got in some trouble over it. About five years ago, I was pulled over after attending a party, and when I opened the glove compartment to get my registration, some coke Richard gave me fell out. Well, the police officer saw it and when he searched my car, he also found a necklace I'd taken from the party. I was convicted of possession and petty theft. Since then, I went to rehab and have been clean ever since.

I still partly blame Richard for my arrest; it was his coke and I never did coke until I started going to his beach house parties. If that wasn't enough, I almost got a big part in a horror movie, produced by Five Peaks, but Richard refused to hire me. He said my scream did not sound terrified enough. I never understood why Cheryl would be into a guy like Richard. Not only was he married, but he was also egotistical and kind of a creeper. I tried to convince her a couple times to break it off with him, but there was no getting through to her; he had some kind of hold on Cheryl.

Cheryl confided in me about everything, so I know things started to get real tense two weeks before Cheryl died. She sent me daily text messages about how worried she was because she was pregnant and Richard told her to have an abortion. She told him over and over how she wanted to keep the baby because she didn't believe in abortion, but the more she protested the angrier he got. I think I saved at least one of the texts. She told me he even promised to pay her $10,000 if she got it "taken care of" and kept her mouth shut. Then she said he told her something that gives me chills even now. He said, "One way or the other, I am not going to let this pregnancy ruin my life!"

Cheryl called me a few minutes after 1:00 a.m. on July 2, CY-1. She was crying when I picked up the phone and said she heard a noise outside of her condo. Cheryl was afraid it was Richard because they got in a big fight over dinner since she refused to get an abortion. A minute later she yelled out, "Oh no, I think I hear a key in the lock! He's the only one with a key to my place! I can't let him find me!" She sounded so terrified and kind of drunk because she was slurring her words, but I could still understand what she said. I told her to lock herself in her bedroom and I would be right there. I only live about twenty minutes away from Cheryl's condo. I figured I could maybe talk some sense into Richard, if he really was there. Now I wish I would have called 911 as soon as I got off the phone.

I threw on a pair of jeans and a t-shirt as fast as I could and drove to Cheryl's place. I got there a few minutes before 2:00 a.m., but no one answered the door and I got really worried. That's when I called the cops. Not long after, I got that terrible phone call that Cheryl's body had been found. On my way to the site where Cheryl's car was, I couldn't stop myself from calling that bastard, Richard. I blamed him for killing Cheryl. He didn't even deny it. He just swore at me and hung up the phone. Since her family is all out of state, and I was her closest friend, the police had me identify her body. It was so awful. It was the worst thing that has ever happened in my life. I still can't believe that Cheryl is gone. I just wish she would have listened to me and not gotten mixed up with that jerk, Richard.

I have read the above statement. It is complete, accurate, and true.

Signed: Jordan Summers
                 Jordan Summers

Witness: Cameron Hastings
                 Detective Cameron Hastings

Statement of Dr. Toni Cooke

My name is Dr. Toni Cooke. I have worked for the Maliwood County Coroner's Office for nine years and have been the lead physician on hundreds of procedures. I attended the University of Jackson Hall for my undergraduate studies, where I received my Bachelors in Biology. I attended Smith University in Washington, D.C. for medical school before moving to San Diego, California to do a three-year residency in anatomic pathology at University of Nirvana Medical Center. Upon completion of my residency, I did a one-year fellowship in forensic pathology, again at Nirvana Medical. In the fellowship I was trained in diagnosing causes of death and have assisted on over two hundred procedures involving all forms of injuries and disease.

I examined the body of Cheryl Byron at 9 a.m. on July 2, CY-1, and ruled her death to be a homicide. The autopsy procedure involved a physical assessment of the deceased, X-ray, MRI, and toxicological analysis.

Immediately upon the commencement of the autopsy it was evident that the decedent had suffered a great amount of trauma to the left side of her body. This was clear because of the large amount of bruising and several hematomas on her left arm and abdomen, as well as lacerations caused by broken glass on her left arm.

The police informed me that the decedent was found inside of her vehicle, which was turned on its left side, at the base of Maliwood Canyon. The injuries to her body seem to be consistent with a car accident where the impact was on the driver's side. The head injury, however, is inconsistent with all the other injuries.

Inspection of the skull revealed a depressed fracture in the vicinity of the left temporal lobe. The size and shape of the injury indicates it was made by something approximately two inches by four inches. The depth of the wound along with the depression and fracturing of the skull indicate the impact was one of significant force, applied to a specifically targeted area. There was no other bruising or fracturing present on the tissues and bones of the face. In my opinion, if the head had struck against the interior of the vehicle during the crash, the injury would not be so focused on one impact point.

The separated shoulder, broad bruising, hematomas, and large fracture areas are consistent with such an accident. The force of the body landing on the left arm against the car door as the vehicle rolled likely caused the fractures and separation at the joints, as well as in the ribcage. However, none of these injuries were fatal. The fatal wound was the depressed skull fracture, which caused internal bleeding and bone fragments to lacerate parts of the brain. Given the size, shape, and depth of the wound, as well as the type of accident, the decedent was more likely struck by a blunt object with a focused amount of force directed specifically at her head. While the time of death cannot be more specifically targeted than a range of several hours, such an injury is likely to cause death in a matter of minutes. The severity of the injury undoubtedly would have caused the decedent to fall unconscious immediately, and she would have been unable to operate a vehicle.

For these reasons, I have ruled that Cheryl Byron was killed before her vehicle went off the cliff.

I have read the above statement. It is complete, accurate, and true.

Signed: *Toni Cooke*
                Toni Cooke

Witness: *Cameron Hastings*
                Detective Cameron Hastings

Statement of Jessie Waters

My name is Jessie Waters and I am twenty-five years old. I moved to Oceana eight years ago to attend college at the Santa Ana University to pursue a degree in Child Studies. I haven't finished my degree just yet because I have had some personal struggles along the way that have required me to take some time off from school. I started working at Sunset Shadows after the birth of my daughter, Angela, about five years ago. It has been hard balancing school and work as a single parent, but I've adjusted. I usually work the late shift so I can take Angela to and from school.

On the night of July 1, CY-1, I was working, and I remember Richard and Cheryl came in to have dinner. Richard is one of my regular customers; he always asks to be seated in my section, and we have developed a kind of friendship over the years. I've noticed that in the last two years or so he has come into the restaurant more often, maybe a couple times a week. It is usually only for a light snack or a glass of wine—he is quite the wine connoisseur. I'd met Cheryl a number of times, but I hadn't spoken to her that much. She was kind of cold and got jealous whenever Richard talked to other women.

It is hard to remember all the details of that evening. I started my shift at 4:00 p.m. It was a pretty long day and I was exhausted because Angela was sick with a fever the night before and I didn't get much sleep. I remember Richard and Cheryl came in around 9:00 p.m. and sat out on our deck overlooking the ocean. It can get chilly out there at night with the ocean breeze so we have a number of heated lamps on the deck. Soon after they sat down, Cheryl started to complain about it being too cold. I noticed that she did not have a sweater or a jacket. To make her happy, I positioned two heat lamps at both her sides.

They didn't seem like their usual selves that night; I could tell from across the room their conversation was tense. When I came to take their drink orders, I noticed Richard had a big band-aid on his arm. It's the kind of band-aid I have at home because my daughter Angela is always coming home from preschool with scrapes from the playground. Anyway, Cheryl ordered an apple martini and asked me to make it strong. Usually, she drinks whatever wine Richard orders, so I thought that was a little strange. Richard ordered a bottle of wine for the table.

I could tell that with each course their conversation got more and more serious and emotional. I didn't know what they were discussing, but at one point during the main course, I couldn't help but hear Cheryl yell out, "I won't do it; I won't." She kept repeating that and getting angrier and angrier. I think she also added something like she didn't believe in doing that sort of thing. She yelled so loudly, the entire restaurant heard. It was pretty embarrassing and uncomfortable for everyone. Halfway through dessert, Cheryl began yelling at Richard again, saying something about it not ever being about the money, and then she stormed out of the restaurant crying. That was right around midnight. I remember I kept looking at my watch, just waiting for them to leave because they were scaring away customers in my section.

Understandably, Richard was pretty embarrassed by the whole thing. He came back in after chasing after her, apologized for the whole mess, and left a big tip. I think the alcohol went to Cheryl's head and kind of made her go crazy for a moment. She was raving mad at him, and as far as I can tell he is a pretty sweet guy. I was sorry to hear about what happened to Cheryl. Richard was devastated when he told me a couple days later when he came by the restaurant. I hope everything works out for Richard, and I feel awfully bad about Cheryl.

I have read the above statement. It is complete, accurate, and true.

Signed: *Jessie Waters*
            Jessie Waters

Witness: *Cameron Hastings*
            Detective Cameron Hastings

Statement of Dr. Shane Chaves

I am an orthopedic surgeon currently practicing at St. Monica's Medical Center in San Andreas, Oceana. I received my undergraduate degree in organic chemistry at the University of Frankland. I attended medical school at Ivory University where I became well-versed in general medical knowledge and graduated magna cum laude. I then did my residency in orthopedic surgery, which included one year of general surgery and four years specifically working on surgery involving the musculoskeletal system at Oakwood Regional in San Andreas. I have been practicing at St. Monica's for the past fifteen years, and have used both surgical and non-surgical means to heal thousands of patients, ranging from minor sports injuries to serious accidents.

All of the relevant documents in the case of Cheryl Byron's death were made available to me. This included the autopsy, accident photographs, X-rays, and the coroner's report. After an extensive review, I cannot reach the same conclusion as Dr. Cooke in this matter. While Dr. Cooke correctly identified the injuries suffered by the decedent, the diagnosis as to their cause was most likely mistaken, particularly with regard to the bone fractures.

The photos and X-rays clearly show that the decedent suffered blunt force trauma to the head. The lack of life-threatening severity in the other injuries, added to the depth and width of the wound and presence of bone fragments that broke into the brain, make this strike the ultimate cause of death. However, it could have been suffered by any number of things during the accident itself. In my experience, I have seen various parts of cars create roughly semicircular-shaped wounds. Furthermore, the fact that the vehicle's window was shattered makes it very possible that the deceased struck her head on a rock or some other debris as the vehicle rolled down into Maliwood Canyon. This would account for the sand, dust, and dirt found impacted in the wounds.

The X-rays also revealed hairline fractures on the ulna and humerus at the point of the elbow joint, as well as a dislocated shoulder. These injuries are more consistent with someone raising their arm to brace themselves for an impact, or shielding herself from flying glass, than an individual whose arm would be lying limply at her side because she was unconscious. Had Cheryl Byron been dead before the accident and the car rolled on its left side, there would be fractures running across the shoulder bones, humerus, ulna, or radius, if there were any breaks at all. In this case, the hairline fractures were found at the elbow joint. Whether bracing against the window or attempting to shield herself, the elbow joint is probably the point of the body which would strike the window, ground, or car first. The force of the impact created the fractures and then separated the shoulder. The fact that no lacerations were found on the face only serves to support the conclusion that the left arm, likely shielding the decedent's face, bore the brunt of the damage when the window shattered.

There are any number of scenarios in a crash that could have resulted in the decedent's injuries, but the medical evidence available demonstrates it is likely that Cheryl Byron was alive at the time of the crash because the bone fractures in her left arm are not consistent with a person being unconscious or deceased prior to the crash. She suffered blunt force trauma to the head during the crash. This caused the depression in her skull and projected bone fragments into the brain tissue. Sadly, she then succumbed to death before help could arrive on the scene.

I have read the above statement. It is complete, accurate, and true.

Signed: *Shane Chaves*
               Shane Chaves

Witness: *Cameron Hastings*
               Detective Cameron Hastings

Exhibit A

Office of the Maliwood County Coroner

DATE and HOUR AUTOPSY PERFORMED: 7/2/(CY-1); 09:00 hours by Toni Cooke, M.D. 555 Jackson Avenue Maliwood, OC 555-4906 (FAX 555-4907)	Full Autopsy Performed

SUMMARY REPORT OF AUTOPSY

Name: BYRON, Cheryl	Date of Birth: 8/30/(CY-30)
Date of Death: 7/1/(CY-1) – 7/2/(CY-1)	Body Identified by: Jordan Summers, friend of deceased
Case # MW043652	Investigative Agency: Maliwood County Sheriff's Department

EXTERNAL EXAMINATION:

The autopsy commenced at 09:00 hours on July 2, (CY-1). The body is presented in a black body bag. The body is that of a normally developed female measuring 67 inches, weighing 127 pounds, and appearing generally consistent with the stated age of 29 years.

The eyes are partially open. The irises are blue. The corneas are cloudy. The hair is blond, straight, and approximately 14 inches in length. The hair is encrusted with what appears to be blood.

On the left temporal region of the scalp, there is a deep semi-circular wound to the skull approximately 4 cm in diameter.

The chest, abdomen, limbs, and back are symmetrical and intact, but with bruising and large hematomas on the left side of the abdomen, left shoulder, and forearm, as well as the outer, upper left thigh.

The external genitalia are that of an adult female, and there is no evidence of injury. Limbs are equal, symmetrically developed, and intact.

INTERNAL EXAMINATION:

HEAD--CENTRAL NERVOUS SYSTEM: The blunt force injury to the left side of the head was made by contact with a blunt object with a semi-circular shape having a diameter of approximately 4 cm. The wound path is approximately 2 cm in length and penetrates the skin and subdermal tissues. The force creating the wound was significant enough to depress and fracture the skull. Bone fragments have caused lacerations and bruising to the brain in the area of the fracture. Microscopic examination of the wounds reveals what appear to be grains of dirt, sand, or dust. The brain weighs 1,325 grams and is within normal limits.

SKELETAL SYSTEM: A depressed fracture to the left temporal area of the skull is observed by X-ray.

X-ray also reveals that the left shoulder was dislocated and hairline fracturing is exhibited at the elbow (ulna and humerus) as well as in the left 3rd, 4th, 5th, and 6th ribs.

RESPIRATORY SYSTEM--THROAT STRUCTURES: The organs, glands, and cartilages of the respiratory system are intact and show no damage. The lungs weigh: right, 350 grams; left, 360 grams. The lungs are unremarkable.

CARDIOVASCULAR SYSTEM: The heart weighs 249 grams, and has a normal size and configuration. No evidence of atherosclerosis is present.

GASTROINTESTINAL SYSTEM: The organs of the gastrointestinal system are intact.

URINARY SYSTEM: The kidneys weigh: left, 120 grams; right, 115 grams. The kidneys are anatomic in size, shape, and location and are without lesions.

FEMALE GENITAL SYSTEM: The structures are within normal limits. Examination reveals that the decedent was pregnant at the time of death. Fetal weight and development is consistent with 7 weeks. There are no signs of recent sexual activity.

TOXICOLOGY: A sample of right pleural blood was submitted for toxicological analysis.

Drug Screen Results:

Urine screen {Immunoassay} was NEGATIVE.

Ethanol: 80 mg/dl, Blood (BAC: .08%)

EVIDENCE COLLECTED:

1. One (1) black cocktail dress.

2. Ten (10) samples collected from under the deceased's fingernails.

3. Samples of Blood (type A+) and Tissue (heart, lung, brain, kidney, liver, spleen).

4. Nine autopsy photographs.

5. One postmortem CT scan.

6. One postmortem MRI.

MANNER OF DEATH:

Homicide

IMMEDIATE CAUSE OF DEATH:

Blunt force injury to the head made with an instrument with a semi-circular end four cm in diameter and at least two cm in length.

TIME OF DEATH:

Body temperature, rigor mortis, and liver mortis approximate the time of death between 23:00 hours, 7/1/CY-1 and 03:00 hours, 7/2/CY-1.

Toni Cooke

Toni Cooke, M.D.
Maliwood County Coroner's Office
July 2, CY-1

Exhibit B

Maliwood County Sheriff's Department
Office of Forensic Investigation
Computer Crimes Unit
16437 Glenhurst St
Maliwood, OC 90120

July 6, CY-1

Re   People v. Brooks
       Case # MW043652

Detective Hastings,

I analyzed the contents of victim Cheryl Byron's cellular telephone,
specimen #8675309. The following text messages were recovered from
the SIM card found inside the telephone.

Outgoing Message
>To: Jordan (555)289-0210
>>>Sent on: July 1 CY-1 2:23 p.m.

Get this I'm meetn R tonight for dinner at Sunset Shadows. He has
gone bizzurk! I told him he better do the right thing by me, n he
kinda freaked! I'll call u after w/ details

Incoming Message
>From: R<3 (555)576-1302
>>>Received: June 24, CY-1 1:46 a.m.

Just think about it babe. 10k is a lot of money. I need a decision
ASAP, we have to get things rolling.

Sincerely,

Danica Pryor
Danica Pryor
Forensic Analyst
Serial #10187

Exhibit C

SUPERIOR COURT OF THE STATE OF OCEANA

COUNTY OF MALIWOOD

STATE OF OCEANA,	Plaintiff,	Case No. MW02626
v.		**CHARGE(S):** 11350 Possession of Cocaine 1 count
JORDAN SUMMERS,	Defendant.	484 Petty Theft 1 count

CERTIFIED JUDGMENT OF CONVICTION

On September 21, CY-6, Maliwood County District Attorney being present and Defendant having appeared in person with counsel, being the date fixed by the Court for pronouncement of judgment and sentence upon a verdict of Guilty of the offenses of possession of cocaine in violation of Health and Safety Code § 11350 and petty theft in violation of Penal Code § 484, Defendant was sentenced to twenty-four months of summary probation, thirty days in Maliwood County Jail commencing at 12:00 o'clock noon on September 26, CY-6, Narcotics Anonymous meetings twice a week for six months, and a fine of five hundred dollars.

IT IS FURTHER ORDERED that the Clerk of this Court deliver a certified copy of the Judgment and Commitment to the Sheriff or other appropriate officer as a commitment of Defendant.

IT IS SO ORDERED.

O. Wright

Judge O. Wright

Date: September 21, CY-6, State of Oceana

Exhibit D

SUPERIOR COURT OF THE STATE OF OCEANA

COUNTY OF MALIWOOD

STATE OF OCEANA,		Case No. MW015763
	Plaintiff,	
v.		**CHARGE(S):**
		23152(a)
RICHARD BROOKS,		Driving Under the Influence of Alcohol
	Defendant.	1 count

CERTIFIED JUDGMENT OF CONVICTION

On January 12, CY-10, Maliwood County District Attorney being present and Defendant having appeared in person with counsel, being the date fixed by the Court for pronouncement of judgment and sentence upon a verdict of Guilty of the offense of driving under the influence in violation of Vehicle Code § 23152(a), Defendant was sentenced to thirty-six months of summary probation, a fine of one-thousand three hundred dollars, a ninety-day Oceana state driver's license restriction, and a three-month alcohol education program.

IT IS FURTHER ORDERED that the Clerk of this Court deliver a certified copy of the Judgment and Commitment to the Sheriff or other appropriate officer as a commitment of Defendant.

IT IS SO ORDERED.

M. Roberts

Judge M. Roberts

Date: January 12, CY-10, State of Oceana

Exhibit E

Exhibit F

Exhibit G

Exhibit H

Exhibit I

Exhibit J

Exhibit K

Exhibit L

Jury Instructions

Members of the jury, I thank you for your attentiveness during this trial. Please pay close attention to the instructions I am about to give you.

In this case, Defendant Richard Brooks is charged with murder in the first degree. A person who unlawfully kills another person with malice aforethought is guilty of the crime of murder in violation of Oceana Penal Code section 187. To prove the crime of murder, the State must prove the following elements beyond a reasonable doubt:

1. A human being was killed;

2. The killing was unlawful; and

3. The killing was done with malice aforethought.

Unlawful means that a killing is neither justifiable nor excusable.

Malice may be either expressed or implied. Malice is expressed when there is a manifested intent to unlawfully kill a person. Malice is implied when:

1. The killing is the result of an intentional act;

2. The natural consequences of the act are dangerous to human life; and

3. The act was deliberately performed with knowledge of the danger to, and with conscious disregard for, human life.

When it is shown that a killing resulted from the intentional doing of an act with expressed or implied malice, no other mental state need be shown to establish the mental state of malice aforethought. The mental state constituting malice aforethought does not necessarily require any ill will or hatred of the person killed. The word *aforethought* does not imply deliberation or the lapse of substantial time. Rather, it only means the required mental state must precede rather than follow the act.

Defendant has entered a plea of not guilty. This means that you must presume or believe that Defendant is not guilty unless and until the evidence convinces you otherwise. This presumption stays with Defendant as to each material allegation in the indictment through each stage of the trial until it has been overcome by the evidence to the exclusion of and beyond a reasonable doubt.

To overcome Defendant's presumption of innocence, it is the State's burden to prove the following:

1. The crime with which Defendant is charged was committed.

2. Defendant is the person who committed the crime.

Defendant is not required to prove anything.

The State has the burden to prove the elements beyond a reasonable doubt. Whenever the words *reasonable doubt* are used, you must consider the following: A reasonable doubt is not a mere possible doubt, because everything relating to human affairs is open to some possible or imaginary doubt. Reasonable doubt is the state of the case that, after hearing and considering all the evidence, leaves the minds of the jurors in the condition that they cannot say they feel an abiding conviction of the truth of the charge.

It is to the evidence introduced during this trial, and to it alone, that you are to look for that proof. A reasonable doubt as to the guilt of Defendant may arise from evidence, a conflict in the evidence, or a lack of evidence. If you have a reasonable doubt, you should find Defendant not guilty. If you have no reasonable doubt, you should find Defendant guilty.

You must decide this case on the evidence and the law. It is up to you to decide what evidence is reliable. You should use your common sense in deciding what evidence is reliable and what evidence should not be relied upon in considering your verdict.

A witness is a person who has knowledge related to this case. You will have to decide whether you believe each witness and how important each witness's testimony is to the case. You may believe all, part, or none of a witness's testimony. In deciding whether to believe a witness's testimony, you may consider, among other factors, the following:

1. The extent of the witness's opportunity to see, hear, or otherwise become familiar with any matter about which the witness testified.

2. The ability of the witness to accurately recall or communicate any matter about which the witness testified and the character and quality of that testimony.

3. The witness's manner and demeanor while on the stand.

4. Whether or not the witness has bias, an improper motive, or an interest in the outcome of the case.

5. The witness's attitude toward this trial or toward testifying.

6. Whether the witness's testimony was consistent or inconsistent with other testimony or evidence presented in this case.

7. Any previous statements made by the witness that are consistent or inconsistent with the witness's testimony.

8. The witness's character for honesty or veracity, or their opposites.

9. Whether the witness was offered money, preferred treatment, or any other benefit to testify or whether the witness received any threats or was under any pressure that might have affected the truth of the witness's testimony.

10. The witness's previous conviction of a felony or past criminal conduct amounting to a misdemeanor.

You may rely upon your own conclusions about each witness. A juror may believe or disbelieve all or any part of the evidence or the testimony of any witness.

There are some general rules that apply to your deliberations. You must abide by these rules in order to return a verdict that is consistent with the law:

1. You must follow the law as it is explained to you in these instructions. If you fail to follow the law or disregard the law, any verdict you reach will be a miscarriage of justice.

2. You must decide the case only upon the evidence that you have heard from either the testimony of witnesses or exhibits that you have seen.

3. You must not decide the case for or against anyone because you feel sympathy for that person, or because you are angry at that person.

4. You must not decide the case based on your feelings about the lawyers in this case. The lawyers are not on trial.

5. You must not consider any potential sentence Defendant might receive. It is not your duty to consider punishment. Your only duty is to determine guilt or innocence. It is the judge's job to determine the proper sentence if you find Defendant guilty.

6. Whatever verdict you render must be unanimous; that is, each juror must commit to the same verdict. The verdict must be the verdict of each juror as well as that of the jury as a whole.

7. It is entirely proper for a lawyer to talk to a witness about what testimony the witness would give if called into the courtroom. The witness should not be discredited for talking to a lawyer about his or her testimony.

8. You must not decide this case based on feelings of prejudice, bias, or sympathy. Any verdict you may reach should be based on the evidence and the law contained in these instructions.

Deciding a proper verdict is exclusively your job. I cannot participate in that decision in any way. Please disregard anything I might have said or done that made you think I preferred one verdict over another.

Only one verdict may be returned for the crime charged. The verdict must be in writing and the verdict form has been prepared for you. It is as follows:

(READ JURY VERDICT FORM)

In just a few moments, the Bailiff will escort you to the jury room. Once inside the jury room, the first thing you should do is elect a foreperson, who will preside over your deliberations. It is the foreperson's job to sign and date the verdict form when all of you have agreed on a verdict in this case and to bring the verdict back to the courtroom when you return.

In conclusion, let me remind you that it is imperative that you follow the law as I have explained it to you in these instructions. Regardless of how you feel about the laws, you must apply them.

SUPERIOR COURT OF THE STATE OF OCEANA

FOR THE COUNTY OF MALIWOOD

STATE OF OCEANA,	Plaintiff,	Case No. MW043652
v.		**CHARGE(S):**
RICHARD BROOKS,	Defendant.	187 Murder in the first degree 1 count

VERDICT

As to the charge of murder in the first degree, in violation of Oceana Penal Code section 187, we, the jury, find the Defendant, Richard Brooks:

_____   GUILTY

_____   NOT GUILTY

So say we all.

_____
Foreperson of the Jury

_____
Date

CASE FILE No. 2

STATE OF OCEANA

V.

CLIFFORD JACKSON

(Attempted Murder)

SUPERIOR COURT OF THE STATE OF OCEANA

COUNTY OF SAN ANDREAS

STATE OF OCEANA,		Case No. SA101811
	Plaintiff,	
v.		**FELONY COMPLAINT**
CLIFFORD JACKSON,		
	Defendant.	

COUNT 1

On or about June 25, CY-1, in the City of San Andreas, San Andreas County, State of Oceana, a felony, in violation of section 664(a)/187 of the Oceana Penal Code, commonly referred to as ATTEMPTED MURDER, was committed by the above named defendant, who at the time and place last aforesaid, did willfully and with malice aforethought attempt to murder Antonio Villalobos.

It is alleged that the crime was committed by the above defendant for the furtherance of a criminal street gang, as defined in Oceana Penal Code 186.22(a).

IT IS SO ORDERED.

Ellen Woods

Ellen Woods
District Attorney, County of San Andreas

Witness List

Witnesses for the State:

1.   Antonio Villalobos*

2.   Alex Paulson***

Witnesses for the Defense:

1.   Clifford Jackson*

2.   Kiarra Washington**

Each side must call both witnesses listed for their respective party, and both parties stipulate that each party's expert witness would testify consistently with his or her provided statement.

*This witness must be played by a male.

**This witness must be played by a female.

***This witness may be either gender.

Stipulations

1. Both the Federal Rules of Criminal Procedure and Federal Rules of Evidence apply.

2. Assume each witness who gave an interview reviewed the officer's report of his or her interview and signed the interview to verify for accuracy.

3. All exhibits included in the file are authentic and, unless otherwise stated, are the original of that document.

4. Other than what appears in the officer's report of the interviews, there is nothing exceptional or unusual about the background of any of the witnesses that would bolster or detract from their credibility.

5. All dates are denoted by CY (current year) or CY-*n* (current year minus *n* years).

6. All pretrial motions shall be oral.

7. No party may invent witnesses or evidence that is not specifically mentioned in this case file.

8. "Beyond the record" is not a proper objection. Rather, the attorneys shall use cross-examination as the means of challenging a witness whose testimony strays beyond the facts contained in the case file.

9. The physical description of a witness, e.g., clothing, should be tailored to that of the student playing the witness, except for height, weight and age.

10. Antonio Villalobos is an admitted member of the Los Diablos Locos gang.

11. The knife found in the alley belongs to Antonio Villalobos and was not tested for fingerprints because both parties stipulate that the Defendant, Clifford Jackson, used the knife.

12. Oceana Penal Code Section 664/187(a) states that a person is guilty of attempted murder if
    A. A direct, but ineffective, act was done to kill the person and;
    B. The attempted killing was unlawful; and
    C. The attempted killing was done with malice aforethought.

13. The parties stipulate to the admittance of the emergency room physician's report of Antonio Villalobos and the statement given by Reverend Greg Boyd. These exhibits can be used by either side. The parties have waived hearsay objections for only these exhibits.

14. All witness statements were given under oath.

15. All witnesses called to testify who have identified the Defendant Jackson or any tangible evidence can, if asked, identify the same at trial.

16. The text messages are authenticated under the Federal Rules of Evidence 902(11) and are admissible as certified business records under Federal Rules of Evidence 803(6).

17. The expert witnesses' reports are stipulated to as being an accurate reflection of what each expert would testify to if called as a witness. Either side may constructively read into the record the expert

witnesses' testimony in whole or in part or move the testimony into the record. Any such testimony by the stipulated experts is subject to objections pursuant to the Federal Rules of Evidence.

18. The prosecution and defense may only call the two witnesses listed on their respective witness list.

19. The prosecution and defense have stipulated that the proper foundation has been laid for the medical report and they have stipulated that the medical expert would testify pursuant to his report. However, either side is free to dispute the contents of the report.

20. The witnesses Clifford Jackson and Antonio Villalobos must be male. The witness Kiarra Washington must be female. The witnesses may be called in any order.

COUNTY OF SAN ANDREAS SHERIFF'S DEPARTMENT
INVESTIGATION REPORT

RECORDS & STATISTICS BUREAU'S USE ONLY			DATE: 6/25/CY-1	PAGE: 1 OF 3

ACTION	ACTIVE (X) INACTIVE ( ) PENDING ( )	INDEX Yes (X) INFO No ( )	N of Adult Arrests 1	No of Subject Detentions 1	URN (File No.) SA101811

CLASSIFICATION
ATTEMPTED MURDER INVESTIGATION

DATE, TIME OF OCCURRENCE
06/25/CY-1, 01:25 HOURS

LOCATION OF OCCURRENCE 2142 S CENTRAL BLVD, DOWNTOWN SAN ANDREAS, OC	TYPE OF LOCATION ALLEY	TRACT

CODE: V - VICTIM, W - WITNESS, I - INFORMANT, R - REPORTING PARTY, P - PARTY

CODE V NO. 1 OF 1	LAST NAME VILLALOBOS, ANTONIO	FIRST	MIDDLE	SEX M	AGE 15	RACE HISPANIC

RESIDENCE ADDRESS 1320 IMPERIAL AVE, DOWNTOWN SAN ANDREAS, OC	RES. PHONE (AREA CODE) N/A

BUSINESS ADDRESS	RES. PHONE (AREA CODE)

CODE W NO. 1 OF 1	LAST NAME WASHINGTON, KIARRA	FIRST	MIDDLE	SEX F	AGE 25	RACE BLACK

RESIDENCE ADDRESS 817 VAN SYLVAN ST, DOWNTOWN SAN ANDREAS, OC	RES. PHONE (AREA CODE)

BUSINESS ADDRESS	RES. PHONE (AREA CODE)

CODE: S - SUSPECT, SJ - SUBJECT, M - PATIENT, S/V - SUSPECT/VICTIM, SJ/V - SUBJECT / VICTIM

CODE S No 1 OF 1	LAST NAME JACKSON, CLIFFORD	FIRST	MIDDLE	DRIVER'S LICENSE (STATE & No) OC59458019

RESIDENCE ADDRESS 817 VAN SYLVAN ST, DOWNTOWN SAN ANDREAS, OC	RES. PHONE (AREA CODE)

BUSINESS ADDRESS	BUS. PHONE (AREA CODE)

SEX M	RACE BLACK	HAIR BR	EYES BR	HEIGHT 6'0''	WEIGHT 250 LBS	DOB 07/06/CY-28	AGE 28	WHERE DETAINED MALIWOOD CANYON

OBSERVABLE PHYSICAL ODDITIES/TATTOOS/SCARS "K4L" TATTOO, RIGHT FOREARM	AKA / NICKNAME "TRIGGER"	BOOKING No. OC

CLOTHING WORN BLACK SWEATSHIRT, BLUE JEANS, WHITE SHOES	MAIN

CHARGE ATTEMPED MURDER	WEAPON USED KNIFE

CODE No OF	LAST NAME	FIRST	MIDDLE	DRIVER'S LICENSE (STATE & No)

RESIDENCE ADDRESS	RES. PHONE (AREA CODE)

BUSINESS ADDRESS	BUS. PHONE (AREA CODE)

SEX	RACE	HAIR	EYES	HEIGHT	WEIGHT	D.O.B.	AGE	WHERE DETAINED OR CITE No.

OBSERVABLE PHYSICAL ODDITIES	AKA / NICKNAME	BOOKING No.

CLOTHING WORN	MAIN

CHARGE	WEAPON USED

VEHICLE USED IN CRIME YES ( ) NO (X) UNKNOWN ( ) STORED ( ) IMPOUNDED (X)	YR 1992	MAKE HONDA	BODY TYPE CIVIC	COLOR TEAL	BY DEPUTY GARCIA	BADGE No. 2157

LICENSE (STATE & No.) OC 552SRA5	V.I.N./ FRAME No.	DEPUTY	BADGE No.

REGISTERED OWNER CLIFFORD JACKSON	STATION DSV	UNIT / CAR No. 4240	SHIFT NIGHT

IDENTIFYING CHARACTERISTICS	APPROVED PAULSON	BADGE No. 2019	TIME NIGHT

O.H.P. 180 SUBMITTED YES ( ) NO ( )	GARAGE NAME & PHONE	ASSIGNMENT GANG VIOLENCE TASK FORCE

Narrative Report – URN SA101811

At 01:20 hours on June 25, CY-1, emergency operators received an anonymous call reporting that a young male was bleeding heavily at the intersection of Central Blvd. and Crenshaw Ave. The caller gave the location as 2142 South Central Blvd.

Officers responded to the scene at approximately 01:30 hours. They found an unconscious Hispanic male, later identified as Antonio Villalobos, lying on the sidewalk. Villalobos was bleeding profusely and appeared to have several puncture wounds on his chest and lower abdomen. Paramedics were called and Villalobos was transported to Holy Cross Hospital.

The first responding officers reported a trail of blood droplets leading from an alley to the location of Villalobos's body, a distance of about six feet. Upon inspecting the alley, the officers observed and measured a four-inch switchblade. The switchblade appeared to have blood on it. Because this attack occurred in the 2100 block of South Central Blvd, a notorious high crime area plagued with gang violence, I was contacted as a detective with the Gang Violence Task Force to respond and initiate an investigation.

I arrived at the scene at approximately 02:10 hours. The scene had been cordoned off and secured by the initial responding officers. The letters "LDL" were spray painted in red over the letters "CBK" on the bus stop sign, about ten feet from the alley where Villalobos had been located (see attached Exhibit B). Upon touching the graffiti, I noticed it was still relatively fresh. Given my experience working in the gang violence task force, I formed the opinion that the attack on Villalobos was most probably a gang related retaliatory attack. The fresh paint led me to form the opinion that Villalobos crossed out the CBK graffiti and replaced it with LDL graffiti, an aggressive action that likely drew retaliatory gang violence.

On that same day at 06:00 hours, following a call from Holy Cross Hospital that Villalobos had regained consciousness, I interviewed Villalobos. Initially, he was hostile and uncooperative, but eventually named his attacker as Clifford "Trigger" Jackson, a CBK gang member. Villalobos, a member of LDL, told me that he was spray-painting his gang's insignia on the bus stop when Jackson approached

him from behind and began yelling at him. He said Jackson knocked the spray paint out of his hand and

then flashed the CBK gang sign. Jackson then told Villalobos to leave and when Villalobos refused,

Jackson threatened him and showed him his "shot-caller" tattoo to illustrate his elevated status in the

CBK gang. Villalobos then said Jackson challenged him to a fight and the two walked into the alley,

where Villalobos alleges Jackson came at him from behind with a knife, pushed him up against a wall and

stabbed him several times. Villalobos's own knife was knocked out of his hand during the struggle and

was recovered in a search of the alley (See attached Exhibit I). The knife that Jackson allegedly used was

not found in the alley or in the area immediately surrounding the crime scene.

A search of Jackson in our computers revealed that he's currently on parole. At 08:00 hours I

gathered a team of three officers to go to Jackson's home to arrest him and conduct a search of his home.

He was at his residence along with Kiarra Washington, who identified herself as Jackson's girlfriend. We

arrested Jackson and searched his apartment. No knife was recovered. A cell phone was found in

Jackson's bedroom that contained incriminating text messages between him and another member of CBK.

At the station, Jackson, with counsel present, waived his Miranda rights and relayed that he works

as a gang interventionist and claimed that he confronted Villalobos with the intention of encouraging him

to give up the gang life. He further claimed that since he believed Villalobos was armed and because

Jackson's girlfriend was present, he wanted to move the conversation into the alley. Jackson stated he

wanted to protect his girlfriend. He claimed Villalobos was unwilling to listen to him and attacked him.

Two days later, after receiving the emergency room physician's report, which stated that the stab

wounds sustained by Villalobos did not match Jackson's story of self-defense, Jackson was arrested for

the attempted murder of Villalobos.

Signed,

Alex Paulson

Detective Alex Paulson

Statement of Antonio Villalobos

Detective Paulson (DP): The date is June 25, CY -1 at approximately 11 a.m. and we are at Holy Cross Hospital in San Andreas. Antonio, tell me what happened.

Antonio Villalobos (AV): I got stabbed.

DP: Tell me what happened.

AV: I have nothing to say. Leave me alone.

DP: We need to know what happened.

AV: I already told the doctors I didn't want to talk to the cops. Things will be taken care of.

DP: Who attacked you?

AV: A cowardly piece of shit. Now go.

DP: I'm not going anywhere. I'll be here all day if it means I'll get the answers I need.

AV: Get comfortable then.

DP: I know how it is on the street. They tell you, "Don't snitch, don't talk to the cops." That's not the case here. I'm not trying to bust you. I'm just trying to do my job and make my arrest.

AV: Whatever.

DP: I'll be straight with you; we've already got a guy arrested. Turns out, I don't even need to talk to you.

AV: Why are you wasting my time then?

DP: Because there are two sides to every story. And right now, the other guy is telling us he acted in self-defense. He says you attacked him.

AV: Screw that! I'm not about to go to jail for a CBK. It was Trigger.

DP: So you knew your attacker?

AV: Trigger? Man, everybody knows who he is.

DP: What were you doing in the 2100 block at that time of night?

AV: The 2100 block is our territory.

DP: Cut the shit, what were you doing that night before you got attacked?

AV: Maybe I found a bus stop that looked like it needed some artwork.

DP: What time was this?

AV: I don't know. Maybe one or two in the morning.

DP: Did this bus stop already have some artwork on it?

AV: You mean did it have CBK tagging on it? Yeah it did. Some CBK asshole tagged up a wall in the 2100 block like they owned it.

DP: So you're tagging up a bus stop and then what happens?

AV: I was just about to finish when someone called for me. It was that fool and some skank.

DP: What'd he say?

AV: He told me to get out of there and that I should know what CBK could do to me.

DP: Was he hot?

AV: He flashed the c-gun. He got right up in my face and knocked the spray paint out of my hand.

DP: When you say "the c-gun", do you mean CBK's gang hand symbol?

AV: Yeah.

DP: Did you say anything back?

AV: I wasn't about to let some burnout tell me what to do, especially on our turf. I told him to f-off and get out of my face before I called my homeboys over. I said he was a wuss that couldn't handle the gang life anymore so he tried to get others to quit to make his pathetic self feel better.

DP: Were you carrying a weapon the night you were attacked?

AV: Of course I was. We always have to watch our backs, even in our own turf. I had my switchblade with me. Can't leave home without it.

DP: So one of the most dangerous gangsters comes up to you in the middle of the night and sees you cross out his gang's graffiti. You're not feeling the least bit worried?

AV: I told him he didn't scare me for one second. After he got out of prison he said he had changed his ways or some bullshit like that. I don't believe it for a second. I heard he ratted out his own homies just to get released earlier. I said I wasn't leaving and I asked him what he was going to do about it. Then he rolled up his sleeve and showed me a tattoo.

DP: What did the tattoo look like?

AV: It was dark so I couldn't really see.

DP: Did he say anything when he showed you the tattoo?

AV: Yeah he said, "You see this? You don't know who you're talking to." By this point, I knew this guy wanted to fight. So I put my hand in my pocket and grabbed my blade. I didn't take it out because I didn't want him to know I was strapped. But I wanted to be ready.

DP: All right, then what happened?

AV: There was an alley across from the bus stop and he went inside and told me to follow him if I wanted to prove how tough I was.

DP: You followed him inside?

AV: Hell yeah I did. You know how it is on the streets. I'm a LDL; we never back down. I had to follow him into that alley. I didn't really have a choice.

DP: What happened in the alley?

AV: He ran towards me and slammed me into a wall. I lost my knife and went down. He was on me and got me with his knife.

DP: Where did he stab you?

AV: He stabbed me in the stomach and in the chest, like the homies teach you in jail, to do the most damage. You don't stab nobody in the chest and stomach to protect yourself. You stab them there to make sure they really bleed. My homeboys will put that badass Trigger down!

DP: What did you do after you got stabbed?

AV: I kept blacking out and coming back. The last thing I remember was walking out of the alley and then I fell onto the street.

DP: Okay, I think we have everything we need.

[END OF TAPE]

Statement of Alex Paulson

My name is Alex Paulson. I have been a detective for the San Andreas Police Department for the past fifteen years. In CY-8, I was promoted to the Gang Violence Task Force. In CY-7, I was assigned to blocks 1800-2400 of inner city San Andreas as the resident gang expert.

To become a gang expert in the city's Gang Violence Task Force, a police officer has to serve a minimum of ten years in the police department, five of which have to be in violent crimes. Gang experts receive one year of apprentice-style training and then become certified as experts to testify as expert witnesses in court. The Gang Violence Task Force takes three approaches to gather intelligence against criminal street gangs. The first is street patrol, which is primarily observation of the gangs in their claimed territories ("turfs"). The second is informal contacts with gang members, through either non-confrontational stops or conversations. The third is through post-arrest interviews, where we train our gang experts to coax information out of gang members after they have been arrested.

As a gang intelligence officer, my expertise is in the culture of the criminal street gangs that claim my assigned blocks as their turf. Currently, there are two rival gangs that claim the 1800-2400 blocks: the Cold Blooded Killers (CBK) and the Los Diablos Locos (LDL). CBK claims the 1800-2000 blocks, while LDL claims the 2200-2400 blocks. The 2100 block is the subject of the bitter rivalry between the two gangs, and they have been engaging in deadly gang warfare for the past six years. Since both CBK and LDL finance their gang activities with revenue from drug sales, they feud over who will control the lucrative drug market in the 2100 block. My partner and I patrol the 1800-2400 blocks on a daily basis to observe members of LDL and CBK. By regularly patrolling these streets, we have gathered substantial intelligence on each gang's respective culture.

CBK is a violent street gang that was founded in CY-30. We have been gathering intelligence on them since CY-10, and we believe they have committed ninety-eight homicides. They are an extremely violent gang that recruits young males, as early as eleven, and primarily recruits members through familial connections, with older siblings initiating their younger siblings into the gang. The gang has a loose two-tiered structure. CBK members who have been in the gang for a long time, or who have paid considerable "service" to the gang, usually in the form of killings, are called "shot callers." Shot callers are the only ones allowed to get the special shot caller tattoo, K4L, which stands for "killer for life." This tattoo differentiates them from the lower level members, who are expected to obey orders from the shot callers. The younger members are primarily responsible for selling narcotics.

CBK's members are required to wear the gang's colors of black and yellow at all times in order to demonstrate CBK's presence. Gang members are very territorial and if a rival gang member enters into another gang's territory sporting his gang's colors, it is an open invitation for confrontation. CBK also has a gang hand sign, which is made by curving one hand to form a "C" and extending the thumb, middle, and pointer fingers of the other hand to form a "gun;" this is called the "c-gun." If a gang member "flashes" his gang sign at a member of another gang, it is an act of aggression, which, in gang culture, is seen as a challenge to fight. Gang members who do not accept the challenge to fight are seen as weak and, in turn, their gang is seen as weak. No gang wants to be perceived as weak because they lose their intimidating status in street politics. Another way that gang members challenge one another is through graffiti use. Gangs paint their graffiti all over their turf to symbolize their dominion. It is a significant sign of disrespect to cross out another gang's graffiti and paint your own over it. Often times it is retaliated against with brutal physical force, even killings.

LDL is the other major criminal street gang that occupies inner city San Andreas. It was founded in CY-17. Although LDL is much younger than CBK, LDL has become very influential on the streets of San Andreas because of their extremely violent tendencies. This is also due to LDL's ties to South American drug cartels. Since much of San Andreas street crime is financed by narcotics sales, LDL's narcotics trafficking is facilitated by these ties, giving them an advantage which has allowed them to dominate narcotics sales in inner city San Andreas. Because of their influence in narcotics trafficking, LDL has been clashing with CBK. As LDL is getting bigger and recruiting more members, they are slowly encroaching onto CBK's turf. This is the reason why the 2100 block is so heavily contested between the two gangs. LDL is not organized into two levels of membership like CBK because they believe they are all brothers and are therefore equal; however, younger or newer members must prove themselves to be loyal to the gang before they can become a full-fledged member allowed to wear the LDL colors (red and black) or tattoo themselves with LDL's insignia. Thus, younger or newer members are prone to be violent because they are eager to prove themselves.

I am familiar with Clifford Jackson from my work in the Gang Violence Task Force. I know him by his gang moniker, "Trigger." He is a very revered figure in the CBK gang network, and his status as a shot caller makes him an authority figure. Consequently, he is known in the Gang Violence Task Force as one of the most dangerous criminals on the streets of inner city San Andreas. He has been the primary suspect in several felony investigations I have conducted, two of which resulted in convictions. Clifford Jackson is a violent, hardened criminal and it is my professional opinion as a gang expert that he committed this attempt on Antonio Villalobos's life in retaliation. I have based this opinion on a comprehensive investigation of this case, particularly on the following factors:

1. The attack occurred in the contested 2100 block of South Central Boulevard;

2. Jackson witnessed Villalobos cross out CBK graffiti and replace it with LDL graffiti;

3. Jackson confronted the victim first by knocking the spray paint out of his hand;

4. Jackson flashed Villalobos his gang sign, showed him his gang tattoo, and threatened him; and

5. Jackson challenged Villalobos to a fight in the alley so there could be no witnesses.

I swear under penalty of perjury that the foregoing is true and accurate.

Signed,

Alex Paulson

Alex Paulson
Detective, San Andreas Police Department
Gang Violence Task Force

Clifford Jackson Interrogation

Detective Alex Paulson (AP): This is Detective Alex Paulson of the San Andreas Police Department's Gang Violence Task Force. I'm here with Clifford "Trigger" Jackson of the Cold Blooded Killers gang. He has been read his rights and he has agreed to talk to me with his attorney, Mr. Reed, present. The date is July 1, CY-1 and the time is 11:00 a.m. Trigger, state your name for the record.

Clifford Jackson (CJ): My name is *Clifford* Jackson. I don't go by Trigger anymore. I quit the game a long time ago.

AP: Touching story, but that's not what I asked you. Focus on giving answers to only the questions I ask. You've been in here enough times to know the way it works.

CJ: That Trigger stuff is ancient history. I'm an interventionist now.

AP: Whatever, let's hear your side. What went down?

CJ: You should be hauling that kid into this interrogation room and asking him.

AP: Who said anything about a kid? Come on, Jackson. I thought you didn't do anything?

CJ: I didn't. He attacked me.

AP: I've got a fifteen-year-old kid that's lying in a hospital bed, badly injured, and you put him there. And now you're looking me in the eye and telling me that you're the one that got attacked?

CJ: Clearly you've talked to him first.

AP: Of course I talked to him first. They found him in a pool of his own blood. They thought he was going to die. I needed to get the ID of the person who did that to him. And he pointed me right to you.

CJ: He's lying.

AP: Yeah? Lay it out for me.

CJ: Give me a minute.

Mr. Reed: My client, Mr. Jackson, is not at fault in this incident. He wants to cooperate with the authorities to ensure the real person responsible is brought to justice. However, he will only continue to do so if he is treated with respect.

AP: He'll get it if he gives it. Now let's take this from the top. Where were you last night?

CJ: At a concert with my girlfriend, Kiarra.

AP: Where was the concert?

CJ: At the Sundown Club on Central and Florence.

AP: That's on the 2100 block of Central. A lot of bad stuff happens there, Jackson. Your CBK buddies and LDL have been warring over the 2100 block.

Mr. Reed: That has nothing to do with my client.

AP: We'll see about that. What time did the concert get out?

CJ: Well it was supposed to end at 2:00 a.m. but my girlfriend, Kiarra, and I left around 1:00 a.m.

AP: You left before everyone else. No witnesses?

CJ: It's not like that, man. Kiarra and I only had our babysitter until 1:30 a.m. so we had to get back to our son. I told you, I don't gangbang no more.

AP: If you say so. Did you see the kid?

Mr. Reed: We need to take a break so I can talk to my client.

AP: Fine. This is Detective Paulson. We're going to take a break. The interview will continue shortly.

[END OF TAPE]

AP: This is Detective Paulson. We're back on the record with Clifford Jackson and his attorney, Mr. Reed. It's currently 11:45 a.m. Now, Jackson, answer the question: did you see the kid when you and your girl came out of the concert?

CJ: Yes.

AP: Where was he in relation to you?

CJ: Across the street.

AP: How far away?

CJ: I don't know. Just the width of South Central Blvd., I guess.

AP: Did he see you?

CJ: No, his back was turned to me because he was tagging up a bus stop.

AP: Ah. So you caught this punk kid tagging. Did you go over and show him what was up?

CJ: No, I didn't.

AP: No?

CJ: I went over to talk to him.

AP: Go on.

CJ: I wanted to tell him that tagging and all these other gang activities just lead to trouble. Like I said before, I'm an interventionist now. I had to spend my youth in and out of jail and I had to miss my son's birth before I finally realized the gang life leads you nowhere. I was just trying to help him get on the right track.

Mr. Reed: It's true, Detective. Rev. Greg Boyd of Turnaround Ministries can verify that my client has been working as a gang interventionist for about a year. Mr. Jackson is reformed and now he devotes his time to helping kids transition out of gangs.

AP: Does your work as a gang interventionist involve stabbing fifteen-year-old kids in alleys and leaving them there to die?

CJ: Forget it; this is pointless. You don't believe a damn word I say.

AP: Honestly, Jackson, I'd like to believe you. But it simply isn't adding up. Something's missing here, and I need you to fill me in. That's why we're here. Now tell me, why did you think it was a good idea to confront a kid from LDL of all gangs in the middle of the night while nobody else was around? Do they teach you that in Turnaround Ministries?

CJ: First of all, I didn't confront him. I told you I just wanted to talk to him. Second, Kiarra was there. And you're right, the reason I wanted to talk to him then and there was because nobody was around. He wasn't with one of the older homies, who are bad influences on these kids. I figured he'd be more willing to talk to me if he was at ease and he didn't feel like he had to be a tough guy in front of one of the older LDL members.

AP: So you just strolled on over to him and tapped him on the shoulder then?

CJ: Come on man, do you really think I'd pick a fight in front of my girlfriend?

AP: You're the infamous Trigger of CBK. You're not exactly known for being calm. Just admit it. You were pissed. You wanted to show him what's what. This guy was disrespecting your gang's territory. That had to strike a nerve with you.

CJ: Hell yeah I was pissed! I was pissed because this kid is becoming another statistic. First, he's tagging up a bus stop. Next he'll be selling drugs then doing robberies, and eventually, shootings. I thought I could help him and I had him alone, which is rare, so I took the opportunity.

AP: So what'd you say to him?

CJ: I just said, "Take it from me, man. This is a waste of your time." I said I was tired of seeing kids around the 2100 block and that he should go before he gets seen by CBK. It's dangerous and he should know what they're capable of. That's all.

AP: I know LDL rookies. They need to prove they're tough. I'm guessing he didn't take to that too kindly.

CJ: He was hostile at first. But I looked him in the eye and I knew that I could get through to this kid. He was cussing me out and he even threatened to call some of his homies over. I saw right through his tough guy act. I knocked the paint out of his hand and told him to stop it. I told him that this wasn't who he was and that he could find better uses for his time.

AP: Did he know who you were?

CJ: I told him I was an interventionist. After spending years gangbanging and even reaching shot caller status, I turned my life around. I even showed him my tattoo so he could see it's never too late to change. These kids think that once they're in, they're in for life.

AP: So you come up to this kid when he's alone, you knock the spray paint out of his hand, you show him your tattoo and you tell him to get out of there? I don't know Jackson. You're telling me you don't gangbang anymore but that sounds an awful lot like gangbanging to me.

CJ: I'm telling you, man! That's how it went down.

AP: So what did he do next?

CJ: He put his hand in his pocket and I expected him to pull out a gun. The mother of my child was across the street and in harm's way, so I told him we should move this conversation to the alley. Plus, it'd be safer to talk in the alley because we wouldn't have to worry about CBK or LDL members driving by and seeing us.

AP: So what happened in the alley?

CJ: I walked in first because I wanted to show him I wasn't looking for a fight. If I walked in behind him he wouldn't trust me. That's how it is in the streets. Anyone that walks behind you is looking to stab you in the back. But that backfired because the minute we disappeared into the alley, he ran toward me with his knife.

AP: Did he stab you?

CJ: I dodged. I ducked. I tried to get the knife out of his hands. He stabbed me in the arm. Finally, I managed to wrestle the knife away from him but the whole time I was struggling with him, I felt another bulge in his pocket. I thought it was a gun or another knife or something. He kept coming at me even though I kept pushing him off me, so I didn't have a choice. I gave him a few quick jabs, just enough to get him to back up so I could run away. My only intention was to get back to Kiarra so we could get the hell out of there.

AP: Where did you go after?

CJ: Straight home. I wanted to get back to my son.

AP: Why didn't you call the cops?

CJ: Come on, Paulson. You know you wouldn't believe me worth a damn. Besides, why should I call the cops if I was the one who got attacked? He stabbed me first, man!

AP: You've got a nasty cut there on your arm. Why didn't you go to the ER?

CJ: Kiarra and I don't have health insurance. We can't afford it.

AP: Yeah and the fact that they can tell whether wounds were acquired offensively or defensively had nothing to do with that decision, I'm sure.

Mr. Reed: Watch it, Detective. I won't warn you again.

AP: Give me a second. I want to show you something. This is Antonio Villalobos's medical report. It tells an entirely different story than the one you just told me. This kid lost four pints of blood and has six very deep stab wounds. Six! He's got one in the stomach, one in the chest and he even has one in his back. And you know what the real clincher is? The ER physician says these were inflicted in such a way that there's no way someone defending himself "with a few quick jabs" would be able to cause the severe injuries suffered by the patient. What do you have to say about that?

CJ: Man, this is ridiculous. This is all because kids these days have no respect. If he just listened to what I had to say, we wouldn't be in this mess and I wouldn't have had to do what I did to—

Mr. Reed: That's enough! I'm cutting this off. This is attorney Fletcher Reed and this interview is officially over.

[END OF TAPE]

Statement of Kiarra Washington

My name is Kiarra Washington. I'm twenty-five years old, and I have been with Clifford Jackson for nine years. He's had a rough past and he's done some bad things, but he's a changed man now. We have a ten-month-old baby boy together, Clifford Jr. Ever since Clifford Jr. was born, Cliff quit gangbanging, and now he's trying to help other kids around the hood do the same. Cliff has changed the lives of so many kids by working for Turnaround Ministries.

I was with Cliff on June 25, CY-1. We had gone to a concert together that night. It was late, around 1:00 in the morning. We were walking to our car parked on the 2100 block of South Central when we saw a kid across the street tagging up a bus stop. He was wearing red and black, the LDL colors. I couldn't really see what he was writing on the bus stop, but I'm almost positive he was one of them. Cliff said, "Wait here," and walked toward the kid. I begged Cliff not to go because I knew there could be trouble, but he didn't listen.

Cliff walked over to the kid and yelled at him to stop. The kid just flipped him off and kept tagging. I couldn't hear what he and Cliff were saying to one another, but I could tell things were about to get ugly because Cliff knocked the spray paint out of the kid's hand. I saw the kid put his hand inside his front pants pocket. At that point, I was terrified because he had a bulge like there was some long object in his pocket; I thought it was a gun. Cliff did not have a weapon. Cliff looked around and motioned to me to stay where I was. He and the kid walked into an alley together. I don't know what happened in there; all I know is that I was afraid for Cliff's life.

After what seemed like hours, Cliff finally came out of the alley. His hands were bloody and he had tears in his shirt and jacket. Cliff's arm was badly cut and bleeding a lot. He grabbed my hand and we ran towards the car. I don't know if the kid came out of the alley. I didn't look back. We got in the car and we drove straight home. Cliff was really shaken up about the fight. He said the kid knifed him. He had quite a few cuts and his arm looked bad, but he didn't want to go to the emergency room because we don't have health insurance. I felt so bad for Cliff. I didn't think we needed to call the cops or anything since Cliff was the one that got attacked. I grew up in inner city San Andreas; I know the cops don't do anything for us besides create more trouble. Besides, that gang officer has it out for Cliff, always trying to pin some crime on him so he can send Cliff back to prison. Cliff just wanted to sleep it off, so we went to bed after I cleaned and bandaged his arm.

The next morning the cops showed up. It was about 7:00 a.m. when I heard someone practically banging down our door. I got up and went to answer the door. Cliff was still asleep. It seems like the minute I unlocked the door they pushed it open and barged their way into our apartment. I was told to lie on the floor with my hands over my head while I was still barely dressed in my nightgown and bathrobe. One of the officers stood guard over me with a gun while the others went to get Cliff. They wouldn't even let me go get my crying baby. They dragged Cliff out of the bedroom handcuffed while he was only wearing boxers, saying he was under arrest for attempted murder. Unbelievable! Cliff was attacked by some LDL and now he was the one taking the rap? Cliff demanded to see their warrant but the officer got up in his face and said they didn't need a warrant to search a parolee. They searched our apartment for what seemed like forever, throwing our stuff on the ground recklessly. They knocked over and broke a framed photograph of our baby. They said they were looking for a knife, but the only knives we have are kitchen knives. The cops finally let Cliff put some clothes on, and they took him away.

My family is devastated by this case. Our son keeps asking for his daddy and it breaks my heart to tell him that his daddy will be gone for a while. This will be Cliff's third strike and the cops know it. They want to convict him of one more felony so that he will go to prison for life. Cliff is innocent; he only defended himself! The LDL kid knifed him!

I swear under penalty of perjury that the foregoing is true and accurate.

Signed,

Kiarra Washington

Kiarra Washington

Statement of Greg Boyd

My name is Reverend Greg Boyd. I am sixty years old, and I am the founder of Turnaround Ministries. I am a thirty-six-year resident of San Andreas and I have seen firsthand the gang turmoil that plagues the inner city. My calling in life is to do the Lord's work, and that's what led me to establish Turnaround in 1995. Turnaround works in two ways. First, we rehabilitate older gang members who have been in gangs for years. We get them substance abuse counseling, job training and even tattoo removal to help them reenter society as productive members of the workforce. Second, we train and employ these former gang members as "gang interventionists." Our gang interventionists serve as mentors and counselors to help kids who are gang members transition out of gangs. Our gang interventionists use their previous gang authority to persuade the younger kids to avoid making their mistakes. The kids listen to former gang members. Since its inception, Turnaround has helped over 500 gang members leave a life of crime behind.

I met Cliff Jackson in CY-1. He had just been released from prison and came to me looking for a job as a gang interventionist. He told me he had to miss his son's birth because of his incarceration and that was what it took for him to change. Plus, his girlfriend, Kiarra was begging him to quit the gang. I knew of Cliff before he ever came into my office because of his reputation on the streets as one of the most dangerous gang members of inner city San Andreas. It only took a couple of minutes of conversation with Cliff to realize how charismatic and magnetic he was. It was clear that had Cliff channeled his talents into work or school, he would have had a completely different life. In spite of his rough history, I knew Turnaround could cultivate his talents and use them for good. The fact that his girlfriend wanted him to stop the gang-life helped too. I hired him on the spot. Cliff was a hit with the kids. Turnaround had never seen passion and dedication like his. He was like a big brother to those kids and they admired him. Cliff even drove across the county at three in the morning to pick up an abused youth who had run away from home. It was easy giving him the mentor of the year award (See attached Exhibit H).

Cliff only worked with CBKs. I have a no-rival-gang policy at Turnaround that forbids gang interventionists from reaching out to the young members of their former rival gangs. The temptation is just too strong. There was, however, a tragedy about a month ago. Treyvon Jones, a sixteen-year-old CBK that Cliff had developed a close bond with, was killed in a drive-by shooting committed by a couple of LDLs. The loss was devastating to everyone at Turnaround, but especially Cliff. Cliff once told me he regarded himself as a father figure in Treyvon's life. After Treyvon passed, Cliff became very persistent about reaching out to LDL youth. Cliff felt that the murder of Treyvon was the last straw, and he wanted to put an end to the violence between CBK and LDL. I told him I'd consider it because I know that Cliff was extraordinarily gifted when it came to working with kids.

Aside from his duties as an interventionist, he always showed up on time to his substance abuse support groups and actively participated in discussions. All his drug tests were negative. He enrolled in auto repair classes and expressed a desire to open up his own auto body shop. Before he was wrongfully accused of this crime, Cliff had even applied for our tattoo removal services to get rid of his K4L tattoo.

We miss Cliff at Turnaround Ministries. I am absolutely 100% confident that Cliff has left that part of his life in the past and that he's reformed. Being an interventionist isn't an easy job and kids aren't always willing to listen to my interventionists' advice; oftentimes they can be hostile. I stand by Clifford Jackson and I'm willing to help the authorities in any way. I know that this was a case of self-defense. Cliff is a changed man. There is no way that he would have attacked a kid. I am sure that Cliff was just trying to talk that kid into quitting the gang life.

I swear under penalty of perjury that the foregoing is true and accurate.
Signed,

Greg Boyd
Reverend Greg Boyd
Founder and President, Turnaround Ministries

Exhibit A

Holy Cross Hospital ✝
EMERGENCY UNIT & TRAUMA CENTER
16251 Compton Dr
San Andreas, OC, 90119

Patient Name: Villalobos, Antonio
Address: 1320 Imperial Ave, San Andreas, OC
Phone Number: (555)555-4444
DOB: 12/22/CY-15 (Age 15)
SSN: 123-45-6789
Height: 5'6''
Weight: 145
Blood Type: B+
Insurance: UNINSURED

Emergency Room Physician's Report

Date: June 25, CY-1
Time: 7:00 a.m.

Summary: Antonio Villalobos ("Patient") was brought into the emergency room by paramedics after being found bleeding and unconscious on the street. The patient is a Hispanic male of average height and small build. Patient was still bleeding on arrival, had a weak pulse, and was pale. I immediately ordered an IV and began to prepare him for surgery. The patient had lost approximately four pints of blood and his blood pressure dropped while his heart rate was rapidly increasing, so I ordered a blood transfusion to be performed to resuscitate him.

The patient had several puncture wounds scattered across his upper body, specifically on his abdomen, chest and back. The wounds were about an inch wide and deep enough to cause hemorrhaging of the soft tissue. Two of the stab wounds on the lower abdomen were assymetrical in nature. This was most likely due to the twisting of the puncturing object once it made contact with the patient's flesh. The twisting of the puncturing object not only led to the assymetricality of the wounds but also quickened the patient's profuse bleeding. Given the number, length and depth of these marks, I formed the opinion that these were stab wounds caused by several rapid jabs made at a close distance. Also, upon closer examination, I formed the opinion that the wounds were most likely made by an elongated sharp object approximately eight to ten inches in length and approximately eight centimeters wide. The angle at which they appear on the patient's body does not appear to support self-infliction. The stab wounds appear to have been made by the person inflicting them standing directly in front of the patient and making upward stabbing motions, with the exception of the stab wound on the patient's back. He also had three superficial cuts on his right hand. It appears they were made by being grazed by something sharp, such as the edge of the blade of a knife.

Diagnosis: The patient suffered severe hemmorhaging and soft tissue trauma caused by six stab wounds to his body.

Treatment:
- Blood IV-type B+
- Fluid resuscitation with crystalloid solution
- Blood transfusion-type B+
- Robaxin, tetanus antibiotic

FRONT/BACK

LEFT/RIGHT

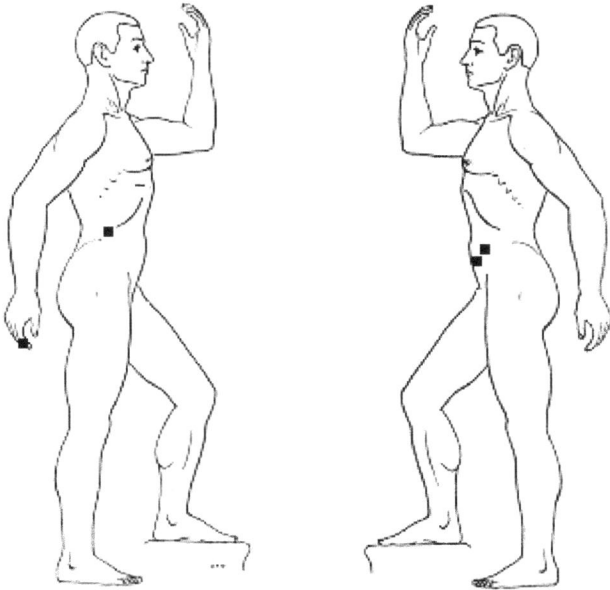

Injury Type: Stab Wounds

Head: 0
Neck/Shoulders:0
Chest: 1
Right Arm: 0
Left Arm: 0
Right Hand: 3 (cuts only)
Left Hand: 0
Upper Back: 0
Lower Back: 1
Abdomen: 1
Right Side: 1
Left Side: 0
Pelvic Region: 2
Right Upper Leg: 0
Right Lower Leg: 0
Right Foot: 0
Left Upper Leg: 0
Left Lower Leg: 0
Left Foot: 0

Total Number: 6

Exhibit B

★ SAPD

SAN ANDREAS POLICE DEPARTMENT
17381 Temple Hill Blvd
San Andreas, OC, 90119

GANG MEMBER

RECORD OF ARRESTS AND PROSECUTIONS

NAME: Jackson, Clifford
SSN: 987-65-4321
DOB: 07/06/CY-28
HEIGHT: 6'0''

WEIGHT: 250 lbs
RACE: B
GANG AFFILIATION: Cold Blooded Killers
MONIKER: Trigger

JUVENILE

Charge: SAMC 104.7 (Vandalism of Public Property)
Date: 04/25/CY-15
Description: Minor was seen tagging gang insignia on a liquor store wall. Was let off with a warning.
Disposition: Warning.

Charge: SAMC 77.6 (Violation of Mandatory Curfew for Minors)
Date: 08/13/CY-14
Description: Minor was out on the street at 12:30 a.m., two and a half hours after mandatory curfew.
Disposition: Released into the custody of the minor's parents.

Charge: SAMC 1648.3 (Truancy)
Date: 12/20/CY-14
Description: Minor was walking the streets at 11:00 in the morning during school hours without a valid doctor's note or signed excuse form from the school.
Disposition: Returned to school and given citation.

Charge: OC112300 (Possession of Less Than One Ounce of Marijuana)
Date: 02/14/CY-13
Description: As part of a routine school search of lockers, minor's locker was searched and he was found to be in possession of two marijuana cigarettes. Arrested and taken to station.
Disposition: One year of probation.

Charge: OC415 (Assault)
Date: 05/02/CY-12
Description: Minor and three other youths were arrested in connection with a group assault on another minor at school. The minor was severely beaten and needed stitches.
Disposition: Six months in the juvenile detention facility.

Charge: OC11230 (Possession of Cocaine Base for Sale)
Date: 03/18/CY-11
Description: The minor was loitering in front of a liquor store on South Central Blvd., which is a notorious area for narcotics trafficking. Apprehended by police and discovered to be in possession of two rocks of cocaine base and several denominations of dollar bills, which is indicative of narcotics selling. Arrested and taken to the station.
Disposition: One year in the juvenile detention facility.

ADULT

Charge: OC225 (Robbery)
Date: 06/29/CY-12
Description: Subject robbed a man who was jogging in Griffin Park at gunpoint. Subject took the man's wallet, mp3 player and watch, totaling $800 in loss.
Disposition: Convicted; sentenced to 2 years in state prison.
NOTE: released after one year, three months due to prison overcrowding

Charge: OC446 (Discharging a Firearm into an Occupied Dwelling/Vehicle)
Date: 11/28/CY-10
Description: Subject was riding in the passenger seat of a vehicle that pulled up next to another vehicle driven by members of a rival gang. The subject fired two shots into the adjacent vehicle. No one was injured.
Disposition: Convicted; sentenced to three years in state prison.
NOTE: released after two years due to prison overcrowding*

Charge: OC422.6 (Criminal Threats); OC664/187 (Attempted Murder)
Date: 04/12/CY-8
Description: Subject was driving a vehicle when one of his gang associates committed a drive-by shooting on two members of a rival gang. The two members of the rival gang were injured but survived.
Disposition: Convicted; sentenced to seven years state prison.
NOTE: released after six years due to early release credits earned for good behavior

Exhibit C

★ SAPD

SAN ANDREAS POLICE DEPARTMENT
Computer Crimes Unit
21250 6th St.
San Andreas, OC, 90119

July 3, CY-1

Re: People v. Clifford Jackson
        Case # SA101811

Detective Paulson,

The contents of defendant Clifford Jackson's cellular telephone, specimen #875660, were deconstructed and subsequently analyzed. The following text messages were recovered from the SIM card found inside the telephone.

Incoming Message
>From: Lil Weezy (555) 555-5555
>>>Received: June 24, CY-1 3:43 p.m.

Hey man how you been? I haven't seen you since the funeral. You going to the concert tomorrow?

Outgoing Message
>To: Lil Weezy (555) 555-5555
>>>Sent: June 24, CY-1 3:50 p.m.

Hey Weezy. I'm doing ok. Still trying to get back into the swing of things. Kiarra and I are going if we get a babysitter. How are you?

Incoming Message
>From: Lil Weezy (555) 555-5555
>>>Received: June 24, CY-1 3:55 p.m.

Yeah it's crazy. Treyvon was so young. I'm sorry man. I knew he was like your little brother. Damn LDLs shooting up our turf.

Outgoing Message

>To: Lil Weezy (555) 555-5555
>>>Sent: June 24, CY-1 4:14 p.m.

He's in a better place now. Those damn LDLs cut his life short just as I was getting through to him. You know he had a chance to get a basketball scholarship?

Incoming Message
>From: Lil Weezy (555) 555-5555
>>>Received: June 24, CY-1 3:55 p.m.

Damn that sucks. RIP Trey. They'll get theirs in the end. I know they will. Damn LDLs.

Outgoing Message
>To: Lil Weezy (555) 555-5555
>>>Sent: June 24, CY-1 4:14 p.m.

Oh I know they will. You best believe it. I'll keep fighting the good fight until they learn some respect. See you at the concert tonight.

>>END OF RECOVERED MESSAGES<<

Sincerely,

Danica Pryor

Danica Pryor
Forensic Analyst
Serial #10187

Exhibit D

★ SAPD

SAN ANDREAS POLICE DEPARTMENT
17381 Temple Hill Blvd
San Andreas, OC, 90119

GANG MEMBER

RECORD OF ARRESTS AND PROSECUTIONS

NAME: Villalobos, Antonio
SSN: 123-45-6789
DOB: 12/22/CY-15
WEIGHT: 145 lbs
HEIGHT: 5'6''

RACE: H
GANG AFFILIATION: Los Diablos Locos
MONIKER: N/A

JUVENILE

Charge: OC415 (Assault)
Date: 04/11/CY-2
Description: Minor was arrested in connection with an assault on another minor at school. The minor was severely beaten.
Disposition: Six months in the juvenile detention facility

Exhibit E

Exhibit F

Exhibit G

Exhibit H

Turnaround Ministries

This is to Certify that

Clifford Jackson

Has Earned This Service Award for

Mentor of the Year.

Signed,

G Boyd

Reverend Gregory Boyd
Founder and President, Turnaround Ministries

April 1, C.Y.-1

Exhibit I

Jury Instructions

Members of the jury, I thank you for your attentiveness during this trial. Please pay close attention to the instructions I am about to give you.

In this case, Defendant Clifford Jackson is charged with attempted murder in the first degree. A person who unlawfully attempts to murder another person with malice aforethought is guilty of the crime of attempted murder in violation of Oceana Penal Code section 664(a)/187. To prove the crime of attempted murder, the State must prove the following elements beyond a reasonable doubt:

1. A direct, but ineffective, act was done to kill the person; and

2. The attempted killing was unlawful; and

3. The attempted killing was done with malice aforethought.

Unlawful means that a killing is neither justifiable nor excusable.

Malice may be either express or implied. Malice is express when there is a manifested intent to unlawfully kill a person. Malice is implied when:

1. The attempted killing is the result of an intentional act; and

2. The natural consequences of the act are dangerous to human life; and

3. The act was deliberately performed with knowledge of the danger to, and with conscious disregard for, human life.

In deciding whether or not such an act was done, it is necessary to differentiate between mere preparation for the act and the actual commencement of doing the act itself. Mere preparation is not enough to constitute an attempt. To be an attempt, the act must be an immediate step in the execution of the criminal act, the progress of which was interrupted by some unforeseen circumstances not present in the original plan.

When it is shown that an attempted killing resulted from the intentional doing of an act with express or implied malice, no other mental state need be shown to establish the mental state of malice aforethought. The mental state constituting malice aforethought does not necessarily require any ill will or hatred of the person killed. The word *aforethought* does not imply deliberation or the lapse of substantial time. Rather, it only means the required mental state must precede rather than follow the act.

Clifford Jackson has entered a plea of not guilty. This means that you must presume or believe that Clifford Jackson is not guilty unless and until the evidence convinces you otherwise. This presumption stays with Clifford Jackson as to each material allegation in the indictment through each stage of the trial until it has been overcome by the evidence to the exclusion of and beyond a reasonable doubt.

To overcome the Defendant's presumption of innocence, it is the State's burden to prove the following:

1. The crime with which Defendant is charged was committed.

2. Defendant is the person who committed the crime.

The State has the burden to prove the elements beyond a reasonable doubt. Whenever the words *reasonable doubt* are used, you must consider the following: A reasonable doubt is not a mere possible doubt, because everything relating to human affairs is open to some possible or imaginary doubt. Reasonable doubt is the state of the case that, after hearing and considering all the evidence, leaves the minds of the jurors in the condition that they cannot say they feel an abiding conviction of the truth of the charge.

It is to the evidence introduced during this trial, and to it alone, that you are to look for that proof. A reasonable doubt as to the guilt of the Defendant may arise from evidence, a conflict in the evidence, or a lack of evidence. If you have a reasonable doubt, you should find Defendant not guilty. If you have no reasonable doubt, you should find Defendant guilty.

You must decide this case on the evidence and the law. It is up to you to decide what evidence is reliable. You should use your common sense in deciding what evidence is reliable and what evidence should not be relied upon in considering your verdict.

A witness is a person who has knowledge related to this case. You will have to decide whether you believe each witness and how important each witness's testimony is to the case. You may believe all, part, or none of a witness's testimony. In deciding whether to believe a witness's testimony, you may

consider, among other factors, the following:

1. The extent of the witness's opportunity to see, hear, or otherwise become familiar with any

    matter about which the witness testified.

2. The ability of the witness to accurately recall or communicate any matter about which the

    witness testified and the character and quality of that testimony.

3. The witness's manner and demeanor while on the stand.

4. Whether or not the witness has bias, an improper motive, or an interest in the outcome of the

    case.

5. The witness's attitude toward this trial or toward testifying.

6. Whether the witness's testimony was consistent or inconsistent with other testimony or

    evidence presented in this case.

7. Any previous statements made by the witness that are consistent or inconsistent with the

    witness's testimony.

8. The witness's character for honesty or veracity, or their opposites.

9. Whether the witness was offered money, preferred treatment, or any other benefit to testify or

    whether the witness received any threats or was under any pressure that might have affected

    the truth of the witness's testimony.

10. The witness's previous conviction of a felony or past criminal conduct amounting to a

    misdemeanor.

You may rely upon your own conclusions about each witness. A juror may believe or disbelieve

all or any part of the evidence or the testimony of any witness.

There are some general rules that apply to your deliberations. You must abide by these rules in

order to return a verdict that is consistent with the law:

1. You must follow the law as it is explained to you in these instructions. If you fail to follow

    the law or disregard the law, any verdict you reach will be a miscarriage of justice.

2. You must decide the case only upon the evidence that you have heard from either the testimony of witnesses or exhibits that you have seen.

3. You must not decide the case for or against anyone because you feel sympathy for that person, or because you are angry with that person.

4. You must not decide the case based on your feelings about the lawyers in this case. The lawyers are not on trial.

5. You must not consider any potential sentence Defendant might receive. It is not your duty to consider punishment. Your only duty is to determine guilt or innocence. It is the judge's job to determine the proper sentence if you find Defendant guilty.

6. Whatever verdict you render must be unanimous; that is, each juror must commit to the same verdict. The verdict must be the verdict of each juror as well as that of the jury as a whole.

7. It is entirely proper for a lawyer to talk to a witness about what testimony the witness would give if called into the courtroom. The witness should not be discredited for talking to a lawyer about his or her testimony.

8. You must not decide this case based on feelings of prejudice, bias, or sympathy. Any verdict you may reach should be based on the evidence and the law contained in these instructions.

Deciding a proper verdict is exclusively your job. I cannot participate in that decision in any way. Please disregard anything I might have said or done that made you think I preferred one verdict over another.

Only one verdict may be returned for the crime charged. The verdict must be in writing and the verdict form has been prepared for you. It is as follows:

(READ JURY VERDICT FORM)

If you find that Clifford Jackson committed the crime of attempted murder alleged in count 1, you must then decide whether the Prosecution has proved the second allegation of whether the crime was done for the furtherance of a criminal street gang. To prove this allegation, the Prosecution must show that:

1. Clifford Jackson is a member of a criminal street gang AND

2. Clifford Jackson attempted to murder Antonio Villalobos for the furtherance of a criminal street gang.

A criminal street gang is any association of four or more individuals, formal or informal, the purpose of which is to promote criminal activity, supported by a pattern of criminal activity by the members, either acting alone or in concert. *Criminal activity* is defined as any of the acts that are considered crimes under the Oceana Penal code.

In just a few moments, the Bailiff will escort you to the jury room. Once inside the jury room, the first thing you should do is elect a foreperson, who will preside over your deliberations. It is the foreperson's job to sign and date the verdict form when all of you have agreed on a verdict in this case and to bring the verdict back to the courtroom when you return.

In conclusion, let me remind you that it is imperative that you follow the law as I have explained it to you in these instructions. Regardless of how you feel about the laws, you must apply them.

SUPERIOR COURT OF THE STATE OF OCEANA

FOR THE COUNTY OF SAN ANDREAS

STATE OF OCEANA,	Case No. SA101811
Plaintiff,	
v.	**CHARGE(S):**
	664(a)/187
CLIFFORD JACKSON,	Attempted murder in the first degree
Defendant.	1 count
	186.22(a)
	Criminal street gang enhancement
	1 count

VERDICT

As to the charge of attempted murder in the first degree, in violation of Oceana Penal Code section 664(a)/187, we, the jury, find the Defendant, Clifford Jackson:

____   GUILTY

____   NOT GUILTY

As to the enhancement of sentence for criminal activity done in furtherance of a criminal street gang, pursuant to Oceana Penal Code section 186.22(a), we, the jury, find the Defendant, Clifford Jackson:

____   GUILTY

____   NOT GUILTY

So say we all.

_____

Foreperson of the Jury

_____

Date

STATE OF OCEANA

V.

JAIME RAMIREZ

(Robbery and Residential Burglary)

SUPERIOR COURT OF THE STATE OF OCEANA

COUNTY OF MALIWOOD

STATE OF OCEANA,		Case No. MW122408
	Plaintiff,	
v.		**FELONY COMPLAINT**
JAIME RAMIREZ,		
	Defendant.	

COUNT 1

On or about July 1, CY-1, in the City of Maliwood, State of Oceana, a felony, in violation of section 211 of the Oceana Penal Code, commonly referred to as first degree ROBBERY was committed by the above defendant, who at the time and place last aforesaid, did willfully take the property of Kelly Sims by threat of force.

COUNT 2

On or about July 1, CY-1, in the City of Maliwood, State of Oceana, a felony, in violation of section 459 of the Oceana Penal Code, commonly referred to as first degree RESIDENTIAL BURGLARY, was committed by the above defendant, who at the time and place last aforesaid, entered the home of Kelly Sims with the intent to commit a felony therein.

IT IS SO ORDERED.

Simon Luna

Simon Luna
District Attorney, County of Maliwood

Witness List

Witnesses for the State:

1.   Taylor Green***

2.   Kelly Sims**

Witnesses for the Defense:

1.   Jaime Ramirez*

2.   Randy Granger***

Each side must call both witnesses listed for their respective party, and both parties stipulate that each party's expert witness would testify consistently with his or her provided statement.

*This witness must be played by a male.

**This witness must be played by a female.

***This witness can be played by either gender.

Stipulations

1. Both the Federal Rules of Criminal Procedure and Federal Rules of Evidence apply.

2. Assume each witness who gave an interview reviewed the officer's report of his or her interview and signed the interview to verify for accuracy.

3. All exhibits included in the file are authentic and, unless otherwise stated, are the original of that document.

4. Other than what appears in the officer's report of the interviews, there is nothing exceptional or unusual about the background of any of the witnesses that would bolster or detract from their credibility.

5. All dates are denoted by CY (current year) or CY-*n* (current year minus *n* years).

6. All pretrial motions shall be oral.

7. No party may invent witnesses or evidence that is not specifically mentioned in this case file.

8. "Beyond the record" is not a proper objection. Rather, the attorneys shall use cross-examination as the means of challenging a witness whose testimony strays beyond the facts contained in the case file.

9. The physical description of a witness, e.g., clothing, should be tailored to that of the student playing the witness, except for height, weight and age.

10. All witness statements were given under oath.

11. All witnesses called to testify who have identified Defendant Ramirez or any tangible evidence can, if asked, identify the same at trial.

12. The expert witnesses' reports are stipulated to as being an accurate reflection of what each expert would testify to if called as a witness. Either side may constructively read into the record the expert witnesses' testimony in whole or in part or move the testimony into the record. Any such testimony by the stipulated experts is subject to objections pursuant to the Federal Rules of Evidence.

13. The prosecution and defense may only call the two witnesses listed on their respective witness list.

14. Oceana Penal Code section 211 states that a person who takes the property of another person by force or threat of force is guilty of the crime of robbery.

15. Oceana Penal Code section 459 states that a person who enters a residence with the intent to commit a felony therein is guilty of the crime of residential burglary.

16. The parties stipulate to the admittance of Detective Alice White's statement and the statement given by Investigator Paul Burns. These exhibits can be used by either side. The parties have waived hearsay objections for only these exhibits.

17. The witness Jaime Ramirez must be male. The witness Kelly Sims must be female. The remaining witnesses may be either gender. The witnesses may be called in any order.

COUNTY OF MALIWOOD SHERIFF'S DEPARTMENT
INVESTIGATION REPORT

RECORDS & STATISTICS BUREAU'S USE ONLY					DATE: 7/1/CY-1	PAGE: 1 OF 4

ACTION	ACTIVE (X) INACTIVE ( ) PENDING ( )	INDEX Yes (X) INFO No ( )	N of Adult Arrests 1	No of Subject Detentions 1	URN (File No.) MW122408	

CLASSIFICATION
ROBBERY/RESIDENTIAL BURGLARY INVESTIGATION

DATE, TIME OF OCCURRENCE
7/1/CY-1, 15:07 HOURS

LOCATION OF OCCURRENCE 5962 SANDSTONE PL., MALIWOOD, OC	TYPE OF LOCATION PRIVATE BEACH	TRACT

CODE: V - VICTIM, W - WITNESS, I - INFORMANT, R - REPORTING PARTY, P - PARTY

CODE V NO. 1 OF 1	LAST NAME SIMS, KELLY	FIRST	MIDDLE	SEX F	AGE 55	RACE WHITE
RESIDENCE ADDRESS 5962 SANDSTONE PL., MALIWOOD, OC				RES. PHONE (AREA CODE) (555) 555-3976		
BUSINESS ADDRESS MALI FINE ARTS, 24255 PALMERO ST, MALIWOOD, OC				RES. PHONE (AREA CODE) (555) 555-3976		

CODE NO. OF	LAST NAME	FIRST	MIDDLE	SEX	AGE	RACE
RESIDENCE ADDRESS				RES. PHONE (AREA CODE)		
BUSINESS ADDRESS				RES. PHONE (AREA CODE)		

CODE: S - SUSPECT, SJ - SUBJECT, M - PATIENT, S / V - SUSPECT/VICTIM, SJ / V - SUBJECT / VICTIM

CODE S No 1 OF 1	LAST NAME RAMIREZ, JAIME	FIRST	MIDDLE	DRIVER'S LICENSE (STATE & No) OC 7251987
RESIDENCE ADDRESS 415 HIGHLAND ST, EASTLAKE VILLAGE, OC				RES. PHONE (AREA CODE)
BUSINESS ADDRESS				BUS. PHONE (AREA CODE)

SEX M	RACE HISPANIC	HAIR BROWN	EYES BROWN	HEIGHT 5'9''	WEIGHT 225 LBS	DOB 02/26/CY-25	AGE 25	WHERE DETAINED MALIWOOD CANYON
OBSERVABLE PHYSICAL ODDITIES/TATTOOS/SCARS N/A						AKA / NICKNAME N/A		BOOKING No. MW329110
CLOTHING WORN BLUE JEANS, WHITE T-SHIRT, BROWN SHOES								MAIN
CHARGE ROBBERY, RESIDENTIAL BURGLARY								WEAPON USED KNIFE, BASIN WRENCH

CODE No OF	LAST NAME	FIRST	MIDDLE	DRIVER'S LICENSE (STATE & No)
RESIDENCE ADDRESS				RES. PHONE (AREA CODE)
BUSINESS ADDRESS				BUS. PHONE (AREA CODE)

SEX	RACE	HAIR	EYES	HEIGHT	WEIGHT	D.O.B.	AGE	WHERE DETAINED OR CITE No.
OBSERVABLE PHYSICAL ODDITIES						AKA / NICKNAME		BOOKING No.
CLOTHING WORN								MAIN
CHARGE								WEAPON USED

VEHICLE USED IN CRIME YES (X) NO ( ) UNKNOWN ( ) STORED ( ) IMPOUNDED (X)	YR 2002	MAKE TOYOTA	BODY TYPE TACOMA	COLOR BLACK	BY DEPUTY ROBINSON	BADGE No. 78391
LICENSE (STATE & No.) OC 552SRA5	V.I.N./ FRAME No.				BY DEPUTY GREEN	BADGE No. 31229
REGISTERED OWNER JAIME RAMIREZ			STATION MWD	UNIT / CAR No. 1302	SHIFT DAY	
IDENTIFYING CHARACTERISTICS			APPROVED	BADGE No.	TIME	
O.H.P. 180 SUBMITTED YES ( ) NO ( )	GARAGE NAME & PHONE		ASSIGNMENT			

Narrative Report – URN MW122408

On July 1, CY-1, at 15:12 hours, my partner, Deputy Robinson, and I were patrolling the Maliwood University area when we got a call from dispatch alerting officers of a home invasion robbery that had just occurred on Sandstone Place. The robber, described as a Hispanic male, had reportedly fled in a black Toyota Tacoma pickup truck and was armed with a knife. He was seen fleeing northbound from Sandstone Place towards Maliwood Canyon Road.

My partner and I were within two minutes of Maliwood Canyon Road and immediately proceeded to that location. Approximately five minutes after we entered the canyon, I observed a black Toyota Tacoma ahead of our position travelling approximately 65 miles per hour in a 45 miles per hour zone. I maneuvered my vehicle to a position behind the suspect vehicle and activated my overhead lights, solid forward-facing red light, and siren. I had to exercise caution as I maneuvered my car past the vehicles between me and the pickup truck because Maliwood Canyon is a dangerous, curvy road. I got on my loudspeaker and instructed the truck to pull over immediately and the driver complied.

My partner and I exited the vehicle with our guns drawn but at our sides. I approached the suspect's window as my partner approached the passenger side. The suspect, a young Hispanic male, was alone. He appeared agitated, drumming his fingers on the steering wheel. I noticed his forehead was sweaty.

Before I had the chance to identify myself or tell him why I pulled him over, the suspect stated: "I didn't do anything! Why are you pulling me over? I just went for a walk on the beach. That's all man!" I commanded him to put his hands on the steering wheel and keep his hands where I could see them at all times and not to reach for anything or make any sudden movements. During this time, the suspect kept asking why he was stopped. Backup deputies arrived within two minutes. The suspect was instructed to exit his vehicle and lie face down on the ground with his hands behind his head. My partner then conducted a pat-down search for weapons, which came up negative. My partner placed the suspect in our vehicle.

I then searched the suspect's vehicle. A wallet in the glove compartment revealed the suspect to be 25-year-old Jaime Ramirez of Eastlake Village. Also inside was $700 cash in $100 bills. (See Exhibits J & K). On the front passenger seat was a long metal object with a claw (See Exhibit C). A pair of striped worker's gloves and a knife were located in the truck bed toolbox (See Exhibits H & L). I had one of the backup deputies run a search for warrants on the pickup truck's license plate, which came back negative.

Given the fact that Ramirez was speeding in a vehicle matching the description of the robber's vehicle in the vicinity of the robbery area minutes after the call came in, and also given that Ramirez's demeanor and resemblance matched the description of the robber given by dispatch, as well as the fact that he appeared to have a burglar's tool and a large amount of cash, I formed the opinion that he was the suspect in the Sandstone Place robbery.

I instructed one of the backup officers to go to the victim's residence and bring her to our location to see if she could identify Ramirez as the man who robbed her. In the meantime, I began to read him his rights. Before I could ascertain whether Ramirez wanted to waive his rights, he spontaneously stated: "What the hell is going on? I didn't do anything! You can't arrest me for a speeding ticket!"

I told him he matched the description of the robber, but this only further angered him. He continued to yell: "I haven't done a thing! I don't know what you all are talking about! You're just harassing me because I'm a Hispanic driving in Maliwood!"

At 15:30 hours, my partner arrived with the victim and removed Ramirez from our unit. I instructed the victim to look at the suspect and ascertain if he was the man that robbed her. She appeared very anxious, only glanced briefly at the suspect, and then backed away. I put Ramirez back in my squad car and walked over to the victim to speak to her privately. I asked her if she recognized Ramirez; she replied that she was unsure because the robber had a ski mask on. I urged her to think long and hard about it because the faster we identify a suspect after a crime has been committed, the better the chances of conviction. She said the suspect had a similar height and build and the skin tone seemed to match. Also, she stated that the white t-shirt, blue jeans, and work boots Ramirez was wearing were similar to what the robber had worn. I told her that Detective White would be visiting her shortly for a subsequent investigation.

Before leaving the location, I radioed dispatch to ask if any other black Toyota pickup trucks were seen or stopped by any deputies around the time of the robbery. There were none. I then returned to the location where we first spotted the suspect speeding and passing other cars. I inspected the roadsides and trash bins to see if he had thrown the ski mask out of the window, but I was unable to locate any further evidence.

Attached is the supplemental statement of Detective White as well as photos of the crime scene and recovered evidence.

Contents:

1. Photograph of suspect's vehicle, black 2002 Toyota Tacoma pickup truck (See Exhibit A)

2. Photographs of items recovered in search of suspect's vehicle:

   • 11 inch straight blade knife (See Exhibit L)

   • 19 inch basin wrench (See Exhibit C)

   • Striped worker's gloves (See Exhibit I)

   • Seven (7) $100 bills (recovered from wallet in glove compartment) (See Exhibits J & K)

3. Photographs of boots worn by suspect (See Exhibits G & H)

I certify that the foregoing is accurate under the penalty of perjury.

Signed,

Dep. Taylor Green

Deputy Taylor Green

Statement of Kelly Sims

My name is Kelly Sims. I am fifty-five years old and live in Maliwood with my husband, Steven. I'm a full-time artist. My husband and I own an art gallery, Mali Fine Arts. In all the years I've lived in Maliwood, I have never experienced a break-in before. I've always felt safe in my home and loved living there, until the day I was robbed. I still can't believe that someone invaded my home, in the middle of the day, especially in a quiet, safe town like Maliwood. This used to be a small town where everyone knew each other, and now it seems like there's lots of unwanted riff-raff here.

I was alone at my beach house located on Sandstone Place. My husband, Steven, was out of town on a business trip for the week. It was 3:00 p.m. and I was reading in my study. All of the doors were locked. My back door that opens out to the beach has a small doggie door that I had installed years ago when we still had a dog. It is a very small doggie door, and I never thought anyone could use it to open my door. I heard a jimmying sound coming from the family room. I went to check it out when I heard someone walking around in the family room. This is the room with the doggie door that opens to the beach. As I peered around the corner to look into the room I was face to face with a man in a black ski mask. He completely startled me. I was too frightened to move, seeing that he held a big knife in his hand; I'm pretty sure it was a switchblade. He pointed the knife at me and demanded that I give him all my cash, so out of fear I took him to the safe in my study and gave him $500 in $100 bills. The man looked about 5'11", in comparison to me, as I am 5'5". When he spoke to me, I noticed that he had a slight accent, which sounded Hispanic. As I handed him the cash, I noticed that he was wearing striped worker's gloves and that his arms were brown.

Right after I handed him the money, he put it in his back pocket and then took off running. He left through the family room door and onto the beach. I immediately locked my door and phoned 911. As I was making the call, I saw the robber through my window. He was running away wearing the ski mask and carrying a straw beach bag. I tried to describe him to the dispatcher and tell her which direction he was heading toward. I noticed he had a long metal object or tool in his hand. I don't know what it was because I've never seen that type of device. It appeared to be two feet long and had a round shape on the end of it. I saw him get in an older black Toyota pickup truck that was parked about three houses down from mine. I heard his tires screech as he sped off. He drove north toward the canyon. I wasn't able to make out any license plate number or any other distinguishing characteristics on the truck. I'm sure of the make and model, as my gardener has a similar truck.

I was so shaken after the incident that I went upstairs and locked myself in my bedroom. While I waited for the police to arrive, I called my husband. A deputy came to my house about twenty minutes after I called 911. He said they had caught a suspect a third of the way into the canyon and that I should come see if I recognized him. The deputy drove me to the canyon, where there were several police cars and the shoulder was cordoned off with police tape.

The deputy escorted me over to a police car where another deputy was holding the arm of a Hispanic man in handcuffs. The deputies told me to get a good look at him but I was so frightened that I couldn't stand to look at him very long, so I looked at him for a little bit then walked away. The deputy holding onto the man's arm put him back inside the police car then walked over to me and told me that I shouldn't be afraid to say if this was the guy who did it. The deputy then said that the faster a suspect is identified, the faster he can get convicted and I wouldn't have to worry about another criminal on the streets. I told the deputy his height, build, and coloring looked like the man who broke into my house, but I could not ID his face because the man who robbed me had a ski mask on.

A couple hours later, Detective White came to my house with some evidence in bags. She brought a long metal object with a gripping claw at the end, some other types of wrenches, a knife, a pair of boots, and some gloves. She asked me if I recognized any of the items. I told her the long metal object with the claw looked like the object that the robber had in his hand when he got in his truck, but I couldn't be sure. I then walked her over to the area where I saw the robber and I showed her the door I think he came through. Detective White put on gloves, and took the long object out of the evidence bag and went outside. She told me to close and lock the door. Then she attempted to open the door by putting the object through the doggie door and tried using the claw to grip the doorknob. It took her several minutes but she got the door to open. She then asked me to show her around outside, but I told her I was very tired after the incident and I just wanted to go upstairs and rest. Detective White said I could go and rest. She informed me that she was going to search the perimeter of my house for footprints or boot prints. She stated that I should lock my doors and that after she conducted her search of the exterior area of my home, she would be on her way. She advised me to get a cover for the doggie door to help prevent future break-ins. She also provided me with her business card in case I had any questions or problems, or in case I remembered any other details about the robbery.

I hope the deputies arrested the right guy. I've never had such a traumatic experience in my life. I've been too frightened to stay in my home alone ever since the robbery. I have trouble falling asleep; I'm so afraid of someone breaking in again.

I swear under penalty of perjury that the foregoing is true and accurate.

Signed,

Kelly Sims

Kelly Sims

Statement of Alice White

My name is Alice White, and I have been a detective with the Maliwood Police Department for the last seventeen years.

On July 1, CY-1, I went to 5926 Sandstone Place, the home of Kelly Sims at 17:15 hours to investigate whether Sims's conclusion that someone broke into her home via her doggie door was plausible. I took several different kinds of tools with me including: a basin wrench (recovered from Jaime Ramirez's truck) (see Exhibit C), a crescent wrench, lead pipe, a strap wrench, and a pipe wrench. I wanted to make sure that she was able to identify the tool that we recovered from the truck of Jaime Ramirez. Sims identified the basin wrench as looking similar to the object she saw the suspect holding when he ran out of her home. I also took the boots Ramirez was wearing to see if I could use them to compare any boot prints I might find in the sand.

Sims's back door had a fairly small doggie door measuring one foot by one foot at the base of the door. The door itself is seven feet high. The doorknob is about three feet from the bottom of the door and the top of the doggie door is about eighteen inches below that (See Exhibit B).

With the help of Sims, we closed and locked the door. From the outside, I used the basin wrench recovered from Ramirez's truck to see if I could open the door by sticking my arm and the wrench through the doggie door and around the doorknob.

I was able to open the locked door on the third try. I kneeled from the outside and stuck my whole arm through the doggie door with the wrench and approximated where the inside knob would be by looking at the knob on the outside. That was easy to do. The hardest part was getting the claw around the doorknob; however, as long as the claw was raised slightly above the knob and then pulled down, it closed around the knob. While the basin wrench slipped off the knob on my first and second attempts, it did not on the third attempt. Once the claw was around the knob, it was fairly easy to open. In fact, we timed the whole process. It took me three minutes and forty-eight seconds to open the door. Given my height, 5'7'', it is likely that Jaime Ramirez would not have experienced any physical impediments to opening the door by inserting a basin wrench through the doggie door. It should also be noted that I am unfamiliar with using a basin wrench, so it is safe to assume that the process would be easier for someone who regularly uses this type of tool.

Next, I asked Sims to show me around outside, as I wanted to search for any other evidence, such as boot prints that the perpetrator might have left behind. Sims said that she was exhausted from her ordeal, and that if I did not have any more questions of her, she wanted to go and take a nap. I gave her my business card and some safety tips to help her prevent a future robbery, and then I went outside to investigate on my own. I was looking for footprints or boot prints in particular. Since the Sims residence is a beach house and is surrounded by sand, it was the ideal location to observe footprint or boot print evidence. I found two trails of boot prints right outside the house. Based on the direction of the prints, it was clear that one set led up to the house and one led away from the house. The prints started and ended at the doggie door. The boot brand *ecco* was clearly delineated in the sand. I took photos of the boot prints (See Exhibits E & F). It appears that someone wearing *ecco* boots walked up to the doggie door of the house and then ran away from the same door. I base this conclusion on the clear imprint in the sand of the *ecco* brand, and on the fact that the set of prints leading up to the house was not as deep as the one set that led away from the house. Running in sand leaves a deeper print impression. It is my conclusion that the person who broke into the house was thus most likely wearing a pair of *ecco* boots (See Exhibits G & H). It should be noted that when the defendant was arrested he was wearing *ecco* brand boots.

I certify that the foregoing is accurate under the penalty of perjury.

Signed,

Alice White

Deputy Alice White

Interrogation of Jaime Ramirez

Deputy Taylor Green (TG): Alright, we're on the record in case number MW122408. This is Deputy Taylor Green, the date is July 1, CY-1 at 16:00 hours and I have the suspect in custody at Maliwood County Sheriff's Department. State your name and age for the record.

Jaime Ramirez (JR): My name is Jaime Ramirez, and I am 25 years old. I'm innocent. I haven't done nothing wrong.

TG: Just give me the answer to the question I ask. I'm going to advise you of your rights: You have the right to remain silent, anything you say can and will be used against you. You have the right to have a lawyer present. If you can't afford a lawyer, one will be provided for you at no cost to you. Do you understand and give up these rights?

JR: Uh, okay. I guess.

TG: Where are you from?

JR: I'm not illegal. I'm American, man. I live alone in Eastlake Village. Been here for 10 years since my family moved from Mexico.

TG: Don't give anything else but the answer to the question I ask you. Are we clear?

JR: Didn't you say I get a lawyer or something? You couldn't care less about my side of the story.

TG: You just waived your right to a lawyer. Do you want to talk to me now or not?

JR: I want to talk to you, but it seems to me like you aren't interested in what I have to say. Maybe I should get a lawyer? I don't know. All I know is that I didn't do nothing.

TG: You can get a lawyer all right, but as soon as he comes in here, that's it. Your chance to tell me your side of the story is gone forever. So, you still want that lawyer?

JR: Well . . . umm . . . I need some time to think it over becau—

TG: I take that as a yes. I'll go call one up. You just wait here until he shows up. I'm going to go prepare the documentation for a robbery prosecution.

JR: Man, I'm telling you I haven't done nothing wrong! I didn't rob nobody! I'm an honorable man and have been a U.S. Citizen for over ten years!

TG: You made your choice. If you'll excuse me, I have to find some public defender that will drive all the way down here to try to dig you out of this mess. This is Deputy Taylor Green and this concludes the interview with robbery suspect Jaime Ramirez.

[END OF TAPE]

TG: This is Deputy Taylor Green and we're back on the record in case MW122408. It is now 16:25 hours and Mr. Ramirez has changed his mind and he wants to speak to me regarding this incident. Right, Jaime?

JR: Yeah, I guess. I just want to get this straightened out. I've been hurt in so many ways by being accused of stealing this money.

TG: Well, that's what we're here for. Tell me what happened. What were you doing in Maliwood today? You don't live in this area.

JR: Today's my day off, man. I work really hard and I just wanted to go to the beach to chill for a day. Do you know how hot it gets in Eastlake Village in July? There ain't nothing wrong with that.

TG: Well, it seemed like you were pretty eager to get out of Maliwood when I pulled you over. You were going pretty fast and passing cars on Maliwood Canyon; that's a curvy, dangerous road, Jaime.

JR: Man, when you pulled me over I wasn't even going fast. Everybody goes at that speed and passes cars on the canyon. Unless there's a code section for driving with dark skin in Maliwood.

TG: You sure don't look like you were dressed for a day at the beach. Blue jeans and work boots? Come on, Jaime. Make it easier for yourself. Where's the ski mask? Just tell me where you dumped it.

JR: I don't know what you're talking about. I don't got a ski mask. I don't ski, so I have no use for one. I'm too busy working because I have a responsible job. I sure as hell didn't rob anyone.

TG: So, tell me Jaime, do you always go for a walk on the beach carrying $700 in cash?

JR: Look, I had a lot of cash on me today because I just got paid yesterday on June 30th. I always get paid at the end of the month.

TG: My brother-in-law is a plumber, and he doesn't carry that much cash around with him.

JR: My boss's name is Randy Granger. You need to talk to him. He'll back me, man. I was paid $1,000 in $100 bills for a plumbing job. It was a big job on a new house construction. I had worked on it six days a week for the whole month of June.

TG: You were paid that much in cash?

JR: Believe me, I'm sure of this, 'cause my rent is due on the first of each month, and I'm always just scraping by, trying to pay the rent on time. That's why I had all that cash and didn't put it in the bank. I was just going to pay the landlord in cash. Randy always pays in cash. I don't ask why—he's the boss. I just do my work, and I do a good job.

TG: Well, what about pay stubs or records or something?

JR: I don't have nothing like receipts; it's not that kind of business. Just ask Randy, he'll back me up. I've been working for Randy since I was 18. He helped me get my citizenship. He's a good guy.

TG: That still doesn't explain why you would walk on the beach with $700 in cash.

JR: Look man, I got paid yesterday and I put the cash in my wallet as soon as I got it. My rent is due today and I was going to drop it off on my way home after the beach. To be honest, I forgot I even had it on me when I went to the beach to beat the heat and get some fresh air. I wasn't planning on going swimming, so the money was safe.

TG: You drive a black Toyota Tacoma pickup?

JR: You saw me driving one.

TG: The victim said that the man who robbed her sped away in a black pickup truck.

JR: Wow. So you're trying to base a case on cash, which doesn't prove a damn thing, and a truck that's one of the most common ones on the road. Did the victim get a plate number?

TG: We have lots of physical evidence connecting you to the robbery, plus an eyewitness.

JR: Oh really? Well I hope she did get a plate number, because then we'd know for sure that it wasn't my truck.

TG: No other black Toyota pickup trucks were stopped by me or my other deputies today after the robbery. You were seen in your truck, speeding, leaving the area of the robbery, right after it happened. How do you explain that?

JR: Man, a lot of people have black Toyota trucks around Maliwood. There's no reason to accuse me of a crime just because I drive the same kind of truck as some robber. I was just making my way home from the beach. I can't help it if someone was robbed there.

TG: That's really interesting, Jaime. I didn't say anything about the robbery occurring at the beach. I wonder how you would know that if you weren't the robber?

JR: What? What are you talking about? You're just messing with me, trying to get me to admit to something that I didn't do! You're the one that just said it was the beach area!

TG: I never mentioned the beach.

JR: You said you saw me leaving the area of the robbery and obviously I was driving from the beach area through the Canyon.

TG: Let's move on. How many of those trucks had a knife, gloves, basin wrench, and cash that match the descriptions given by the victim?

JR: So? I already told you I got paid that day. Besides, every plumber has those things. The basin wrench is a common plumber's tool that we use to install sinks and tighten faucets and knobs and stuff that is hard to reach. Just ask Randy. I wouldn't have the slightest idea how to enter a house with a basin wrench. That is ridiculous! And every worker has gloves like that. It doesn't mean jack. Why don't you go look for the real robber and find the ski mask and a lock pick?

TG: What about the knife? I can't think of any reason a plumber would need one of those.

JR: All plumbers have knives of one type or another. Mine's longer than most. Ok, so what? I don't know; I just had it. Still, it doesn't mean a thing. This is such bull! You people are just blaming this on me because of the color of my skin. I swear all these snobby rich Maliwood people are the same. They just stare at me like I don't belong there because I'm Latino. But they don't mind if I've got my tools with me; they think, "That's okay because the Mexican's just doing a job and he'll be out of there soon."

TG: Any feelings of racism you may have are delusional and self-inflicted. Let's get back to the reason you're here: the robbery you committed.

JR: Man, this is unbelievable. You're already convinced I did it. Stupid me. I should have gone with that lawyer.

TG: Well, it's not too late. Although if I were you, I'd finish telling me your side of the story. I've already got enough though to send to the DA's office. You don't want to cut it off now.

JR: This is so unfair! I'm a hard worker. I'm an honorable man, and I didn't do nothing wrong!

TG: Okay, this is obviously going nowhere. We're done here. This concludes the interview with robbery suspect Jaime Ramirez. It is now 16:32 hours.
[END OF TAPE]

Statement of Randy Granger

My name is Randy Granger. I am fifty-eight years old. I've been married for thirty-six years. My spouse and I have four children, and three beautiful grandchildren. I was born and raised in Oceana, where I am a plumbing contractor and owner of my own company, Paradise Plumbers. I started the business sixteen years ago. This is the first time one of my guys has gotten in trouble. My company has a great reputation, and I'm very particular about who I hire. I never get complaints about any of my workers; I stand by all of them. We're a small business, and we all work well together and trust one another. My guys are honest and hardworking—ask anyone in town.

Jaime Ramirez has worked for me for seven years. He's always reliable and punctual. I've never had a problem with him. None of my clients have ever had a problem with him. Jaime takes pride in his work and my customers love him. I remember one time last year when this one lady tried to give him a hundred bucks for a tip because she was so happy with the job he did. She told me that he refused to take it, saying that my company paid him a fair amount. There's no way Jaime robbed that lady. Jaime's more concerned with doing a good job than he is with making a lot of money. He lives by himself and doesn't even have a wife or kids to support, so he's not hurting for money. He's a plumber, which is skilled work, so he makes good money. No way he would steal.

I usually pay my workers by check, but every once in a while I just pay them in cash. On this particular occasion, I remember paying him in cash because a homeowner had just given me a large payment in cash for a large job. That's not usually the norm. I don't know why the homeowner chose to pay in cash. I don't ask questions of my good clients; I'm just happy to have the work. Jaime worked on that home construction project for most of June. Well, I pay my guys at the end of each month, and the amount varies depending on the job. The June construction job was a big one. Like I said, I usually pay by check but that time I paid him in cash. I remember clearly because it was only last week and I got paid so much cash for that job that I was uncomfortable carrying that much money around until I got it in the bank. I know I paid Jaime $800 in $100 bills. I am positive about these denominations because all of the money that I received from the job was in $100 bills. I don't have written paperwork for the amount I paid Jaime. We just work on a trust basis. Jaime worked several hours a day on the job so I paid him $200 per week for four weeks, that's how I know it was $800. I'm sure about that.

I was informed that the police think the robber might have used a long tool with a claw at the end to break into the home. Of course Jaime has a tool like that; all of my boys have one. Actually, every plumber has this tool—it's called a basin wrench. It is a common tool to install a sink; the handle extends and there is a claw-like grip on the end to get to hard to reach areas, like wall outlets. Basin wrenches are as common to plumbers as hammers are to carpenters. I don't think a robber would use a basin wrench to break into a house. That would be difficult to do, and it doesn't make sense.

It's not like he had someone's jewels or something personal to the victim. Having cash on him doesn't prove anything. I need Jaime to get back to work. I think the cops are picking on him because he is Hispanic. I've always been proud to live in Oceana, but Maliwood can be really snobby and sometimes the cops pull people over because they're not white. That's just not okay. In fact, this isn't the first time I've heard of that detective targeting Hispanics. Green pulled over my Guatemalan brother-in-law once and accused him of stealing the BMW he was driving. Green refused to believe that he was a successful business owner who bought it himself. It's embarrassing.

I feel bad that someone got robbed, but believe me, Jaime didn't do it. He should never have been arrested. The cops got the wrong guy! This case needs to get dismissed so Jaime can get back to work.

I swear under penalty of perjury that the foregoing is true and accurate.

Signed,

Randy Granger

Randy Granger

Statement of Paul Burns

My name is Paul Burns, I am the founder and president of my own company, Burns Investigative Agency. I have been a private investigator for the past twenty-six years. I have been retained by the defense in the case of People v. Jaime Ramirez.

On July 7, CY-1, I was escorted by a deputy in the Maliwood Sheriff's Department to the home of Kelly Sims, the complaining witness of this alleged robbery. My goal was to test the Sheriff Department's theory as to how the suspect entered the house. The complainant showed me the door she claims the robber entered her home through that day.

I brought a standard basin wrench, about twenty inches long, with me to the complainant's home. The door is approximately seven feet tall. The doggie door is located approximately eighteen inches below the doorknob. It is a standard doggie door made for small to medium sized dogs. The door is made of solid wood and has no windows; the only way to see inside is through the doggie door. I asked the complainant to close the door and lock it so I could test the detective's theory. I positioned myself at the foot of the door. First, I attempted to open the lock by kneeling at the doggie door and pushing my arm with the basin wrench inside. This proved impossible to do because it was very difficult to maneuver the basin wrench at that angle. I then attempted to lie down on my back and extend the basin wrench straight up. This also proved very difficult. I tried to unlock the door seven times before I was able to unlock it. It is one hurdle to get the basin wrench to reach the doorknob, but it is an entirely separate hurdle to get the claw to close around the doorknob. Also, the process itself is very noisy, with the wrench clanging against the metal doorknob and the screeching sound the metal claw makes when grinding against the metal doorknob.

I have formed the opinion that it is very implausible that Jaime Ramirez was able to use the basin wrench to unlock the complainant's back door and break into her home. He is 5'9", and I am 5'11". I had difficulty reaching through the doggie door, and as Jaime Ramirez is two inches shorter than me, he would have had even more difficulty. Also, even if he were the same height as me, the process of unlocking the door with the basin wrench is way too complicated and noisy. As noted, I was only able to unlock the door with the basin wrench on my seventh try. I also noted that the scratches I observed around the doorknob are inconsistent with the theory that the basin wrench was used to unlock the door. The scratches resemble those made by a lock-picking tool that burglars commonly use. In all the attempts that I made to open the door, I did not make one scratch with the basin wrench. It is much more likely that a robber used burglar tools, such as a lock-pick, to quickly unlock the door from the outside.

I swear the forgoing is true and accurate.

Signed,

Paul Burns

Paul Burns
Private Investigator

Exhibit A

Exhibit B

Exhibit C

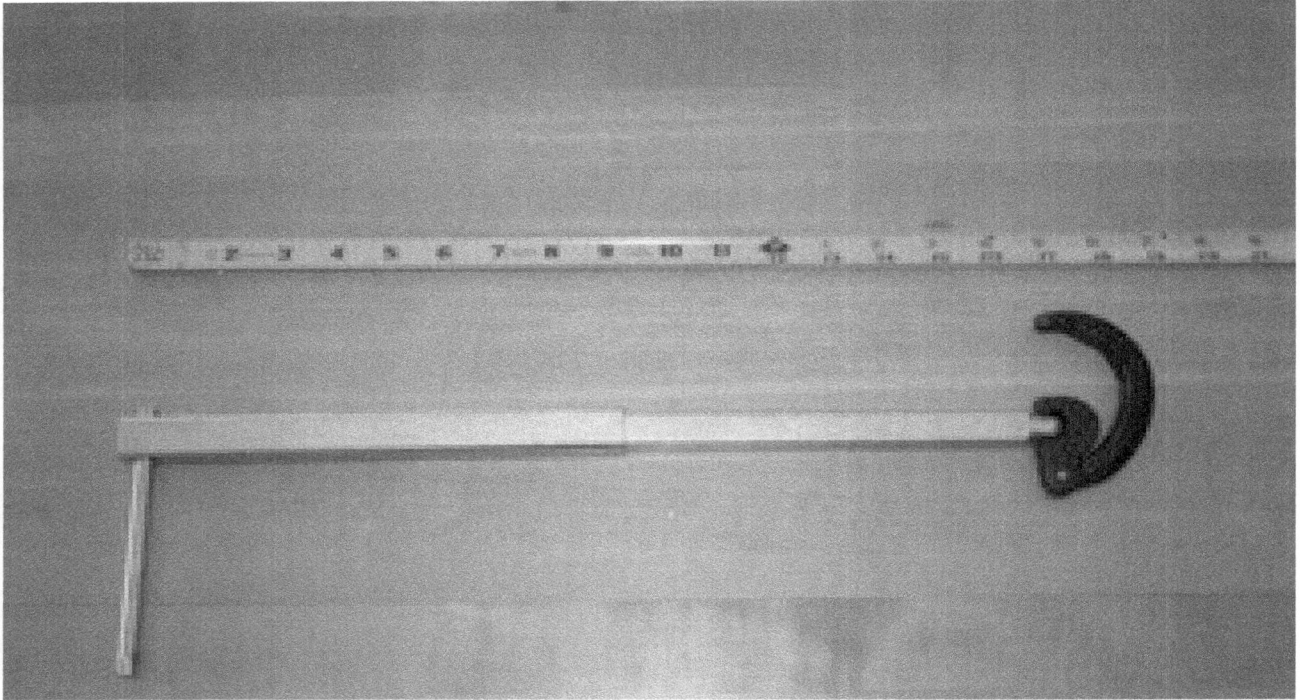

Exhibit D

Exhibit E

Exhibit F

Exhibit G

Exhibit H

Exhibit I

Exhibit J

Exhibit K

Exhibit L

Jury Instructions

Members of the jury, I thank you for your attentiveness during this trial. Please pay close attention to the instructions I am about to give you.

In this case, Defendant, Jaime Ramirez, is charged with robbery in the first degree and burglary in the first degree. A person who takes the property of another person by force or threat of force is guilty of the crime of robbery in violation of Oceana Penal Code section 211. A person who enters a residence with the intent to commit a felony therein is guilty of the crime of residential burglary in violation of Oceana Penal Code section 459.

To prove the crime of robbery, the State must prove the following elements beyond a reasonable doubt:

1.   Defendant made a threat or show of force against the victim; and

2.   The threat or show of force induced the victim into relinquishing his or her property.

A threat of force may be actual or implied. It does not matter whether or not Defendant actually had the ability to carry out the threat. Rather, it depends on whether the victim reasonably believed Defendant could carry out the threat.

To prove the crime of residential burglary, the State must prove the following elements beyond a reasonable doubt:

1.   Defendant unlawfully entered the victim's residence; and

2.   Defendant entered the victim's residence with the intent to commit a felony therein.

Defendant has entered a plea of not guilty. This means that you must presume or believe that Defendant is not guilty unless and until the evidence convinces you otherwise. This presumption stays with Defendant as to each material allegation in the indictment through each stage of the trial until it has been overcome by the evidence to the exclusion of and beyond a reasonable doubt.

To overcome Defendant's presumption of innocence, it is the State's burden to prove the following:

1.   The crime with which Defendant is charged was committed; and

2.   Defendant is the person who committed the crime.

Defendant is not required to prove anything.

The State has the burden to prove the elements beyond a reasonable doubt. Whenever the words *reasonable doubt* are used, you must consider the following: A reasonable doubt is not a mere possible doubt, because everything relating to human affairs is open to some possible or imaginary doubt. Reasonable doubt is the state of the case that, after hearing and considering all the evidence, leaves the minds of the jurors in the condition that they cannot say they feel an abiding conviction of the truth of the charge.

It is to the evidence introduced during this trial, and to it alone, that you are to look for that proof. A reasonable doubt as to the guilt of Defendant may arise from evidence, a conflict in the evidence, or a lack of evidence. If you have a reasonable doubt, you should find Defendant not guilty. If you have no reasonable doubt, you should find Defendant guilty.

You must decide this case on the evidence and the law. It is up to you to decide what evidence is reliable. You should use your common sense in deciding what evidence is reliable and what evidence should not be relied upon in considering your verdict.

A witness is a person who has knowledge related to this case. You will have to decide whether you believe each witness and how important each witness's testimony is to the case. You may believe all, part, or none of a witness's testimony. In deciding whether to believe a witness's testimony, you may consider, among other factors, the following:

1.   The extent of the witness's opportunity to see, hear, or otherwise become familiar with any matter about which the witness testified.

2.   The ability of the witness to accurately recall or communicate any matter about which the witness testified and the character and quality of that testimony.

3.   The witness's manner and demeanor while on the stand.

4.   Whether or not the witness has a bias, an improper motive, or an interest in the outcome

of the case.

5.   The witness's attitude toward this trial or toward testifying.

6.   Whether the witness's testimony was consistent or inconsistent with other testimony or

        evidence presented in this case.

7.   Any previous statements made by the witness that are consistent or inconsistent with the

        witness's testimony.

8.   The witness's character for honesty or veracity, or their opposites.

9.   Whether the witness was offered money, preferred treatment, or any other benefit to

        testify or whether the witness received any threats or was under any pressure that might

        have affected the truth of the witness's testimony.

10.   The witness's previous conviction of a felony or past criminal conduct amounting to a

        misdemeanor.

You may rely upon your own conclusions about each witness. A juror may believe or disbelieve all or any part of the evidence or the testimony of any witness.

There are some general rules that apply to your deliberations. You must abide by these rules in order to return a verdict that is consistent with the law:

1.   You must follow the law as it is explained to you in these instructions. If you fail to

        follow the law or disregard the law, any verdict you reach will be a miscarriage of justice.

2.   You must decide the case only upon the evidence that you have heard from either the

        testimony of witnesses or exhibits that you have seen.

3.   You must not decide the case for or against anyone because you feel sympathy for that

        person, or because you are angry at that person.

4.   You must not decide the case based on your feelings about the lawyers in this case. The

        lawyers are not on trial.

5.   You must not consider any potential sentence Defendant might receive. It is not your

duty to consider punishment. Your only duty is to determine guilt or innocence. It is the judge's job to determine the proper sentence if you find Defendant guilty.

6.   Whatever verdict you render must be unanimous; that is, each juror must commit to the same verdict. The verdict must be the verdict of each juror as well as that of the jury as a whole.

7.   It is entirely proper for a lawyer to talk to a witness about what testimony the witness would give if called into the courtroom. The witness should not be discredited for talking to a lawyer about his or her testimony.

8.   You must not decide this case based on feelings of prejudice, bias, or sympathy. Any verdict you may reach should be based on the evidence and the law contained in these instructions.

Deciding a proper verdict is exclusively your job. I cannot participate in that decision in any way. Please disregard anything I might have said or done that made you think I preferred one verdict over another.

Only one verdict may be returned for the crime charged. The verdict must be in writing and the verdict form has been prepared for you. It is as follows:

(READ JURY VERDICT FORM)

In just a few moments, the Bailiff will escort you to the jury room. Once inside the jury room, the first thing you should do is elect a foreperson, who will preside over your deliberations. It is the foreperson's job to sign and date the verdict form when all of you have agreed on a verdict in this case and to bring the verdict back to the courtroom when you return.

In conclusion, let me remind you that it is imperative that you follow the law as I have explained it to you in these instructions. Regardless of how you feel about the laws, you must apply them.

SUPERIOR COURT OF THE STATE OF OCEANA

FOR THE COUNTY OF MALIWOOD

STATE OF OCEANA,		Case No. MW122408
	Plaintiff,	
v.		**CHARGE(S):** 211 Robbery in the first degree 1 count
JAIME RAMIREZ,	Defendant.	
		459 Residential burglary in the first degree 1 count

VERDICT

As to the charge of robbery in the first degree, in violation of Oceana Penal Code section 211, we, the jury, find the Defendant, Jaime Ramirez:

_____ GUILTY

_____ NOT GUILTY

As to the charge of residential burglary in the first degree, in violation of Oceana Penal Code section 459, we, the jury, find the Defendant, Jaime Ramirez:

_____ GUILTY

_____ NOT GUILTY

So say we all.

_____
Foreperson of the Jury

_____
Date

CASE FILE No. 4

STATE OF OCEANA

V.

HUNTER ROBINSON

(Driving Under the Influence)

SUPERIOR COURT OF THE STATE OF OCEANA

COUNTY OF MALIWOOD

STATE OF OCEANA,

Plaintiff,

v.

HUNTER ROBINSON,

Defendant.

Case No. MW742834

MISDEMEANOR COMPLAINT

COUNT 1

On or about July 12, CY-1, in the City of Maliwood, Maliwood County, State of Oceana, a misdemeanor, in violation of section 23152(a) of the Oceana Vehicle Code, DRIVING UNDER THE INFLUENCE OF ALCOHOL OR DRUGS, was committed by the above defendant, who at the time and place last aforesaid, did drive a vehicle while under the influence of any alcoholic beverage or drug.

COUNT 2

On or about July 12, CY-1, in the City of Maliwood, Maliwood County, State of Oceana, a misdemeanor, in violation of section 23152(b) of the Oceana Vehicle Code, DRIVING WHILE HAVING A .08% OR HIGHER BLOOD ALCOHOL CONTENT, was committed by the above defendant, who at the time and place last aforesaid, did drive a vehicle with .08 percent or more, by weight, of alcohol in his/her blood.

IT IS SO ORDERED.

Simon Luna

Simon Luna
District Attorney, County of Maliwood

Witness List

Witnesses for the State:

1.   Casey Jones

2.   Taylor Harrington

Witnesses for the Defense:

1.   Hunter Robinson*

2.   Alex Lou

Each side must call both witnesses listed for their respective party, and both parties stipulate that each party's expert witness would testify consistently with his or her provided statement.

*This witness must be played by a male.

Stipulations

1. Federal Rules of Criminal Procedure and Federal Rules of Evidence apply.

2. Other than what appears in the officer's report of the interviews, there is nothing exceptional or unusual about the background of any of the witnesses that would bolster or detract from their credibility.

3. Each witness who gave an interview or statement (collectively "witness statement") reviewed the officer's report of his or her witness statement and verified it was complete and accurate.

4. All exhibits in the file are authentic, and unless otherwise noted, are the original of that document.

5. All dates are denoted by CY (current year) or CY-*n* (current year minus *n* years).

6. All pretrial motions shall be oral.

7. "Beyond the record" is not a valid objection. Attorneys for either party should use cross-examination as the proper means to challenge a witness whose testimony goes beyond the facts provided in the witness's statements.

8. No party may invent witnesses or evidence that is not specifically mentioned in this case file.

9. The physical description of a witness, e.g., clothing, should be tailored to that of the student playing the witness, except for height, weight and age.

10. All witness statements were given under oath.

11. All witnesses called to testify who have identified the Defendant Robinson or any tangible evidence can, if asked, identify the same at trial.

12. Oceana Vehicle Code section 23152(a) reads as follows: "It is unlawful for any person who is under the influence of any alcoholic beverage or drug, or under the combined influence of any alcoholic beverage and drug, to drive a vehicle."

13. Oceana Vehicle Code section 23152(b) reads as follows: "It is unlawful for any person, whose blood alcohol content is .08 percent or above, to drive a vehicle."

14. The prosecution and defense may call only the two witnesses listed on the witness list. They may also introduce into evidence by stipulation the witness statement for each party's expert witness.

15. The expert witnesses' reports are stipulated to as being an accurate reflection of what each expert would testify to if called as a witness. Either side may constructively read into the record the expert witnesses' testimony in whole or in part or move the testimony into the record. Any such testimony by the stipulated experts is subject to objections pursuant to the Federal Rules of Evidence.

16. The prosecution and defense stipulate as to the chain of custody for the blood sample.

17. Scott Montgomery is a certified criminalist and qualified to run analyst tests of blood samples, and ran the test in this case consistent with the training and practice he had received and in compliance with all applicable standards. The result of the blood sample is .17 BAC.

18. Hunter Robinson must be played by a male. All other witnesses can be either gender. The witnesses may be called in any order. Steve Jenson moved out of the country and is unavailable as a witness.

Maliwood County Sheriff's Department
Driving Under The Influence Arrest Report

REPORT TYPE: INVESTIGATION NARRATIVE

OFFICER REPORTING: OFFICER CASEY JONES (initialed: CJ)

DATE: 7/12/CY-1

CASE: MW742834

On July 12, CY-1, I was in uniform driving in a black and white patrol unit. I regularly patrol the Maliwood County area. At 20:16 hours, I received a call from dispatch regarding a traffic collision on the 101 northbound between exits Ocean Breeze Parkway and Shell Lane. I was informed that a vehicle had veered off the highway and struck a tree (see attached Exhibit E). Though I was the nearest and first law enforcement official to arrive, it took about twenty minutes to respond. I arrived at the scene at 20:38 hours.

Although it was dark, I was able to locate the reported vehicle. I pulled directly behind the vehicle off the right side of the highway. The headlights and interior lights were on, and the driver's door was open. The vehicle was a yellow Volkswagen Jetta with the license plate 4JKN531. As I approached the driver's side of the vehicle, I detected an odor of alcohol emitting from inside of the vehicle. No one was inside of the vehicle.

At the scene, I was contacted by Taylor Harrington who witnessed the accident. Harrington reported that he had been driving behind the subject vehicle for approximately two miles prior to the accident, and observed the subject vehicle weaving on the freeway through all four lanes of traffic. There are four lanes on this particular highway at the respective location. The number one lane is the furthest lane on the left. Harrington was traveling in the number three lane, which is the third lane from the left. Harrington estimated that the vehicle was traveling in excess of 70 miles per hour. Harrington informed me that the subject vehicle suddenly swerved, and crossed over two highway lanes onto the dirt shoulder.

Within seconds, Harrington heard a loud bang as the subject vehicle collided with a tree just off the shoulder. Harrington pulled behind the Jetta in order to offer help. Before Harrington was able get out and help, the driver of the Jetta opened his door, crawled out of the car, and appeared to have difficulty walking. Harington heard the driver yell, "What am I going to do now?!" When the driver of the Jetta noticed Harrington, he took off running towards the nearby exit at Ocean Breeze Parkway (see attached Statement of Taylor Harrington).

I contacted dispatch with the license plate of the car. Dispatch informed me that the car was registered to an individual by the name of Hunter Robinson who lived at 25 Shell Lane in Maliwood. The address was roughly two miles from the scene of the accident. I waited for backup to arrive. I helped them secure the scene, and I then proceeded to Robinson's residence, arriving shortly after 21:45 hours.

I approached the front door, knocked, and announced myself as a police officer. After four or five knocks, an individual—later identified as Steve Jenson, the subject's roommate—answered the door. I told him that I was looking for Hunter Robinson and asked whether he was home. Steve turned and leaned his head back towards the house, paused, then turned back to me and said, "Yeah, Hunter is here." I then asked Steve if I could come in. Steve opened the door completely, and I went inside the residence. After asking Steve where Hunter was, he hesitated and then said, "I would check one of the bedrooms." Then he pointed down a hallway. I immediately headed down the hallway that took me to two facing bedrooms (see attached Exhibit B). I was able to look inside because both bedroom doors were open. I didn't see or hear anything in the first bedroom on the left so I proceeded down the hallway to the other bedroom on the right. I peered in and saw a messy room with clothes scattered everywhere. After hearing the sound of a flushing toilet, I proceeded through that bedroom to the bathroom door where the sound was coming from. I knocked and announced my presence. Hearing no response, I tried the door that was locked. I retraced my steps and made my way to the same bathroom accessed through the living room. There, in the bathroom, I found Robinson with his face hovering over the open toilet.

Robinson had watery, bloodshot eyes and an obvious odor of alcohol emitting from his person. I asked if he had been driving tonight. Hunter said, "I won't be anymore, I totaled it." I then asked him if he had been drinking. He answered by rolling his eyes and nodded towards the direction of the toilet. Then, spontaneously, Robinson blurted out in a slurred manner, "But I wasn't driving drunk. I had five beers after I got home, but I did not drink any alcohol before driving. Go look in the kitchen, the bottles are on the counter." Thereafter, I looked in the kitchen and observed empty beer bottles on the counter as well as an opened bottle of tequila next to two used shot glasses (see attached Exhibits C and D). I then directed Robinson out of the residence to perform a series of field sobriety tests and to complete an interview.

Following the field sobriety tests (see attached supplemental report), I concluded that Robinson was under the influence of drugs and/or alcohol. I further concluded that Robinson was under the influence of alcohol at the time of the crash based on the odor of alcohol emitting from inside Robinson's vehicle, the eyewitness observations of the crash, and Robinson's obvious state of inebriation.

Immediately following the field sobriety test, I briefly questioned Robinson. I asked, "You really expect me to believe you only drank after the crash? C'mon, I have an eyewitness report that you were drinking an alcoholic beverage at the scene of the crash." Robinson replied, "I thought someone might have seen that." I placed Robinson under arrest, handcuffed him, searched his person, and secured a cell phone, cash, and store receipt (see attached Exhibit A).

I inspected Robinson's cell phone and I observed a text message displayed on the main screen. The text appeared to have been sent to Robinson at 20:19 hours (see attached Exhibit F). The message read, "u alright? I knew you shouldn't have been driving, you need me to pick you up at Sunset Gas?"

At the police station, I advised Robinson of Oceana Vehicle Code section 23612, implied consent. Robinson chose a blood test. Thereafter, Rebecca Richardson, an R.N. with the Law Enforcement Medical Services of Maliwood County, drew blood from Robinson's right arm about an hour after the arrest. The blood sample (BA Kit #203021) was placed in the blood locker and booked into evidence. I also advised Robinson of the *Miranda* rights. Robinson stated that he understood and waived his *Miranda* rights under one condition. He said he was drunk and would only give a statement the next day when he had a chance to "sleep it off and get sober again." He also stated that once he was sober he would be willing to write out a statement of what happened, but he refused to answer my questions. He stated that the police twist things and manipulate people into saying things that hurt their case. He said he wanted a chance to tell his side, but only in the form of a written statement. The day after his arrest he did write out a statement (see attached Statement of Hunter Robinson). I later learned that an inventory search was conducted of Robinson's yellow Volkswagen Jetta. There were no alcohol cans or bottles found. I recommend that this report be forwarded to the Maliwood County District Attorney for review and prosecution of the defendant on the charges of Oceana Vehicle Code 23152(a) & (b).

I certify that the above is true to the best of my knowledge under the penalty of perjury.

Signed,

Officer Casey Jones

Officer Casey Jones

Maliwood County Sheriff's Department
Supplemental Police Report
Field Sobriety Test

Field sobriety tests are administered when an officer suspects an individual to be under the influence of alcohol or drugs. They are administered to test both mental and physical impairment. I conducted these tests at Robinson's residence. Robinson complied and agreed to undergo the field sobriety tests.

ROMBERG TEST

This was the first test that was conducted. In a Romberg test, the subject assumes a position of attention, closes their eyes, tilts their head back, and estimates thirty seconds. The officer is looking for the inability to stand still or steady, body or eyelid tremors, opening eyes to maintain balance, swaying (either front to back or side to side), or any statements made by the accused. The officer is also testing the suspect's internal clock, which will usually be slow in the case of alcohol or depressants, or fast in the case of stimulants. The subject estimated thirty seconds to be forty-three seconds. The results of this test are attached to this report.

HORIZONTAL GAZE NYSTAGMUS

This was the second test performed. In this test, an officer will position an object, in this case a pen, about twelve inches away from the suspect's face. The officer will move the object from side to side while observing the participant's eyes. The officer is looking for a lack of smooth pursuit, involuntary jerking or trembling of the eyeball, and sustained jerking when the eye reaches the furthest point. The officer will also look for the onset of jerking prior to the eye reaching a forty-five-degree angle. Each of these factors or "clues" is counted in each eye. If the officer observes a total of four out of six clues, the officer will conclude that there is a 77% chance that the driver's blood alcohol content is above .10%. The results of this test are attached to this report.

WALK AND TURN

This was the third test performed. In this test, the subject takes nine heel-to-toe steps along an imaginary line, turns, and takes nine heel-to-toe steps back. The officer is looking to see if the accused can keep their balance and follow instructions. The officer also checks to see whether the subject begins too early, stops during the test, leaves space between heel and toe, steps off the line, and loses balance while turning. The results of this test are attached to this report.

STANDING ON ONE FOOT BALANCE

This was the fourth test that was administered. The accused is instructed to stand with heels together, arms at the side, then raise one leg six inches off the ground while counting out loud until the officer directs the accused to stop. The officer is looking for raising of the arms, swaying, hopping, putting the foot down, inability to stand still, body tremors, muscle tension, and any statements made by the accused during the test. The results of this test are attached to this report.

ALPHABET

This was the fifth test that was performed. The accused in this test is given a pad of paper and a pen to write the alphabet. The test is primarily concerned with testing the mental impairment of the subject. The officer looks to see if the alphabet was correctly written, whether the letters vary greatly in size, whether the subject paused, and whether the subject ran out of room. The results of this test are attached to this report.

Signed,

Officer Casey Jones

Officer Casey Jones

Maliwood County Sheriff's Department
Supplemental Police Report

At the request of the Maliwood County District Attorney's Office, I am providing a supplemental report detailing my experience and history as a peace officer. My name is Casey Jones. I am twenty-five years old and married. I have lived in the State of Oceana my entire life. I graduated from the Oceana Police Academy shortly after finishing high school. You could say law enforcement runs in my blood. My father, grandfather, and aunt have all dedicated their lives to serving the public. It was without any hesitation that I chose to do the same.

For the past two years, I have been on my current assignment: nighttime shifts patrolling the Maliwood County area. It's a fairly quiet shift. In fact, if I had to estimate, I would say that I have only performed about seventy-five DUI investigations with twenty-five resulting in arrests. The low numbers are partly because of the laid-back lifestyle of Maliwood County and because prior to this shift assignment, I spent a full year working as a dispatcher. I was reassigned and placed on probation because of some unwise choices I made about three years back. At that time, my marriage was on shaky grounds. I let this affect my work performance. I became an alcoholic, and I even showed up to work intoxicated one day. Off duty, I had been arrested for DUI. Although I was never charged, that experience opened my eyes. Fortunately, I was not fired but reassigned to work as a dispatcher. I have remained sober for over three years now. I think my past experience abusing alcohol and my current sobriety actually gives me an advantage in assessing whether a person is impaired by alcohol.

I certify that the above is true to the best of my knowledge under the penalty of perjury.

Signed,

Officer Casey Jones

Officer Casey Jones

Case No. MW-742834	Arrestee's Name: (Last, First) Robinson, Hunter	DOB 4/15/CY-34

Address, City, Zip Code 25 Shell Lane, Maliwood, 90001	Social Security # 000-00-0001

Height 5'8"	Weight 150 lbs	Age 34	Eye Color Blue	Hair Color Dark Brown

Occupation
Former Lab Technician

MALIWOOD COUNTY SHERIFF'S DEPARTMENT ARREST REPORT

Charge(s)

MC 23152(a) – Driving Under the Influence

MC 23152(b) – Driving with a BAC of .08% or higher

Location of Arrest Defendant's Residence	Date and Time of Arrest July 12th at 9:54 pm

Clothing:	Shirt/Blouse White Tank top	Pants/Shorts Blue basketball shorts	Coat/Jacket N/A	Hat N/A	Shoes Sandals

Property on Person
Cell Phone, Wallet, Sunset Gas Store Receipt

Currency $5.34	Jewelry N/A	Tattoos N/A	Medical Problems Claims Depression

Vehicle License Plate and State 4JKN531 (Oceana State)	Vehicle Description	Make Volkswagen	Model Jetta	Year CY-5	Color Yellow

Vehicle Disposition
Abandoned on Highway 101, Significant Frontal Structural Damage

Reason for Release Signed Promise to Appear, Spent mandatory 24 hours in custody	Released To Jake Gardner (Friend of Defendant)

Arresting Officer (Name & Number) Officer Casey Jones (ID#20221)	Date: 7/12/CY-1	Signature

Maliwood County Sherriff's Department
DUI ARREST REPORT: DUI INTERVIEW

Arrestee's Name (Last, First, MI) **Robinson, Hunter**	Questioning Officer **Casey Jones**
1. Do you have any physical impairments? If yes, explain. ☐ YES ☒ NO	16. Have you had any alcohol since being stopped/the collision? ☒ YES ☐ NO
2. Do you limp? ☐ YES ☒ NO	16a. What kind of alcohol? **Beer**
3. Are you sick or injured? ☐ YES ☒ NO	16b. How much? **5**
4. Are you currently under the care of a dentist or doctor? ☐ YES ☒ NO	17. Time collision occurred? **8 to 8:15 p.m.**
5. Are you diabetic or epileptic? ☐ YES ☒ NO	18. Where were you headed? **Friend's House**
6. Do you take insulin? ☐ YES ☒ NO	19. Without looking, what time do you think it is? **11:15 p.m.**
7. Do you have any prescriptions? ☐ YES ☒ NO	20. What street/highway were you on? **The 101**
8. Do you have any impaired vision? ☐ YES ☒ NO	21. Have you been drinking alcoholic beverages? ☒ YES ☐ NO
9. Do you wear corrective lenses or glasses? ☐ YES ☒ NO	21a. What have you been drinking? **Beer**
10. Were you wearing them when stopped/before collision? ☐ YES **N/A** ☐ NO	21b. When did you start drinking? **8:45 or so**
11. When and how many hours of sleep did you last sleep? **6 hours**	21c. How much did you drink? **5 Beers**
12. Were you driving the vehicle? ☒ YES ☐ NO	21d. Where were you drinking? **My house**
13. To your knowledge is there anything mechanically wrong with the vehicle? ☐ YES ☒ NO	21e. Time of last drink? **I don't know**
14. Have you been injured or involved in any collision in the past 24 hours? ☒ YES ☐ NO	22. Do you believe your ability to drive was affected by your consumption of alcohol? ☐ YES ☒ NO
15. Were you eating/drinking before you were pulled over/the collision? ☒ YES ☐ NO **Chips & Salsa**	23. Have you ever been arrested for DUI before? ☐ YES ☒ NO

PRE-ARREST OBSERVATIONS

1. ATTITUDE	2. COORDINATION	3. EYES	4. FACIAL COLOR	5. ODOR OF INTOXICANTS ON BREATH	6. SPEECH
☒ Cooperative	☐ Good	☐ Normal	☐ Normal	☐ None	☐ Good
☐ Argumentative	☐ Fair	☒ Red/Bloodshot	☒ Flushed	☐ Faint	☐ Fair
☐ Laughing	☒ Poor	☒ Watery	☐ Pale	☐ Medium	☐ Repetitive
☐ Crying	☐ Stumbling	☒ Droopy	☐ Other:	☒ Strong	☐ Fast
☐ Mood Swings	☐ Other:	☐ Pupils Dilated		☒ Obvious	☒ Slow
☐ Other:		☐ Pupils Constricted		☐ Other:	☒ Slurred
		☐ Other:			☐ Other:

7. Officer's Opinion of Subject's Impairment	8. Subject's Native Language
☐ Slight ☐ Obvious ☒ Extreme	☒ English ☐ Other

Maliwood County Sheriff's Department
DUI ARREST REPORT

Case/Citation Number:
MW-742834

☒ On the date, time, and location of this arrest, I had authority to make an arrest pursuant to my agency's jurisdiction.

CONSTITUTIONAL RIGHTS: MIRANDA

1. YOU HAVE THE RIGHT TO REMAIN SILENT.
2. YOU HAVE THE RIGHT AT THIS TIME TO HAVE AN ATTORNEY.
3. ANYTHING YOU DO SAY CAN AND WILL BE USED AGAINST YOU IN A COURT OF LAW.
4. YOU HAVE THE RIGHT TO TALK TO AN ATTORNEY BEFORE ANSWERING ANY QUESTIONS.
5. YOU HAVE THE RIGHT TO HAVE AN ATTORNEY PRESENT DURING THE QUESTIONING.
6. IF YOU CANNOT AFFORD AN ATTORNEY, ONE WILL BE APPOINTED FOR YOU WITHOUT COST IF YOU SO DESIRE.
7. YOU CAN EXERCISE THESE RIGHTS AT ANY TIME.
8. DO YOU UNDERSTAND THESE RIGHTS?

I have read or have had read to me the above explanation of my constitutional rights at this time and I understand these rights.

Subject's Signature _Hunter Robinson_

I understand my constitutional rights. I have decided not to exercise these rights at this time. Any statements made by me are made freely, voluntarily, and without threats or promises of any kind.

_____   _____
Officer's Signature   Subject's Signature

_____
Date/Time/Location

Attorney Requested: Attorney Contacted:
   (CIRCLE ONE)   (CIRCLE ONE)
   YES   NO   YES   NO   UNABLE

Attorney's Name (if applicable) : _____
Attorney's Phone Number (if applicable): (___)___-_____

EXPLANATION (if needed):

Suspect Invoked Right to Silence
Questioning Ended.

Maliwood County Sheriff's Department
DUI ARREST REPORT: FIELD SOBRIETY TESTS/CHEMICAL TEST ADMONITIONMENT

Issuing Officer: Casey Jones	Time & Location/Surface: 9:57, Flat Driveway of Suspect's

FIELD SOBRIETY TEST ADMONITION (given only upon refusal)

The Field Sobriety Tests are given to determine the extent to which alcohol and/or drugs have impaired your mental and physical processes. Your refusal to submit to all/part can be used against you in a court of law. A jury may be instructed that your refusal to submit to the tests demonstrate a consciousness of guilt on your behalf.

Will you perform the Field Sobriety Tests as instructed and demonstrated by the respective law enforcement official?

Response: I guess	Admonition Given By: Officer Casey Jones	Serial # N/A

ROMBERG TEST

- ☐ 1. Sways while balancing
- ☒ 2. Moves feet from original position to balance
- ☒ 3. Uses arms to balance, moves 6 or more inches away from sides
- ☐ 4. Falls
- ☐ 5. Fails to keep eyes closed
- ☒ 6. Subject displays eyelid tremor
- ☒ 7. Fails to tilt head back

HORIZONTAL GAZE NYSTAGMUS

R L
- ☒ ☒ 1. Lack of smooth pursuit
- ☒ ☐ 2. Distinct Nystagmus at maximum deviation
- ☒ ☐ 3. Onset of Nystagmus prior to 45 degrees
- ☐ ☐ 4. Fails to keep head still as instructed
- ☒ ☒ 5. Subject displays eyelid tremors
- ☐ ☐ 6. Fails to follow stimulus

WALK AND TURN

- ☐ 1. Moves feet from original positioning during instruction stage
- ☐ 2. Starts walking before instructed
- ☐ 3. Stops while walking
- ☒ 4. Misses heal-to-toe, by more than ½ inch, while walking
- ☒ 5. Uses arms to balance, moves 6 or more inches away from side
- ☒ 6. Turns improperly
- ☒ 7. Takes the wrong number of steps

ONE LEG STAND

R L
- ☒ ☒ 1. Sways while balancing
- ☐ ☒ 2. Uses arms to balance, moves 6 or more inches away from side
- ☒ ☒ 3. Hopping as means of balance
- ☐ ☐ 4. Puts foot down before 30 seconds/time has elapsed
- ☒ ☐ 5. Fails to point lifted foot as instructed
- ☐ ☒ 6. Fails to look at the lifted foot as instructed
- ☒ ☐ 7. Falls during test

ALPHABET

- ☐ 1. Incomplete/Incorrect alphabet
- ☒ 2. Subject pauses between letters
- ☐ 3. Subject runs out of space for letters
- ☒ 4. Letters vary greatly in size

CHEMICAL TEST ADMONITION (23612 VC)

1. You are required by state law to submit to a chemical test to determine the alcohol and/or drug content of your blood.
2. Because I believe you are under the influence of alcohol and/or drugs, you have a choice of taking a breath or blood test.
3. If you take a breath test, a sample will NOT be saved and you or your attorney will NOT have a breath sample to test for alcohol content.
4. If you want any remaining sample saved for your use, you must choose to take a blood or urine test which will be retained at no cost to you and may be tested by any party in any criminal prosecution
5. If you refuse to submit to, or fail to complete a test, your driving privilege will be suspended for 1 year or revoked for 2 or 3 years. A second offense within ten years of a separate violation of driving under the influence, including such a charge reduced to reckless driving, or vehicular manslaughter will result in a 2 year revocation.
6. Refusal or failure to complete a test may be used against you in court. Refusal or failure to complete a test will also result in a fine and imprisonment if this arrest results in a conviction of driving under the influence.
7. You do not have the right to talk to an attorney or have an attorney present before stating whether you will submit to a test, before deciding what test to take, or during the test.

☐ Refusal	Admonition Given By: Officer Casey Jones	Serial # N/A

Statement of Taylor Harrington

I am forty-four years old and I have lived in Maliwood all my life. I am very familiar with the roads, highways, and stores. My passion is hiking, and I have traveled all over Maliwood County either by vehicle or on foot. On July 12, at around 8:00 p.m., I was driving on the 101 coming back from a hike when I observed a yellow Volkswagen Jetta weaving through traffic. Fortunately, traffic was rather light. I couldn't tell you the exact traveling speed of the car but since I was traveling close to sixty-five miles per hour in the number three lane and it still pulled away, I would guess it was going close to eighty miles per hour or above.

Shortly after watching the Jetta change lanes and maneuver around a few vehicles, the vehicle swerved to the right and onto the dirt and sand shoulder. The driver made no attempt to get in the right lane, and kept driving on the shoulder. It was difficult to see exactly what happened because of the dust, but then there was a loud crash. I was hesitant to approach the vehicle for a couple of reasons. First, due to the erratic driving of the vehicle before it crashed, I was worried about my safety. Second, I had heard that attempting to remove people from car crashes can result in further injury.

Anyways, these thoughts really didn't matter much in the end. Within a few seconds after my 911 call, the driver stumbled out of the vehicle. He said something and appeared frustrated. The driver looked around as if to check whether anyone had observed the crash and that's when our eyes met. He quickly turned, carrying some type of bottle or can in his left hand, and took off. He headed in the direction of the Ocean Breeze Parkway exit, around a half a mile away. Officer Jones arrived about fifteen minutes later, and I gave him my account of the events.

I certify that the above is true to the best my knowledge and recollection under the penalty of perjury.
Signed,

Taylor Harrington

Taylor Harrington

Statement of Scott Montgomery

I am a criminal analyst for the Maliwood County Sheriff's Department. I have been thus employed since CY-5. Prior to my employment, I received my bachelor's degree and master's degree in criminal justice from Oceana State College, and I am certified as a criminal analyst by the State of Oceana. In order to become certified, I completed forty hours of courses on subjects such as crime analysis, criminal intelligence analysis, investigative analysis, and law enforcement research methods and statistics. For the past three years, I have primarily worked in the Drug and Alcohol Detection unit. I have performed over 300 driving under the influence investigations, and have testified ten times in court involving such charges.

On July 14, CY-1, I was assigned to this case. I performed the alcohol analysis of the defendant's blood sample drawn by Rebecca Richardson. I conducted these tests in accordance with proper procedure that I had learned and mastered during my training, certification program, and experience as a criminal analyst. I used gas chromatography in determining the blood alcohol content of the defendant's sample. The result of the test was .17%. Though accurate, this result only provides that at the time the blood sample was drawn, the defendant's blood alcohol content was .17% After speaking with the District Attorney, I found that this conclusion, by itself, was insufficient to render an opinion as to whether the defendant was intoxicated when he was driving.

Following my initial analysis, I was provided additional information. Based on this additional information, I believe that the defendant must have been under the influence of alcohol at the time of the crash. The additional information is as follows: the defendant was arrested by Officer Jones at around 9:57 p.m. on July 12, the defendant was subsequently transferred to the Maliwood County Jail and booked, and the defendant's blood was drawn at approximately 10:54 p.m. The alcohol elimination rate, the rate at which alcohol is eliminated from the body by excretion and metabolism, can range from .012 to .018 per hour depending on the physical characteristics of the subject. I noted that the defendant's height and weight are 5'8" and 150 pounds. Using .015 as the elimination rate, the defendant's blood alcohol content would have been either .18 or .19 at the time of arrest.

The defendant claims not to have had any alcohol in his system prior to the crash. Therefore, in order for the defendant's account to be correct, he must have been at a .00 BAC at 8:54 p.m. and consumed enough alcohol in a forty-five-minute span to register a .17 BAC two hours later. This result is highly improbable. First, a standard size drink will typically raise an individual's blood alcohol content about .02 to .025 BAC. A standard size drink is measured as a twelve-ounce beer, 1.5 ounces of brandy or spirits, or five ounces of wine. In this case, consuming five twelve-ounce beers in a forty-five-minute time span would raise the BAC to levels ranging from .10 BAC to .125 BAC—far below the registered .17 BAC. Moreover, this is assuming that all of the consumed alcohol was actually absorbed into the blood stream. According to the defendant's statement, he had consumed chips and salsa before ingesting any alcohol. Since food in the stomach can slow the absorption rate, it is likely that full absorption of these five beers would have taken between forty-five minutes to an hour. A timeframe that was interrupted by the defendant's arrest but also, more importantly, his vomiting. Though it is unknown how much alcohol was absorbed, it is safe to say that the defendant, by the act of vomiting, disposed of some quantity of alcohol that had not yet been absorbed. Therefore, five beers in this forty-five-minute span with an act of vomiting would likely only raise the defendant's BAC to .09 or lower. The explanation by the defendant does not account for the .18 or .19 calculated BAC at the time of the arrest.

It is important to point out a common myth with regards to blood alcohol content and vomiting. Vomiting will not lower one's blood alcohol content, but it will prevent it from rising more. Consumed alcohol does not affect the blood alcohol content until it has been absorbed by the body. Any alcohol removed from the system by vomiting has not been absorbed and therefore has no effect on the actual blood alcohol content. Alcohol is absorbed from the stomach and small intestine by diffusion. The rate of absorption varies with the emptying time of the stomach and can range from thirty minutes on an empty stomach to upwards of more than an hour. When large amounts of alcohol are consumed over a short time interval, however, or when a large quantity of food is eaten with the alcohol, the absorption phase may not be complete for up to two hours after last consumption. Also, absorption rates typically occur more quickly the greater the level of the beverage's alcohol concentration.

Further, even if the defendant drank much more than the alleged five beers within this forty-five-minute time frame, my conclusion still would remain the same. Assume that the defendant had consumed eight or nine beers, which, at a .02 to .025 BAC per beer, would appear to put him around .20 BAC, a plausible and corroborating result. As stated previously, however, the rate of absorption is greatly affected when an individual consumes a large quantity of alcohol in a short time frame, sometimes taking two hours to reach full absorption. Here, the defendant would not have been able to absorb nine beers at the same pace he would have in the "five beer" scenario above. The slower absorption rate would lead to a greater quantity of unabsorbed alcohol left in the stomach, which is expunged upon vomiting. Thus, this scenario too is effectively ruled out as a viable explanation. The only logical conclusion is that the defendant was under the influence of alcohol at the time of the driving.

I certify that the above is true to the best my knowledge and recollection under the penalty of perjury.

Signed,

Scott Montgomery

Scott Montgomery

Note: Chart is demonstrative. The chart is based off of the information received by Officer Casey Jones that after driving, the defendant consumed five beers. The chart does not account for the defendant's act of vomiting. As per criminal analyst Scott Montgomery, this act likely would have lowered the defendant's cumulative percentage of absorbed alcohol, thus lowering the expected blood alcohol content. The dot represents the tested, stipulated blood alcohol content (.17) of the defendant's blood at 10:54 p.m.

Statement of Hunter Robinson

I am thirty-four years old and a graduate from Cal-Techno where I majored in biomedical engineering. I received my master's degree in biomedical engineering and pharmacology in CY-12. Since June CY-12, I worked as a pharmacist at Jonesha Pharmaceuticals. In CY-10, I married the love of my life and my colleague at Cal-Techno, Lauren Griffin. We were happily married for seven years. We didn't have any children because we wanted to focus on our careers and travel around the world. In the winter of CY-3, however, I returned home one night to find Lauren in bed with someone else. Distraught, I filed for divorce the following week. To add to my troubles, in CY-1, due to the economic collapse, I was laid off from my job at Jonesha Pharmaceuticals. It seemed like my whole world fell apart. I felt so betrayed and I sunk into a depression. I now struggle to make it through every day with the bills piling up, the rent, the car note, etc. I still suffer from depression and have become an alcoholic.

I have gone to psychiatrists off and on, but have not found any medication to lift my despair. I know that drinking alcohol is not a solution, but it numbs the pain. Besides, I don't drink and drive or get into fights, or anything like that. If I tie one on, I am not hurting anyone but myself. Adults should be able to decide how they lead their lives, even if it's self-destructive, as long as it does not hurt anyone else. I would never do anything to jeopardize anyone else's safety. That's why I never drive drunk. I have a cousin who was killed by a drunk driver when he was only seventeen. That was devastating to my family, especially my aunt and uncle. I would never drive drunk, and that is why I know I was not drinking before the crash. I went into biomedical engineering in order to devote my life to helping people. That is the kind of person that I am.

Since losing my job last year, I have had several interviews and have been rejected every time. I have interviewed for positions where I am well qualified, such as lead researcher at Stanford's Biomedical Engineering lab. I have also interviewed for jobs where I am overqualified, such as a clerk in a pharmacy for Right-Aide. After receiving the lowest blow—a rejection letter from Right-Aide-- I hit the wall. My ex-wife's boyfriend even got a job as a scientist and he went to a completely inferior school.

How do you think that makes me feel? It's no wonder I turn to the bottle. It's the only way I can sleep at night.

Getting to what happened yesterday, July 12, CY-1, the night of my arrest—my roommate, Steve, and I were hanging out at the house we rent and we wanted to drink some beer. All we had at home was hard liquor, but no beer. I just wanted to get some beer, so I drove to the liquor store to get a six-pack of Dos Equis. Steve and I really enjoy tossing back beers together. It relaxes us and we don't feel as hung over the next day as we do if we drink hard alcohol. Besides, I was really trying to drink less, so I thought beer would be a better choice than the hard stuff.

It was around 7:30 p.m. and the sun had just set. The canyon was dark. As I was driving back home, I was coming through Maliwood Canyon Drive around the curves. I remember feeling emotional and dazed from my failures these past two weeks in the job search. I was changing the radio stations because every song on the radio made me upset. I must have not been paying close attention to the road because all of a sudden, I saw a shadow of what looked like a deer or coyote, just feet away in front of my car! There is a lot of wildlife in the canyons. I quickly slammed the brakes and made a sharp turn to avoid a collision. I must have lost control. The next thing I knew I was off the side of the highway, in a ditch, and surrounded by airbags.

I was so shocked that I was still alive and still dazed from the events that transpired. Then, I heard a loud bang come from my car. This noise made me jump and fight to get out! I was scared that my car might blow up or something. I squirmed my way from between the airbags, and jimmied the side door open to get out. When I got out, I remember stumbling away from the car. I was shook up, but I had not been drinking. I already had a bottle of Grey Goose in the backseat. I had bought it the day before and just forgot to bring it in the house. The bottle broke during the collision. I was so afraid that the police would think I was drinking and driving, so I took the broken bottle and put it in a bag I had.

I decided to abandon the car and walk to the liquor store and back home. I was too upset, and it was getting too dark to deal with the car until the next morning. Home was only a mile or so away. I walked to the liquor store, threw away the broken bottle and bag, bought a six-pack of Dos Equis and walked home. My roommate Steve was waiting for me at home and let me in. I told him I crashed my car and needed some drinks to settle my nerves. Five beers were not enough, so I opened the bottle of tequila. Just like old college days, I wanted to get trashed. Steve and I hit shot after shot. I don't remember how many we did. Steve always outdid me, so I was on a mission to beat him this time. I don't remember much after that, but that one drink too many sent me to the toilet. I went to my room to recover. I flushed the toilet and looked up. The next thing I knew, a policeman was in my room! He asked if I had been drinking, and I just nodded and put my face back in the toilet.

I knew I was going to get booked. The officer did those crazy tests, a blood test, and then some other stuff. He then told me, "Nice try, let's go." The cop read me my rights. I admitted to the cop that I was drunk, but I tried to explain to him that I did not drink at all until after the crash. He wouldn't listen to me. He had already made up his mind that I was a drunk driver. That's why I refused to answer his questions, but I agreed to write this statement. I want to tell my side and to have the truth come out. The cops try to put words in people's mouths and get them all confused. I feel hung over and lousy today, but I am certain that I was not driving drunk. I had not had one drop of alcohol before the crash that day. The cops can ask the liquor store guy where I bought the beer. I admit that I was drunk when the police found me. It's not a crime to be drunk in your own home, but I wasn't drunk when I crashed the car. I did not drink any alcohol until after the accident.

I have read the above statement and swear, upon penalty of perjury, that the statement is true and accurate.

Signed,

Hunter Robinson

Hunter Robinson

Statement of Alex Lou

My name is Alex Lou, and I have lived in Maliwood for the past twenty years. I have worked at the Maliwood Convenience Store for over ten years. Three years ago, I became the night manager. My hours at work are from 7:30 p.m. until 3:30 a.m. It is a pretty tough shift, but I figure since I don't have anyone at home to tend to, I can make do with that job.

On July 12, CY-1, I was working my usual night shift. Around 8:30 p.m., a customer, who I now know to be Hunter Robinson, came into my store. I remember the time because it was directly after my 15 minute smoke break. I always take a smoke break at 8:15 p.m. It's tough for me to go more than 45 minutes without a smoke. From my perspective, Robinson did not appear drunk at all. He was not staggering, nor did he smell like alcohol. However, he did appear to be very upset. I asked how his night was going, and he told me that he had just been down on his luck. He had just finalized a divorce, and he had just lost his job as a pharmacist. Maybe he confided in me because he could tell I was lonely too. It's kind of like that on the graveyard shift, sometimes strangers just tell you their life story. I felt sorry for him. I know what it's like to be alone. He also said he had just totaled his car trying to swerve away from hitting an animal on the road. In the Maliwood Canyon, there are many deer and coyotes. I asked if he had called the cops or some towing service about his car. He told me that he would be doing that soon. He said he was shook up, needed fresh air, a drink, and just had to walk away from the crash site to clear his head. This made sense to me.

I do recall that he bought a 6-pack of beer. Though he appeared to be of age to purchase the alcohol, I wanted to double-check because of the recent problems we have had. Our store is currently under investigation by the Bureau of Alcohol, Tobacco, and Firearms for the possible sale of alcohol to a minor, so I checked his identification. As I compared his license photograph with his appearance, I noticed that his eyes appeared to be droopy, as if he was tired. He seemed a little confused, but this was entirely consistent with just getting in a car crash. Neither of his eyes appeared red or watery. His speech was not slurred. I have been trained to check for such physical symptoms of intoxication because our store could be held liable if we sell to an intoxicated individual. We also risk the chance of losing our alcohol license, which would cripple our business. In my opinion, Robinson was not intoxicated when he was in my store.

My store has a surveillance camera, and the tape rewinds and runs over after twenty-four hours. I was not contacted about this incident until three weeks after the night in question, so I do not have any recordings of that night. I would have been happy to have saved any tapes, if the police had asked me to. I'll bet the tapes would have shown that Robinson was not staggering or acting drunk.

It came to my attention later, after checking store receipts, that the transaction for beer occurred at 8:54 p.m. I do not believe this is accurate. I have been having some difficulties with my cash register. For instance, the register had incorrectly calculated sales tax on several transactions this month. It also, for whatever reason, would sometimes change the number "five" to the number "three." Because of this, I always double-check the amount of purchases. I never paid much attention to the time listed on the receipt, though; I had no reason to notice it.

I have read the above statement and swear, upon penalty of perjury, that the statement is true and accurate.

Signed,

Alex Lou

Alex Lou

Statement of Olivia Montes

I have been an independently employed criminal analyst for the past eight years. Prior to my employment, I received a bachelor's degree in pharmacology and toxicology and a master's degree in forensics from Oceana City College. I am certified by the State of Oceana in the field of forensic analysis. In order to become certified, I took and completed fifty hours of courses on subjects such as crime scene analysis, biomedical DNA testing, law enforcement research methods, statistics, psychology, and criminal intelligence analysis. For the past six years, I have worked mainly in the Alcohol Detection and Analysis unit. I have performed over 220 driving under the influence investigations and have testified seven times in court for DUI charges.

On July 15, CY-1, I was contacted by the lawyers representing Robinson regarding this case. I was asked to conduct a blood alcohol analysis. I was provided with the relevant and necessary information. It is my professional opinion that Robinson's blood alcohol content of .17 at the time of his arrest is consistent with post accident drinking.

In coming to this conclusion, there are two primary questions that must be answered: first, how much alcohol Robinson consumed; and second, whether or not there was sufficient absorption of this post-accident consumed alcohol such that it represents a BAC reading of .17.

Robinson's blood was drawn at approximately 10:54 p.m. The alcohol elimination rate, the rate at which alcohol is eliminated from the body by excretion and metabolism, can range from .012 to .020 per hour. Using .017 as the elimination rate, Robinson's BAC would have been either .18 or .19 at 9:57 p.m., the time of arrest.

According to the store clerk, Robinson purchased a 6-pack of beer around 8:30 p.m. Though it is unknown exactly what time Robinson returned home, let us assume that Robinson arrived home just before 9:00 p.m. At 9:50 p.m., the arresting officer arrived at Robinson's residence. Therefore, Robinson had about an hour of drinking time. During this time, according to Robinson, he consumed five beers and went "shot for shot" of tequila with his friend. A standard beer will raise one's BAC about .02 to .025.

Five beers would likely put an individual's BAC at about .10 to .125. We do not know how many shots were consumed when Robinson decided to go "shot for shot" with his friend. We do, however, know that Robinson said that Steve Jenson, his friend, would always win drinking games with him. We also know that Jenson has a higher alcohol tolerance, which would explain why Robinson, but not Jenson, was found vomiting when the officer arrived. Second, the "shot for shot" contest led Robinson to consume more alcohol than his body could handle. A standard shot of tequila would raise an individual's BAC .02 to .025. Three shots of tequila here would raise the BAC .06 to .075. Add in the five beers and you would have a BAC in the range of .16 to .20.

It is entirely plausible that Robinson could have consumed five beers and taken three shots of tequila in the hour prior to the officer's arrival. The focus is also on the degree and rate of alcohol absorption that took place prior to vomiting. Vomiting will not lower one's BAC, but it prevents it from rising. By vomiting, the body is refusing to digest excess alcohol in the stomach. Once consumed, alcohol enters the stomach but does not begin entering one's blood stream, thus alcohol does not impact BAC until it either reaches the small intestines or is absorbed into the bloodstream by the stomach's lining. The rate at which alcohol is absorbed into the bloodstream can depend on a number of factors that include whether the individual has recently eaten, how quickly they are drinking, and the concentration of the alcoholic beverage. A standard beer is about 4% of alcohol by volume. A standard shot of tequila is more concentrated than a beer, ranging from about 35%–40% of alcohol by volume. A shot of tequila will absorb at a much greater rate than a beer. How one consumes the alcohol is also important. Chugging a beer versus sipping a beer will lead to a greater rate of absorption. Given how quickly one is able to consume shots, it is possible that Robinson, prior to vomiting, had at least a half-hour to fully absorb the consumed alcohol. The shots of tequila and contest style drinking would have accelerated the rate of absorption. Therefore, it is my professional opinion that Robinson's BAC of .17 is reflective of and directly related to the post accident drinking consumption at his residence.

I am aware of Robinson's statements to the police regarding the type and amount of alcohol he consumed after the accident. Due to his state of inebriation at the time, his recollection of the events is not likely to be accurate. Furthermore, it is common to suffer "blackouts" from excess consumption of alcohol. A blackout is an alcohol related amnesia that affects an individual's ability to create long-term memories or accurately recall memories.

In my years working as a criminal analyst, I have been involved with a great number of cases that involved excess consumption of alcohol based on the experience of traumatic events. Alcohol allows individuals to temporarily get away from their problems. It appears that Robinson's alcohol consumption is another one of these types of cases. There is insufficient information to conclude that Mr. Robinson consumed the alcohol in question before driving. The only fact that is undisputed is that Robinson's BAC was .17 at the time of his arrest. Based on the evidence presented to me in this case, it is a huge leap to try to speculate what his BAC was at the time of driving.

I certify that the above is true to the best of my knowledge and recollection under the penalty of perjury.

Signed,

Olivia Montes

Olivia Montes

Exhibit A

```
                    Sunset Gas

            543 Ocean Breeze Parkway
                 Maliwood County
                 (310)555-0128

              ----CASH RECEIPT---
               7/12/CY-1 8:54 PM
            --------------------
REF ID: 4720-1324
Clerk: Alex

Dos Equis 6 Pack             9.99
Bottle Deposit                .60
------------------------------------

------------------------------------
Subtotal                    10.59
Tax (8.75%)                   .87
                            ------
Total                       11.46

CASH                        20.00

CHANGE                       8.54
------------------------------------

------------------------------------

                  Thank You!
```

Exhibit B

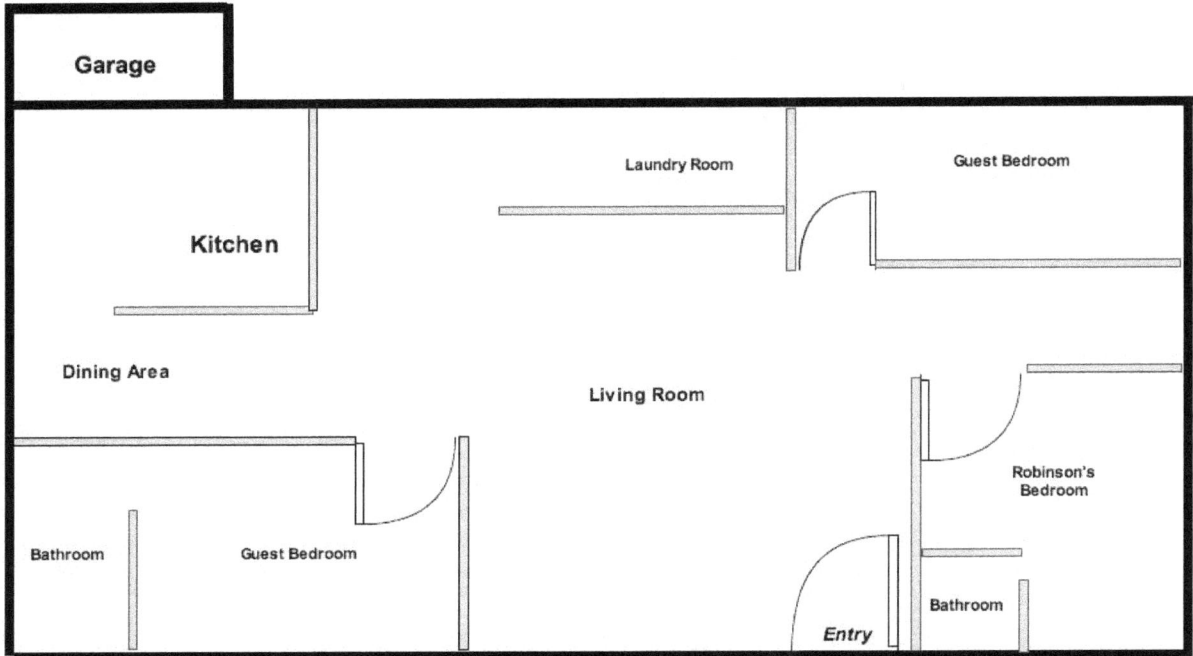

Garage

Kitchen

Laundry Room

Guest Bedroom

Dining Area

Living Room

Robinson's
Bedroom

Bathroom

Guest Bedroom

Bathroom

Entry

Exhibit C

Exhibit D

Exhibit E

Exhibit F

Maliwood County Sheriff's Department
Office of Forensic Investigation
Computer Crimes Unit
16437 Glenhurst St
Maliwood, OC 90120

July 22, CY-1

Re   People v. Robinson
      Case # MW742834

Officer Casey Jones,

I analyzed the contents of Hunter Robinson's mobile, specimen
#8675409. The following text message was recovered from the SIM card
found inside the telephone.

Incoming Message
>From: (555)576-1711
>>>Received: July 12, CY-1 20:19

"u alright? I knew you shouldn't have been driving, you need me to
pick you up at Sunset Gas?"

Sincerely,
Danica Pryor
Danica Pryor
Forensic Analyst
Serial #10187

Jury Instructions

Members of the jury, I thank you for your attention during this trial. Please pay close attention to the instructions I am about to give you.

In this case, Hunter Robinson, Defendant, is charged in two counts. The first count charges the defendant with driving under the influence of an alcoholic beverage in violation of Oceana Vehicle Code section 23152(a). To prove that the defendant is guilty of this crime, the People must prove that:

1. Defendant drove a vehicle; AND

2. When he drove, he was under the influence of an alcoholic beverage.

A person is *under the influence* if, as a result of drinking or consuming alcoholic beverage(s), his or her mental or physical abilities are so impaired that he or she is no longer able to drive a vehicle with the caution of a sober person, using ordinary care, under similar circumstances.

The manner in which a person drives is not enough by itself to establish whether the person is or is not under the influence of an alcoholic beverage. However, it is a factor to be considered, in light of all surrounding circumstances, in deciding whether the person was under the influence.

An *alcoholic beverage* is a liquid or solid material intended to be consumed that contains ethanol. Ethanol is also known as ethyl alcohol, drinking alcohol, or alcohol.

The second count that Defendant is charged with is driving a motor vehicle with a blood alcohol content of .08 percent or higher in violation of Oceana Vehicle Code section 23152(b). In order to prove that Defendant is guilty of this crime, the People must prove that:

1. Defendant drove a vehicle; AND

2. When he drove, Defendant's blood alcohol content was .08 percent, by weight, or higher.

If the People have proved beyond a reasonable doubt that Defendant's blood alcohol level was .08 percent or more at the time of the chemical analysis, you may, but are not required to, conclude that the defendant was under the influence of an alcoholic beverage at the time of the alleged offense.

Defendant has pleaded not guilty to the charges. The fact that a criminal charge has been filed against Defendant is not evidence that the charge is true. You must not be biased against Defendant just because he/she has been arrested, charged with a crime, or brought to trial.

To overcome Defendant's presumption of innocence, the State has the burden to prove the following:

1. The crime with which Defendant is charged was committed.

2. Defendant is the person who committed the crime.

The State has the burden to prove the elements beyond a reasonable doubt. Whenever the words *reasonable doubt* are used, you must consider the following: A reasonable doubt is not a mere possible doubt, because everything relating to human affairs is open to some possible or imaginary doubt. Reasonable doubt is the state of the case that, after hearing and considering all the evidence, leaves the minds of the jurors in the condition that they cannot say they feel an abiding conviction of the truth of the charge.

It is to the evidence introduced during this trial, and to it alone, that you are to look for that proof. A reasonable doubt as to the guilt of Defendant may arise from evidence, a conflict in the evidence, or a lack of evidence. If you have a reasonable doubt, you should find Defendant not guilty. If you have no reasonable doubt, you should find Defendant guilty.

You must decide this case on the evidence and the law. It is up to you to decide what evidence is reliable. You should use your common sense in deciding what evidence is reliable and what evidence should not be relied upon in considering your verdict.

A witness is a person who has knowledge related to this case. You will have to decide whether you believe each witness and how important each witness's testimony is to the case. You may believe all, part, or none of a witness's testimony. In deciding whether to believe a witness's testimony, you may consider, among other factors, the following:

1. The extent of the witness's opportunity to see, hear, or otherwise become familiar with any matter about which the witness testified.

2. The ability of the witness to accurately recall or communicate any matter about which the witness testified and the character and quality of that testimony.

3. The witness's manner and demeanor while on the stand.

4. Whether or not the witness has bias, an improper motive, or an interest in the outcome of the case.

5. The witness's attitude toward this trial or toward testifying.

6. Whether the witness's testimony was consistent or inconsistent with other testimony or evidence presented in this case.

7. Any previous statements made by the witness that are consistent or inconsistent with the witness's testimony.

8. The witness's character for honesty or veracity, or their opposites.

9. Whether the witness was offered money, preferred treatment, or any other benefit to testify or whether the witness received any threats or was under any pressure that might have affected the truth of the witness's testimony.

10. The witness's previous conviction of a felony or past criminal conduct amounting to a misdemeanor.

You may rely upon your own conclusions about each witness. A juror may believe or disbelieve all or any part of the evidence or the testimony of any witness.

There are some general rules that apply to your deliberations. You must abide by these rules in order to return a verdict that is consistent with the law:

1. You must follow the law as it is explained to you in these instructions. If you fail to follow the law or disregard the law, any verdict you reach will be a miscarriage of justice.

2. You must decide the case only upon the evidence that you have heard from either the testimony of witnesses or exhibits that you have seen.

3. You must not decide the case for or against anyone because you feel sympathy for that person, or because you are angry at that person.

4. You must not decide the case based on your feelings about the lawyers in this case. The lawyers are not on trial.

5. You must not consider any potential sentence Defendant might receive. It is not your duty to consider punishment. Your only duty is to determine guilt or innocence. It is the judge's job to determine the proper sentence if you find Defendant guilty.

6. Whatever verdict you render must be unanimous; that is, each juror must commit to the same verdict. The verdict must be the verdict of each juror as well as that of the jury as a whole.

7. It is entirely proper for a lawyer to talk to a witness about what testimony the witness would give if called into the courtroom. The witness should not be discredited for talking to a lawyer about his or her testimony.

8. You must not decide this case based on feelings of prejudice, bias, or sympathy. Any verdict you may reach should be based on the evidence and the law contained in these instructions.

Deciding a proper verdict is exclusively your job. I cannot participate in that decision in any way. Please disregard anything I might have said or done that made you think I preferred one verdict over another.

Only one verdict may be returned for the crime charged. The verdict must be in writing and the verdict form has been prepared for you. It is as follows:

(READ JURY VERDICT FORM)

In just a few moments, the Bailiff will escort you to the jury room. Once inside the jury room, the first thing you should do is elect a foreperson, who will preside over your deliberations. It is the foreperson's job to sign and date the verdict form when all of you have agreed on a verdict in this case and to bring the verdict back to the courtroom when you return.

In conclusion, let me remind you that it is imperative that you follow the law as I have explained it to you in these instructions. Regardless of how you feel about the laws, you must apply them.

SUPERIOR COURT OF THE STATE OF OCEANA

FOR THE COUNTY OF MALIWOOD

STATE OF OCEANA, Plaintiff, v. **HUNTER ROBINSON,** Defendant.	Case No. MW742834 **CHARGE(S):** 23152(a) Driving under the influence of alcohol or drugs 1 count 23152(b) Driving while having a .08% or higher blood alcohol content 1 count

VERDICT

As to the charge of driving under the influence of alcohol or drugs, in violation of Oceana Vehicle Code section 23152(a), we, the jury, find the Defendant, Hunter Robinson:

_____ GUILTY

_____ NOT GUILTY

As to the charge of Driving while having a .08 percent or higher blood alcohol content, in violation of Oceana Vehicle Code section 23152(b), we, the jury, find the Defendant, Hunter Robinson:

_____ GUILTY

_____ NOT GUILTY

So say we all.

_____
Foreperson of the Jury

_____
Date

CASE FILE No. 5

STATE OF OCEANA

V.

ELIN SVENNSON

(Stalking)

SUPERIOR COURT OF THE STATE OF OCEANA

COUNTY OF MALIWOOD

STATE OF OCEANA,		Case No. MW924739
	Plaintiff,	
v.		**FELONY COMPLAINT**
ELIN SVENNSON,		
	Defendant.	

COUNT 1

On or about November 10, CY-1, in the City of Maliwood, Maliwood County, State of Oceana, a felony, in violation of section 646.9 of the Oceana Penal Code, commonly referred to as STALKING, was committed by the above defendant, who at the time and place last aforesaid, willfully, maliciously, and repeatedly followed and harassed Lawrence Wilhoyt and Victoria Beck, and made a credible threat against Lawrence Wilhoyt and Victoria Beck with the intent to place them in reasonable fear of their safety.

COUNT 2

On or about November 10, CY-1, in the City of Maliwood, Maliwood County, State of Oceana, a misdemeanor, in violation of section 166 of the Oceana Penal Code, commonly referred to as VIOLATING A VALID RESTRAINING ORDER, was committed by the above defendant, who at the time and place last aforesaid, came within 100 yards of Lawrence Wilhoyt, Michael Wilhoyt, Samantha Wilhoyt, and Victoria Beck.

COUNT 3

On or about November 10, CY-1, in the City of Maliwood, Maliwood County, State of Oceana, a misdemeanor, in violation of section 422 of the Oceana Penal Code, commonly referred to as MAKING A CRIMINAL THREAT, was committed by the above defendant, who at the time and place last aforesaid, did willfully threaten to commit a crime which would result in death or great bodily injury to

Lawrence Wilhoyt and Victoria Beck with the specific intent that the statement made verbally, in writing, or by means of an electronic communication device, is to be taken as a threat, even if there is no intent of actually carrying it out, which on its face and under the circumstances in which it is made, is so unequivocal, unconditional, immediate, and specific as to convey to the person threatened a gravity of purpose and an immediate prospect of execution of the threat, and thereby causes that person reasonably to be in sustained fear for his or her own safety or for his or her immediate family's safety.

IT IS SO ORDERED.

Simon Luna

Simon Luna
District Attorney, County of Maliwood

Witness List

Witnesses for the State:

1.   Lawrence Wilhoyt*

2.   Victoria Beck**

Witnesses for the Defense:

1.   Elin Svennson**

2.   Alex Villafuentes***

Each side must call both witnesses listed for its respective party, and both parties stipulate that each party's expert witness would testify consistently with his or her provided statement.

*This witness must be played by a male.

**This witness must be played by a female.

***This witness may be either gender.

Stipulations

1. Federal Rules of Criminal Procedure and Federal Rules of Evidence apply.

2. Each witness who gave an interview or statement reviewed the officer's report of his or her witness statement and verified it was complete and accurate.

3. All witness statements were given under oath.

4. All exhibits in the file are authentic and, unless otherwise noted, are the original of that document.

5. All dates are denoted by CY (current year) or CY-*n* (current year minus *n* years).

6. All pretrial motions shall be oral.

7. "Beyond the record" is not a valid objection. Attorneys for either party should use cross-examination as the proper means to challenge a witness whose testimony goes beyond the facts provided in the witness's statements.

8. Oceana Penal Code section 646.9(a) reads as follows: "Any person who willfully, maliciously, and repeatedly follows or willfully and maliciously harasses another person and who makes a credible threat with the intent to place that person in reasonable fear for his or her safety, or the safety of his or her immediate family, is guilty of the crime of stalking."

9. Oceana Penal Code section 166 reads as follows: "Every person guilty of any contempt of court, including willful disobedience of the terms as written of any process or court order, lawfully issued by any court, including orders pending trial, is guilty of a misdemeanor."

10. Oceana Penal Code section 422 reads as follows: "Any person who willfully threatens to commit a crime which will result in death or great bodily injury to another person, with the specific intent that the statement made verbally, in writing, or by means of an electronic communication device, is to be taken as a threat, even if there is no intent of actually carrying it out, which on its face and under the circumstances in which it is made, is so unequivocal, unconditional, immediate, and specific as to convey to the person threatened a gravity of purpose and an immediate prospect of execution of the threat, and thereby causes that person reasonably to be in sustained fear for his or her own safety or for his or her immediate family's safety."

11. Other than what appears in the officer's report of the interviews, there is nothing exceptional or unusual about the background of any of the witnesses that would bolster or detract from their credibility.

12. No party may "invent" witnesses or evidence not specifically mentioned in this problem.

13. The physical description of a witness shall be tailored to that of the student playing the witness, except for height, weight, and age.

14. The statements of Tracy Piaggi and Penélope Campos Arredondo are stipulated to as being an accurate reflection of what each would testify to if called as a witness; it is therefore unnecessary to call either as a witness. Hearsay objections are waived as to these witness statements.

15. The prosecution and defense may only call the two witnesses listed on their respective witness list.

16. The witness Lawrence Wilhoyt must be a male. The witness Victoria Beck must be a female. The witness Elin Svennson must be a female. The other witnesses may be male or female. The witnesses may be called in any order.

17. Lawrence Wilhoyt's cell phone number is (310) 555-3745.

18. Lawrence Wilhoyt's work phone number is (310) 555-0837.

19. Alex Villafuentes's phone number is (310) 555-2567.

20. A valid restraining order was issued against Defendant Elin Svennson stating that she at all times must remain 100 yards from Lawrence Wilhoyt, Victoria Beck, Michael Wilhoyt, and Samantha Wilhoyt as well as 100 yards from Lawrence's home and business.

21. November 10, CY-1 was a Friday.

COUNTY OF MALIWOOD SHERIFF'S DEPARTMENT
INVESTIGATION REPORT

RECORDS & STATISTICS BUREAU'S USE ONLY   DATE: **11/10/CY-1**   PAGE: **1** OF **2**

ACTION	ACTIVE (X) INACTIVE ( ) PENDING ( )	INDEX Yes (X) INFO No ( )	N of Adult Arrests 1	No of Subject Detentions 1	URN (File No.) MW957100		

CLASSIFICATION
STALKING

DATE, TIME OF OCCURRENCE
11/10/CY-1, 14:30 HOURS

LOCATION OF OCCURRENCE 1400 STARFIRE LANE, MALIWOOD, OC	TYPE OF LOCATION PUBLIC PARK	TRACT

CODE: V - VICTIM, W - WITNESS, I - INFORMANT, R - REPORTING PARTY, P - PARTY

CODE V NO. 1 OF 2	LAST NAME WILHOYT, LAWRENCE	FIRST	MIDDLE	SEX M	AGE 37	RACE WHITE

RESIDENCE ADDRESS 595 RIP CURRENT WAY, MALIWOOD, OC	RES. PHONE (AREA CODE) (310) 555-3745

BUSINESS ADDRESS	RES. PHONE (AREA CODE)

CODE W NO. 1 OF 2	LAST NAME BECK, VICTORIA	FIRST	MIDDLE	SEX F	AGE 26	RACE WHITE

RESIDENCE ADDRESS 6472 POSEIDON LANE, MALIWOOD, OC	RES. PHONE (AREA CODE) (310) 555-0837

BUSINESS ADDRESS	RES. PHONE (AREA CODE)

CODE W NO. 1 OF 1	LAST NAME VILLAFUENTES, ALEX	FIRST	MIDDLE	SEX M	AGE 35	RACE WHITE

RESIDENCE ADDRESS 5871, TIDE BREAK DRIVE, MALIWOOD, OC	RES. PHONE (AREA CODE) (310) 555-2567

BUSINESS ADDRESS	RES. PHONE (AREA CODE)

CODE: S - SUSPECT, SJ - SUBJECT, M - PATIENT, S/V - SUSPECT/VICTIM, SJ/V - SUBJECT / VICTIM

CODE S No 1 OF 1	LAST NAME SVENNSON, ELIN	FIRST	MIDDLE	DRIVER'S LICENSE (STATE & No) OC X1285835

RESIDENCE ADDRESS 5871, TIDE BREAK DRIVE, MALIWOOD, OC	RES. PHONE (AREA CODE)

BUSINESS ADDRESS 5871, TIDE BREAK DRIVE, MALIWOOD, OC	BUS. PHONE (AREA CODE)

SEX F	RACE WHITE	HAIR BLONDE	EYES BLUE	HEIGHT 5'7"	WEIGHT 140 LBS	DOB	AGE 26	WHERE DETAINED MALIWOOD

OBSERVABLE PHYSICAL ODDITIES/TATTOOS/SCARS	AKA / NICKNAME	BOOKING No. MW37698

CLOTHING WORN WHITE SUNDRESS, BEIGE SANDLES	MAIN

CHARGE (1) STALKING; (2) VIOLATION OF VALID RESTRAINING ORDER; (3) MAKING A CRIMINAL THREAT	WEAPON USED N/A

CODE No OF	LAST NAME	FIRST	MIDDLE	DRIVER'S LICENSE (STATE & No)

RESIDENCE ADDRESS	RES. PHONE (AREA CODE)

BUSINESS ADDRESS	BUS. PHONE (AREA CODE)

SEX	RACE	HAIR	EYES	HEIGHT	WEIGHT	D.O.B.	AGE	WHERE DETAINED OR CITE No.

OBSERVABLE PHYSICAL ODDITIES	AKA / NICKNAME	BOOKING No.

CLOTHING WORN	MAIN

CHARGE	WEAPON USED

Narrative Report – URN MW924739

At approximately 14:30 hours, dispatch received a call from Lawrence Wilhoyt. Wilhoyt reported that a woman named Elin Svennson was in violation of a restraining order (RO) placed against her on 11/01/CY-1. The RO against Svennson, granted because she left a threatening note on Wilhoyt's red Ferrari on 10/30/CY-1, required that she not contact or go within 100 yards of Lawrence Wilhoyt, his girlfriend Victoria Beck, or his children.

Wilhoyt stated that Svennson had already been in violation of the RO by making numerous calls over the past week (see attached Exhibit B and Statement of Lawrence Wilhoyt); however, he did not contact the police about the phone calls. Wilhoyt also stated that Svennson threatened him, Beck, and his family today in the parking lot behind Maliwood Sushi, where she approached Wilhoyt and Beck after having left another threatening note on his vehicle (see attached Exhibits C and F).

The original note on the car was taken as evidence on 10/30/CY-1 and filed with the RO (see attached Exhibit C). I was sent to inspect the note and vehicle at Maliwood Sushi (see attached Exhibits E–G) as well as to interview Wilhoyt and Beck. Upon speaking to them, I realized I needed to talk to Svennson herself and make sure that the allegations of stalking and making a criminal threat were justified. Wilhoyt told me that Svennson was now under the employment of Alex Villafuentes. At 15:45 hours, I went to the Villafuentes residence. Svennson was not there, but Villafuentes told me that I could find her at the Maliwood soccer field with the Villafuentes children. Villafuentes followed me to pick up the children while I arrested Svennson for violating the RO.

Signed,

Officer Gabriel
Officer Gabriel

Maliwood County Sheriff's Department
Supplemental Police Report

Report Type: Interrogation of Elin Svennson

*Recorded per Maliwood County Sheriff's Department Interrogation Procedures

Interviewer: Officer Thomas Gabriel (TG)

Date and Time of Interview: November 10, CY-1, 16:30 hours

Suspect was arrested at Maliwood soccer field. The following interview took place at the Maliwood County Sheriff's Station at 16:30 hours after I transported Suspect Elin Svennson (ES) to the station in my police cruiser.

TG: Please state your name.

ES: Elin Svennson.

TG: Ms. Svennson, do you understand that you have the right to remain silent and anything you say can and will be used against you in a court of law?

ES: I understand that is the way it works in America.

TG: You have the right to a lawyer and if you cannot afford a lawyer, one will be provided to you at no cost. Do you understand and give up these rights?

ES: I am aware of my rights. Yes, I give them up. I want to talk to you. I have nothing to hide! I also know that I did nothing wrong. I want to set the record straight and tell you what really happened. I don't need a lawyer because I am innocent!

TG: Are you aware that you have been arrested for stalking Lawrence Wilhoyt, his children, Michael and Samantha, and his girlfriend, Victoria Beck, and for violating a restraining order as well as making a criminal threat against them?

ES: Yes, I know that you think I was "stalking," but it is not like that at all. And that restraining order . . . it's bogus. And I didn't threaten anyone!

TG: Let's start from the beginning. Where are you from Ms. Svennson?

ES: Well, I currently live in Maliwood. But originally, I am from Sweden. I moved to the States in January of CY-3.

TG: Why did you come to the United States?

ES: I came here to live the "American Dream." I just love America, especially American television! I watched all the American shows like "Dancing with the Celebs" and "Billionaire Matchmaker." You know, I was on the show "Foreign Love" where girls from around the world try to get a rose from the bachelor and find a rich husband. The other girls on the show were mean.

TG: Why is that?

ES: Well, I think I was a threat to them because the bachelor liked me the most. They all thought I was after money. They used the term "gold-digger." That wasn't the case at all! I really thought I was falling in love with the Maliwood Bachelor.

TG: Let's talk about Lawrence Wilhoyt. How do you know him?

ES: I was his live-in nanny. He was the first person to give me steady employment here in America. I started working for him in February of CY-2. I came to help out after Lawrence's wife died. I really thought Lawrence was an amazing and special person. No one understands Lawrence like I do. This whole thing is a big misunderstanding. I know in my heart that this is all because of Victoria; she's totally poisoned him against me and my fear is that she'll do the same with the kids! I know I was a great nanny! I would never let anything happen to those kids.

TG: So you were a nanny for Lawrence. Let's talk about that. What did being a nanny entail?

ES: Well, I lived in a guesthouse in the back of Lawrence's house. I would wake up in the morning and make breakfast for Lawrence and his kids, Michael and Samantha. We were like a family. I would then take the kids to school and Lawrence would go to work.

TG: Our records show that your cell phone made over twenty calls to Lawrence over the last week. Why so many calls?

ES: Are you sure it's that many? I didn't think that I made *that* many calls. I was trying to explain to Lawrence how I felt and why he was wrong to fire me and that the restraining order was a mistake, but he wasn't returning any of my phone calls. I really just wanted to make sure that the kids were okay.

TG: What about Victoria Beck?

ES: I really don't want to talk about her. At first, I thought we would be really good friends because we were the same age. She even "friended" me on Facebook. I mean, we were Facebook friends until I saw the way she really was. Victoria is a total phony! All Victoria cares about is her job and money. After I found out who the "real" Victoria was, we did not get along. Let me just say that she was not right for Lawrence or his kids. I'll tell you that I tried to talk to Lawrence about her. That's what kind of relationship Lawrence and I had. He liked it when I was honest with him. I wanted what was best for Lawrence and his kids. I couldn't bear to see a cold, distant, and selfish person like Victoria being a mother to Michael and Samantha.

TG: Well, did you ever say anything to Victoria to make her feel uncomfortable?

ES: Absolutely not. I was honest with her too. I didn't think it was good for the kids to see this woman that wasn't their mother sleeping over. It was confusing for the kids. I told her nicely that I didn't think it was a good idea that she sleep over.

TG: Okay, did you ever send Victoria Facebook messages?

ES: Having a Facebook account is not a crime. You know who else has a Facebook account? Victoria! You should see what's on her page. She posted a whole bunch of pictures of herself getting drunk with different guys. At the same time she was dating Lawrence! Can you believe that? But yeah, I sent her messages. Nothing threatening at all, though. I swear.

TG: More specifically, on October 17, CY-1, did you post a cartoon of a girl cutting off a man's head on Victoria's Facebook page?

ES: That was a total misunderstanding! Yeah, I posted that cartoon, but I meant to post it to my other friend's page. I accidentally posted it to Victoria's page. You see, I have another friend named "Victoria." She found out that her boyfriend was cheating on her. I wanted to show my support for her. That's why I wrote, "You'll be happier single." It's crazy to think that the man in the cartoon was Lawrence. Please believe me when I tell you that it was a misunderstanding! You have to understand that I have only been in this country for three years. I am still trying to learn the cultural differences. Things are so different in Sweden. In my country, we are much more direct and upfront with people. I was so worried about Michael and Samantha's safety with Victoria in the house. There was no way I was going to let her become their future stepmother.

TG: And yet, on October 24, CY-1, you were dismissed from your position as nanny to the Wilhoyt children, were you not?

ES: Yes, but it was a stupid mistake. Victoria had been going on and on about how she was going to take the kids shopping for Halloween costumes. She was just all talk and no show. She got their hopes up, and it was clear she was just doing it to pretend like she would be a good stepmother. So on that day, I took them shopping because I kept thinking that all the good costumes would be sold out before she got around to it. After shopping, they asked if I would take them to a movie. So I did. I turned off my phone in the theater. I forgot to turn it back on. After the movie, we went and got ice cream. Then we went straight home. I tried explaining myself to Lawrence, but Victoria has put things in his head. He can't think straight anymore, so he fired me. He fired me for getting his children costumes, ice cream, and taking them out to see a movie.

TG: You do seem pretty mad about being fired, and full of excuses.

ES: Well, obviously. Yes, you could say I'm furious. Victoria is living the life, and I know she doesn't care at all for Lawrence and those kids. If anything, *she* is the gold-digger!

TG: Back to Lawrence, so did you also leave a note on his car on October 30, CY-1, that said, and I quote, "Now that you fired me you're going to suffer—life as you know it is over"? And then today at Maliwood Sushi, did you leave another note that read: "You and your kids are in danger"?

ES: Obviously, when you read them out loud it sounds bad. I wasn't trying to threaten anyone! I was so worried about Michael and Samantha being alone with Victoria. I was also worried about Lawrence. What that first note meant was that, without me as the nanny, life is going to be a lot tougher for Lawrence, Michael, and Samantha. There is no way Victoria will take care of those kids like I did! And that's also why I left the second note. Victoria will be a horrible stepmother, so Lawrence and the kids were in danger. I wasn't putting them in danger; she was!

TG: Did anything else happen at Maliwood Sushi?

ES: No.

TG: Did you say anything to Lawrence or Victoria?

ES: Victoria started it! She was giving me dirty looks. When we went out to the parking lot, she grabbed Lawrence's arm and looked at me with a crooked smile. She is not a nice person. She glared at me the entire time in the restaurant. I made a point of trying to smooth things over, so when I saw them in the parking lot I walked over and asked how Michael and Samantha were doing. Lawrence didn't respond. Then Victoria looked like she was going to hit me. I was scared! I might have said something to put her in her place, so that she wouldn't get any ideas! I just wanted to protect myself.

TG: Did you tell Lawrence, "You should be scared. Now that you fired me, you and your kids are going to suffer! Don't forget that I know where you live"?

ES: That's not what I said. Victoria wants me out of the picture, so she's making up lies about me. I wanted to let Lawrence know that I was worried about the kids' safety around Victoria. I don't trust Victoria. She doesn't have a maternal bone in her body. I was worried she was going to do something to me. Obviously, she hates me. She must have forced Lawrence into getting the restraining order against me.

TG: Why did you pick Maliwood Sushi of all places? I hear that Lawrence goes there for lunch every Friday. You worked for him for a while, so you must have known that he'd be there on a Friday.

ES: Listen. I didn't follow them there. It is total coincidence when I run into Lawrence, his kids, or Victoria. Three days after Lawrence fired me, I started working for a new family in Maliwood. I was hired by the Villafuentes family to look after their children, Bonnie and Max. Bonnie and Max have wanted to try sushi for a while. Today was a pupil free day at their school, so I thought for a special treat, I would take them to Maliwood Sushi for lunch. I wasn't trying to spy on Lawrence or Victoria. I understood there was a restraining order against me, but Maliwood is a small town. What was I supposed to do? Leave the restaurant? That's stupid. Besides, I was sure that Lawrence would eventually speak to me over the phone and have the restraining order removed.

TG: Is there anything else you would like to tell me?

ES: Yeah, you should talk to my current employer, Alex Villafuentes. I started there just three days after Victoria made Lawrence fire me. If I were so dangerous would Alex have hired me right away? Would I still be working for his family? I don't think so.

I have reviewed this transcript. It is a complete and accurate account.

Signed: *Elin Svennson*
                 Elin Svennson

Witnessed: *Officer Gabriel*
                 Officer Gabriel

Statement of Lawrence Wilhoyt

My name is Lawrence Wilhoyt, and I am thirty-seven years old. I have two children, Michael, who is nine, and Samantha, who is six. My wife died of breast cancer three years ago. I work as a real estate investor, which keeps me from being able to spend as much time as I'd like with my kids. I love my kids more than anything though, and I would never let anything hurt them if I could help it.

I met Elin Svennson two years ago. After my wife died, I needed someone to help take care of the kids after school and during the summer. We went through a few nannies, but then hired Elin through an au pair program. My kids immediately loved her, and she fit right in. She took them to swim lessons and their soccer practices. It was a good arrangement. She was able to live in the converted guesthouse, but she was always around to help with the kids if something came up.

About six months ago, things changed. I had started seeing a woman, Victoria Beck. Victoria was the first woman I'd gone out with since my wife passed away. It was nice at first to have Elin around because that provided my children with some stability; it was something that was familiar to them. Elin was a female authority figure whose role they understood, and I thought she would help them get used to me dating someone new. I thought that if Elin started to treat Victoria as my girlfriend, then the kids would adjust too. Unfortunately, that's not how things turned out.

It was small things at first. Since we first started dating, Victoria would tell me that Elin made her uncomfortable—you know, weird looks or off-hand remarks. After a while, I even started to notice the way Elin would look at Victoria and things that she would say when Victoria wasn't around. For instance, she'd periodically tell me that Michael and Samantha didn't like Victoria. She also would regularly say that I'd regret it if I didn't leave Victoria. She'd tell me it was inappropriate for Victoria to be spending the night at my house and that it would send mixed signals to Michael and Samantha. I guess some of it made sense and I tried to see her side of things, but then her behavior became more erratic.

First, the Facebook blow-up happened. I guess Victoria and Elin became Facebook friends when they first met. I don't really know much about Facebook, so I don't know how it all works. One of the postings Victoria showed me said something like, "You'll be happier single." It was a caption to a cartoon that depicted a girl cutting off a man's head. I told Victoria to take a screenshot of it and save it just in case. It was a cartoon that was supposed to be funny, but it scared Victoria. I told her not to worry and that I'd speak with Elin. That was mid-October.

I did speak with Elin and told her that my relationship with Victoria was my business, and that I knew what was best for my children. I also told her that I didn't appreciate her post on Victoria's Facebook profile. For a week, things seemed okay. I thought I'd finally gotten through to her; however, on October 24, she disappeared with my kids.

I got off early from work that day, so I was home about 5:30 p.m., but the kids weren't there. I tried calling Elin, but there was no answer—her phone was turned off. I called the kids' friends' parents, but no one knew where they were. I called the school, and they didn't have any answers. By 10 p.m., I'd even called the police because there was no sign of any of them. I thought my kids had been kidnapped—or worse. Finally, Elin showed up with Michael and Samantha around 11:30 p.m. Elin acted like everything was fine, but I wasn't buying her act anymore.

She'd taken them to get costumes, and they'd gone to a movie and got ice cream. She said that she turned her phone off during the movie and forgot to turn it back on. That was her explanation for not returning my calls. I lost my temper. I started yelling at her. I don't even remember what I said. I just know that I was furious. I fired her on the spot, and I thought that would be it. It's simply unacceptable to me for a nanny to take my kids away for a night without letting me know where they are.

Three days later, she had a job with another family in the area. The new family's children happened to be friends of Michael and Samantha, and it turned out that Elin was still around. And it was shortly thereafter that I found a note that really shook me up.

I was leaving for work on Monday, October 30. I approached my Ferrari in the driveway of my home, and I saw a note placed under the windshield wiper of the car. I opened it up and it had some really disturbing message on it. Something along the lines of, "Now that you fired me, your life is over." I recognized the writing as Elin's. I have seen her writing many times. I called the police immediately, and I filed for a restraining order against Elin. I did it to protect my kids. Because of the nature of the threat, the restraining order applied to Victoria too. I did not press charges at that point because I was hoping that a restraining order would be the end of it all. But I was wrong. The restraining order was granted on November 1. Not long after, though, Elin started phoning me incessantly. I didn't report those calls because I thought she would get the hint and stop when I didn't respond. I didn't want to have her arrested at first because I felt sorry for Elin, and I also didn't want to put Michael and Samantha through an ordeal. They still felt attached to Elin, and they are even fond of her to this day.

The final straw, however, was today at Maliwood Sushi. I go there every Friday for lunch, and since Victoria and I started dating, we go together. Elin knows that if she wanted to run into us, then she'd have a good chance of finding us there around noon. Elin showed up with the children of the new family she was working for. She sat at a table just across from us and was staring at us the entire time. She was obviously violating the restraining order, and to be honest, it creeped me out. Victoria didn't even want to finish her meal. As we were getting our check, we noticed that she did the same. She followed us out into the parking lot. She even had the nerve to approach me and ask me how Michael and Samantha are doing. I told her I wanted her to stay away from my family, and then she threatened me. She told me: "You should be scared. Now that you fired me, you and your kids are going to suffer! Don't forget that I know where you live." I was terrified. Her tone was frightening. She sounded evil. I walked away towards my car. Then, I saw a note on the windshield. I recognized the writing as Elin's. The note confirmed my worst fears. Elin was threatening my family. This note read: "You and your kids are in danger." That's when I decided to come to the police. She's just gone too far this time.

I have read the above statement. It is complete, accurate, and true.

Signed: *Lawrence Wilhoyt*
           Lawrence Wilhoyt

Statement of Victoria Beck

My name is Victoria Beck and I am twenty-six years old. I am an executive assistant for the vice president of a major telecommunications provider in Oceana. I've worked there for the last two years after moving out here from the East Coast. I met Lawrence about a year and a half after I'd been out here and immediately became enthralled. He's such a wonderful and caring man and his two children, Michael and Samantha, are adorable.

I first met Lawrence through my boss, Tyrell. He and Lawrence went to business school together and had remained golfing buddies. Lawrence and I hit it off immediately.

Over the next few months, Lawrence and I fell in love. The only problem was his creepy au pair, Elin. The more time I spent around Lawrence and the kids, the weirder Elin became towards me. She tried to shield Michael and Samantha from me, and she would regularly say negative things about me to them. I know she did because Michael would ask me questions that a boy his age wouldn't typically ask or understand. He'd ask things like, "Do you *really* care about my daddy?" or "Do you like my daddy because he's rich?" Samantha also made comments about whether I just liked her daddy for what he could buy me. Elin regularly asked me if I was with Lawrence for the money, and she would always do this in front of the kids.

She annoyed me, but I wasn't afraid of her until I got this weird message on my Facebook wall. On October 17, she wrote: "You'll be happier single." There was a cartoon that had a woman cutting off a man's head. I showed it to Lawrence and he said he'd talk to her.

She said that she accidentally posted stuff on my wall when she meant to put it on her friend's, whose name conveniently was also Victoria. Honestly, though, who would believe that? It's ridiculous and shows how crazy she is. Lawrence talked to her and gave her the benefit of the doubt. But I didn't trust her, and I wanted him to fire her.

She clearly was jealous of my relationship with Lawrence and the kids. Just before Halloween, she knew I was planning on taking them to get costumes. Before I got a chance to take them, she took them without asking me or telling Lawrence. Then she took the kids to a movie and didn't bring them home until after midnight. That was on October 24. That was a weeknight. Lawrence was so worried about the kids that he fired her.

After Lawrence fired her, I did some snooping on Facebook and started to learn about her past. I guess she was on this reality show; it was called "Foreign Love" or something like that. Before she was an au pair, she competed to go out with this millionaire. The producers kicked her off the show because of some conflict she had with the other contestants. I found a press release about it, but it was vague and only said that she had been acting in ways inconsistent with the agreement she had signed. But I think that she was kicked off the show because she was creeping out the other contestants, which makes perfect sense to me.

I was hoping that once she was fired, we wouldn't have to deal with her anymore. About a week after she was fired, though, she put a note on Lawrence's car. She threatened him and said that he would be sorry for firing her. I mean, how weird is that! Elin is like a character in a scary movie. I told Lawrence we had to get a restraining order against her. I showed him what I found out about her past, and then he agreed with me. On November 1, we got the order against her. Even that didn't work!

Today we saw her at Maliwood Sushi. Shortly after we arrived, Elin walked in with the new kids she was babysitting, which I thought was weird, because it's a really nice sushi restaurant, and what six-year-old likes sushi? Anyway, the hostess sat Elin across from Lawrence and me. I think Elin specifically asked to be sat across from us. Elin was totally violating the restraining order. Elin stared at us for most of the rest of our meal. It was so uncomfortable I told Lawrence to pay the check so that we could get out of there.

Unsurprisingly, she also got her check at the same time and followed us out to the parking lot. She had the nerve to walk up to Lawrence and ask about his kids. I grabbed his arm out of fear. Then, she said to us: "You should be scared. I'm going to hurt both of you and the kids. Don't forget that I know where you live." The weirdest thing was that when she said, "Don't forget that I know where you live," she glared at me. She was definitely threatening me. To make it all the more terrifying, when we got to the car there was another note. This one read: "You and your kids are in danger." Maybe Elin is

angry with the kids for accepting me now. It's all just too much. She knows we go to Maliwood Sushi

for lunch every Friday. She went there on purpose just to threaten us. She is a scary, dangerous person.

I have read the above statement. It is complete, accurate, and true.

Signed: *Victoria Beck*
          Victoria Beck

Statement of Penélope Campos Arredondo

My name is Penélope Campos Arredondo. I am from Barcelona, Spain. I was a contestant on the show "Foreign Love," and was one of the contestants up against Elin Svennson. First of all, I should say that I do not like her at all. Not one bit. She is a very stuck up woman, and she thinks all the men are in love with her.

I couldn't have been happier that she was kicked off the show. We started filming for the show in January of CY-3. I remember that it was early January because I had just come to the States for the show, and I left my family the day after we celebrated *El Día de los Reyes*.

When we started filming, it was obvious from the start that Elin was a gold-digger. All she ever did was ask us girls how we could afford our clothes and jewelry. With that said, all those girls were just there for the money.

That wasn't the issue we had with Elin. Oh, no! She was violent! She slapped one of the girls on the show right in the face. This footage never aired. In fact, all of Elin's scenes were edited out because the producers kicked her off the show. One of the other blondes, Irina—I think she was Russian—was the girl who got in a fight with Elin. I think Elin felt threatened by her because it was obvious that the guy we were all trying to date was most into Irina. I don't know what started the fight. Seemingly, out of nowhere, Elin lunged at Irina, slapped her in the face, and spit on her. The crew was all over Elin in a second. I don't think the producers pressed charges or anything. I think they thought it would be bad publicity.

I have read the above statement. It is complete, accurate, and true.

Signed: *Penélope Campos Arredondo*
Penélope Campos Arredondo

Statement of Alex Villafuentes

My name is Alex Villafuentes, and I am a thirty-eight year old accountant. I have two children, Bonnie, who is nine, and Max, who is six. My spouse works full-time and travels extensively for business. It's very important to my spouse and me to have a very reliable full-time nanny to care for our children because our work is so demanding. I cannot tell you how many nannies we went through. We were so relieved to find Elin.

As soon as I heard Lawrence Wilhoyt had let Elin go, I made sure to hire her before any other parents could. The other parents were jealous that I was able to hire her. I mean, most of the Maliwood parents think Elin is amazing. She did such a great job with Lawrence's kids, Michael and Samantha. When I would take Bonnie and Max to school events I would see how Elin acted with Michael and Samantha. Elin was like a mother to them. You could tell there was a special relationship there. Bonnie and Max participated in some of the same after-school activities as Lawrence's kids—like horseback riding at the Maliwood stables. Sometimes I would see Lawrence with the kids at these places. I do know Lawrence, just not personally. I mean, when I see him I say hello, but we are not close. It is hard not to run into people in Maliwood. It's a pretty small community.

I really don't know why Lawrence let Elin go. I assume that Lawrence didn't need her anymore because he has Victoria now. Before I hired Elin, I would see Victoria taking the kids around Maliwood more and more. I will tell you this though, the kids seemed much happier when they were with Elin than they do when they are with Victoria. Every time I see Victoria around Maliwood with the kids she seems annoyed to be with them. I wouldn't describe Victoria as the "motherly" type.

Bonnie and Max absolutely adore Elin! She has made such a difference in our lives. Having Elin around just gives me peace of mind. I trust her completely with my kids. With her around I can totally concentrate on work. It is true that sometimes I won't hear from or see Elin until late in the evening when she comes home with the kids. I don't worry though, because I know that Elin will take good care of them and not let anything happen to them.

I am fine with Elin taking my kids out to eat, but I was surprised to find out that Elin took Bonnie and Max to a sushi place because I thought my kids hated sushi. When I got home today, Bonnie and Max told me that they were so excited because they had seen their friends from school, Michael and Samantha, at the sushi restaurant. You know, now that I think of it, Bonnie and Max have talked about seeing Michael and Samantha more often since we hired Elin. Maliwood is a small town though.

Elin has been such a great influence on Bonnie and Max. She is like a second mother to them already. She helps them get ready for school in the morning. She makes sure they have their lunches. She takes them to school in the morning. During the day, she helps me with errands like going grocery shopping, dropping off and picking up the dry cleaning, and general chores around the house. To be honest, my spouse and I would be completely lost without Elin. I want to do everything that I can to help Elin with these ridiculous charges. I'm worried that Elin could be deported because of this. I mean, we simply cannot lose Elin.

The only issue I have had with Elin was about using my computer. Elin kept asking to borrow it. This went on during the first week of her employment. She said she had a virus on her laptop. Eventually, I told her that she had to get hers fixed because she couldn't borrow mine anymore. I needed it for work. I checked the web browser's history and noticed that she had been visiting Victoria's Facebook page a lot. I assumed she wanted to see if Victoria had posted anything about Lawrence's children. She genuinely cares about them.

I have read the above statement. It is complete, accurate, and true.

Signed: *Alex Villafuentes*
Alex Villafuentes

Statement of Tracy Piaggi

My name is Tracy Piaggi, and I am the principal of Maliwood Elementary School. I have a daughter in the same class as Bonnie, Alex Villafuentes's daughter. As principal of Maliwood Elementary, I take great pride in ensuring the students' safety. I like to stand outside in the mornings as the students are getting dropped off and again in the afternoons when the students are being picked up. I am familiar with Elin Svennson. I like to get to know each nanny personally so I know which nanny is responsible for each particular student. I remember meeting Elin when she first came to work for Lawrence Wilhoyt. She would drop off Michael and Samantha at school and pick them up in the afternoon. Michael and Samantha would be so excited to see her in the afternoons. From what I saw, it appeared that Elin had a great relationship with Lawrence's children.

Lawrence immediately informed me when he let Elin go. Lawrence seemed very concerned that Elin not be allowed to pick up Michael and Samantha after she was "let go." I really didn't understand what all the fuss was about. Again, from my initial impression of Elin and the way that Michael and Samantha would interact with her, it appeared that she was an excellent nanny and a really good influence on Lawrence's children. I noticed the same interaction with the Villafuentes children, Bonnie and Max. Almost immediately, it seemed as if Elin was part of the Villafuentes family.

Honestly, Lawrence's girlfriend Victoria Beck is actually a very difficult woman. She is not friendly or easy to talk to, and when she picks up the children she is always in a hurry and acts like it is a burden to pick Lawrence's kids up from school. Lawrence's kids always seemed happier when they were with Elin.

I have read the above statement. It is complete, accurate, and true.

Signed: *Tracy Piaggi*
Tracy Piaggi

EXHIBIT A

MALIWOOD SUSHI

```
135 Wave Crest Avenue
    Maliwood County
      555-0177

   ----CASH RECEIPT---
  11/10/CY-1 12:31 PM
  -------------------

REF ID: 9163-3331
Server: Betty

Maliwood Roll              19.99
Sunset Roll                14.99
Japanese Beer (Large)       7.99
Sake                       10.00
California Roll             7.99
Spicy Tuna Roll            10.00
Las Vegas Roll             10.99
------------------------------------

------------------------------------
Subtotal                   81.95
Tax (8.75%)                 7.17
                           ------
Total                      89.12
TIP                        15.00
TOTAL                     104.12

Signature  Lawrence Wilhoyt
------------------------------------

------------------------------------
       CREDIT CARD APPROVED
          Thank You!
```

EXHIBIT B

Maliwood Cellular

DATE	TIME	CALL TO	NUMBER CALLED	MINUTES
11/01	07:01 AM	MALIWOOD	(310) 555-3745	1
11/01	11:03 AM	MALIWOOD	(310) 555-2567	9
11/01	4:58 PM	MALIWOOD	(310) 555-2567	11
11/02	10:11 AM	MALIWOOD	(310) 555-2567	8
11/03	3:02 PM	MALIWOOD	(310) 555-2567	14
11/04	08:52 AM	MALIWOOD	(310) 555-3745	1
11/05	08:55 AM	MALIWOOD	(310) 555-0837	1
11/05	10:27 AM	INCOMING	(310) 555-9232	5
11/05	11:01 AM	MALIWOOD	(310) 555-0837	1
11/05	11:15 AM	MALIWOOD	(310) 555-2567	1
11/05	11:37 AM	MALIWOOD	(310) 555-2567	1
11/05	12:10 PM	INCOMING	(310) 555-1007	11
11/05	01:15 PM	MALIWOOD	(310) 555-3745	1
11/05	02:25 PM	MALIWOOD	(310) 555-3745	1
11/05	03:30 PM	INCOMING	(310) 555-2567	15
11/05	04:49 PM	MALIWOOD	(310) 555-3745	1
11/05	05:14 PM	MALIWOOD	(310) 555-3745	1
11/05	06:55 PM	MALIWOOD	(310) 555-3745	1
11/05	07:39 PM	MALIWOOD	(310) 555-3745	1
11/05	08:25 PM	TEXT MESSAGE	(310) 555-6958	-
11/05	08:27 PM	TEXT MESSAGE	(310) 555-6958	-
11/06	07:30 AM	MALIWOOD	(310) 555-3745	1
11/06	07:45 AM	MALIWOOD	(310) 555-3745	1
11/06	09:37 AM	MALIWOOD	(310) 555-0837	1
11/06	10:10 AM	MALIWOOD	(310) 555-0837	1
11/06	11:39 AM	MALIWOOD	(310) 555-0837	1
11/06	12:15 PM	INCOMING	(310) 555-2567	12
11/06	12:59 PM	MALIWOOD	(310) 555-2567	7
11/06	01:19 PM	MALIWOOD	(310) 555-0837	1
11/06	01:48 PM	TEXT MESSAGE	(310) 555-6859	-
11/06	03:30 PM	INCOMING	(310) 555-2567	17
11/06	04:15 PM	MALIWOOD	(310) 555-3745	1
11/06	04:19 PM	MALIWOOD	(310) 555-3745	1
11/06	05:27 PM	INCOMING	(310) 555-6859	14
11/06	07:59 PM	MALIWOOD	(310) 555-3745	1
11/06	08:41 PM	MALIWOOD	(310) 555-3745	1
11/07	12:31 AM	MALIWOOD	(310) 555-3745	1

11/07	01:15 AM	MALIWOOD	(310) 555-3745	1
11/07	07:25 AM	MALIWOOD	(310) 555-3745	1
11/07	8:11 AM	MALIWOOD	(310) 555-0837	1
11/07	09:59 AM	INCOMING	(310) 555-2567	10
11/07	11:15 AM	MALIWOOD	(310) 555-0837	1
11/07	11:17 AM	MALIWOOD	(310) 555-3745	1
11/07	12:30 PM	MALIWOOD	(310) 555-3745	1
11/07	12:25 PM	MALIWOOD	(310) 555-0837	1
11/07	1:17 PM	MALIWOOD	(310) 555-3745	1
11/07	2:30 PM	MALIWOOD	(310) 555-3745	1
11/07	2:45 PM	INCOMING	(310) 555-2567	17
11/07	3:31 PM	MALIWOOD	(310) 555-3745	1
11/07	3:45 PM	MALIWOOD	(310) 555-3745	1
11/07	4:59 PM	MALIWOOD	(310) 555-3745	1
11/07	7:31 PM	MALIWOOD	(310) 555-3745	1
11/08	7:44 AM	MALIWOOD	(310) 555-2567	4
11/08	11:56 AM	MALIWOOD	(310) 555-0837	1
11/08	3:33 PM	MALIWOOD	(310) 555-3745	1
11/09	9:17 AM	INCOMING	(310) 555-2567	21
11/09	4:31 PM	MALIWOOD	(310) 555-3745	1
11/09	10:16 PM	MALIWOOD	(310) 555-0837	1

(310) 555-3745: Lawrence Wilhoyt's Cell Phone
(310) 555-0837: Lawrence Wilhoyt's Work Phone
(310) 555-2567: Alex Villafuentes's Phone

EXHIBIT C

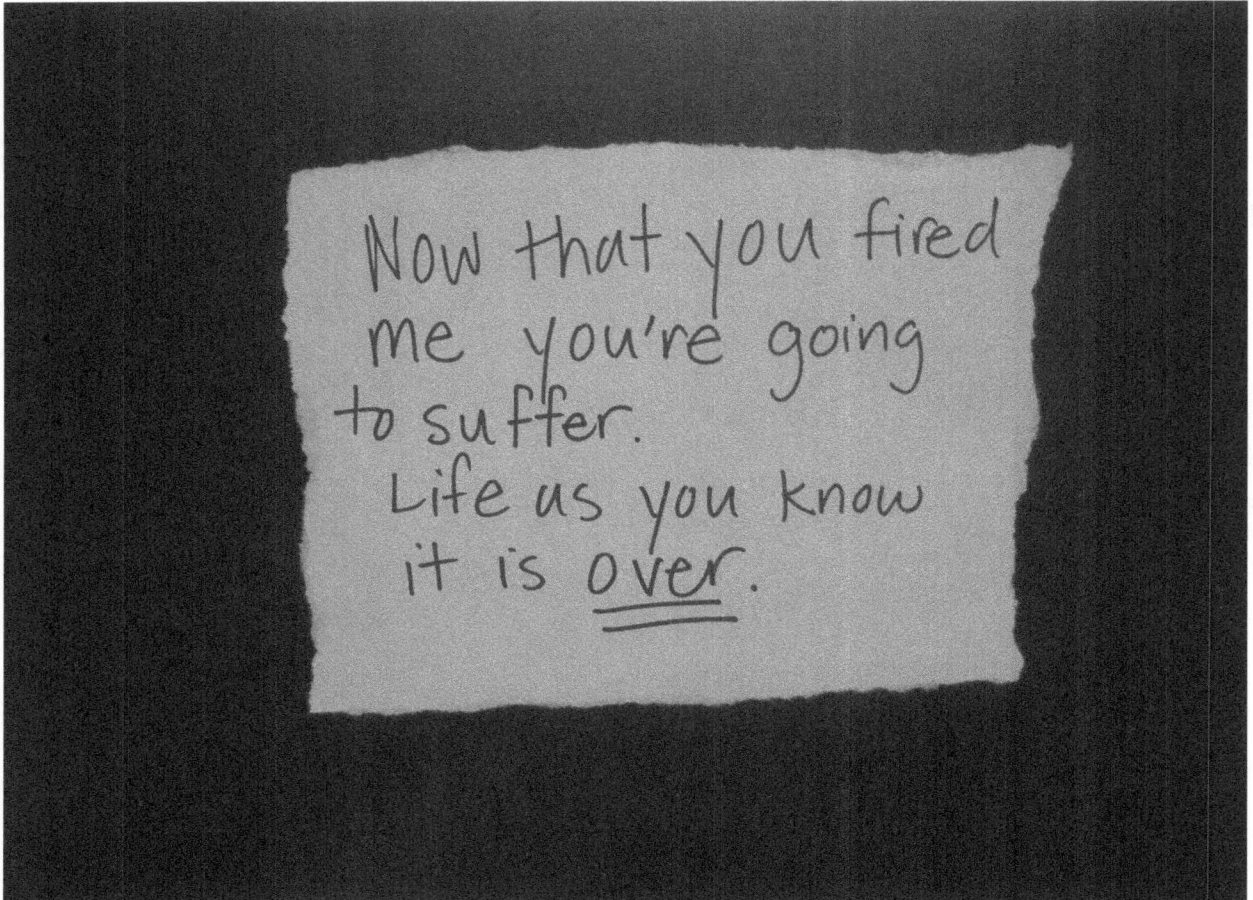

Exhibit D

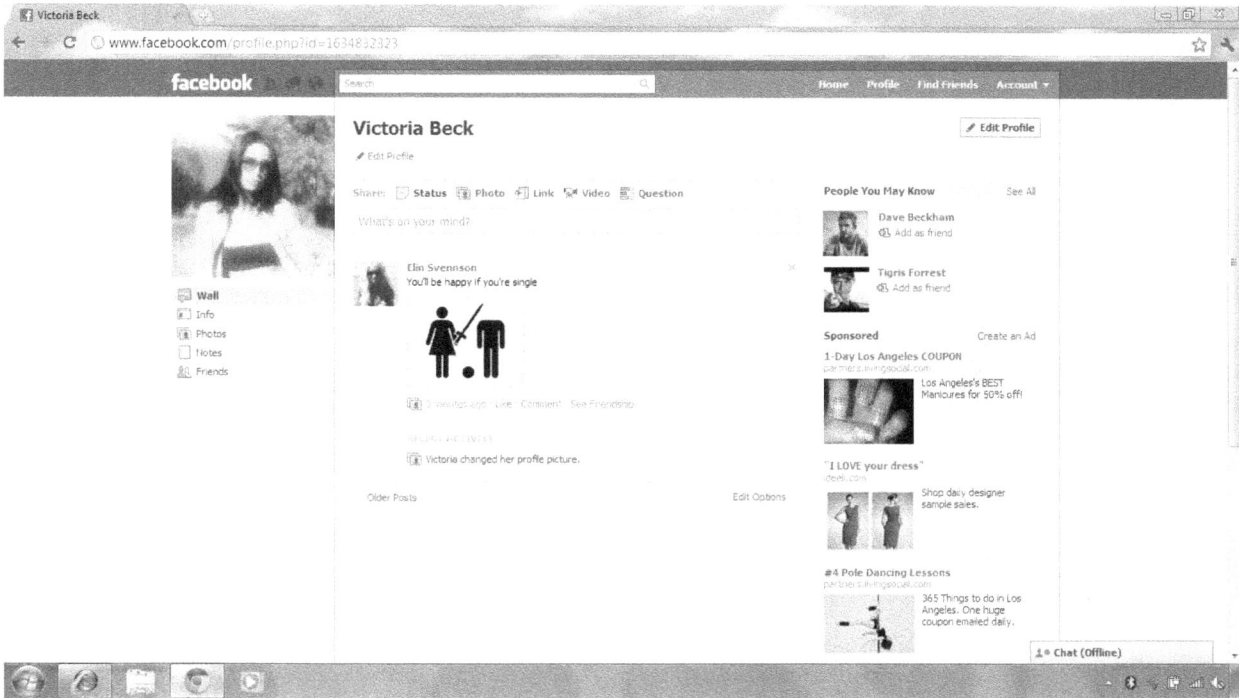

EXHIBIT E

EXHIBIT F

EXHIBIT G

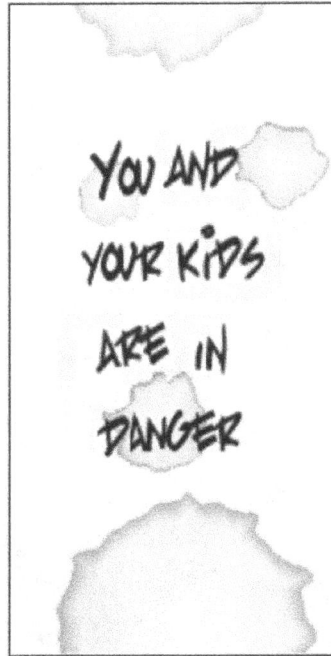

Jury Instructions

Members of the jury, I thank you for your attention during this trial. You have now heard all the evidence and the closing arguments of the attorneys. It is my duty to instruct you on the law that applies to this case. You will have a copy of my instructions with you when you go to the jury room to deliberate. Pay careful attention to all the instructions that I give you.

In this case, Defendant Elin Svennson is accused of stalking. Every person who willfully, maliciously, and repeatedly follows or willfully and maliciously harasses another person and who makes a credible threat with the intent to place that person in reasonable fear for his or her safety, or the safety of his or her immediate family, is guilty of a violation of Oceana Penal Code section 646.9, subdivision (a). To prove the crime of stalking, the State must prove the following elements beyond a reasonable doubt:

1. A person willfully, maliciously, and repeatedly followed or willfully and maliciously harassed another person;

2. The person following or harassing made a credible threat; and

3. The person who made the threat did so with the specific intent to place the other person in reasonable fear for his or her safety or the safety of the immediate family of such person[s].

The word *harass* means to engage in a knowing and willful course of conduct directed at a specific person that seriously alarms, annoys, torments, or terrorizes the person, and that serves no legitimate purpose.

A credible threat means a verbal or written threat, including that performed with the use of an electronic communication device, or a threat implied by a pattern of conduct or a combination of verbal, written, or electronically communicated statements and conduct made with the intent to place the person that is the target of the threat in reasonable fear for his or her safety, or the safety of his or her family, and made with the apparent ability to carry out the threat so as to cause the person who is the target of the threat to reasonably fear for his or her safety or the safety of his or her family. An intent to carry out the threat is not an element of this crime.

In this case, Defendant Elin Svennson is also accused of violating a valid restraining order. Every person guilty of any contempt of court, including willful disobedience of the terms as written of any process or court order, lawfully issued by any court, including orders pending trial, is guilty of a violation of Oceana Penal Code section 166. To prove that Defendant is guilty of this crime, the People must prove the following elements beyond a reasonable doubt:

1.   A court issued a written order that Defendant at all times must remain 100 yards from Lawrence Wilhoyt, Victoria Beck, Michael Wilhoyt, and Samantha Wilhoyt, as well as 100 yards from Lawrence Wilhoyt's home and business;

2.   Defendant knew of the court order;

3.   Defendant had the ability to follow the court order; and

4.   Defendant willfully violated the court order.

In this case, Defendant Elin Svennson is also accused of making a criminal threat in violation of Oceana Penal Code section 422. In order to prove that Defendant is guilty of this crime, the People must prove that:

1.   Defendant willfully threatened to unlawfully kill or unlawfully cause great bodily injury to Victoria Beck and/or Lawrence Wilhoyt or members of his immediate family;

2.   Defendant made the threat orally and in writing;

3.   Defendant intended that her statement be understood as a threat and intended that it be communicated to Victoria Beck and/or Lawrence Wilhoyt;

4.   The threat was so clear, immediate, unconditional, and specific that it communicated to Victoria Beck and/or Lawrence Wilhoyt a serious intention and the immediate prospect that the threat would be carried out;

5.   The threat actually caused Victoria Beck and/or Lawrence Wilhoyt to be in sustained fear for their own safety or for the safety of his immediate family;

AND

6.   Victoria Beck and/or Lawrence Wilhoyt's fear was reasonable under the circumstances.

In deciding whether a threat was sufficiently clear, immediate, unconditional, and specific, consider the words themselves, as well as the surrounding circumstances.

Someone who intends that a statement be understood as a threat does not have to actually intend to carry out the threatened act or intend to have someone else do so.

Great bodily injury means significant or substantial physical injury. It is an injury that is greater than minor or moderate harm.

Sustained fear means fear for a period of time that is more than momentary, fleeting, or transitory.

Immediate family means (a) any spouse, parents, and children; (b) any grandchildren, grandparents, brothers and sisters related by blood or marriage; or (c) any person who regularly lives in the other person's household or who regularly lived there within the prior six months.

Elin Svennson has entered a plea of not guilty. This means that you must presume or believe that Elin Svennson is not guilty unless and until the evidence convinces you otherwise. This presumption stays with Elin Svennson as to each material allegation in the indictment through each stage of the trial until it has been overcome by the evidence to the exclusion of and beyond a reasonable doubt.

To overcome Defendant's presumption of innocence, it is the State's burden to prove the following:

1. The crime with which Defendant is charged was committed.

2. Defendant is the person who committed the crime.

Defendant is not required to prove anything.

The State has the burden to prove the elements beyond a reasonable doubt. Whenever the words *reasonable doubt* are used, you must consider the following: A reasonable doubt is not a mere possible doubt, because everything relating to human affairs is open to some possible or imaginary doubt. Reasonable doubt is the state of the case that, after hearing and considering all the evidence, leaves the minds of the jurors in the condition that they cannot say they feel an abiding conviction of the truth of the charge.

It is to the evidence introduced during this trial, and to it alone, that you are to look for that proof. A reasonable doubt as to the guilt of Defendant may arise from evidence, a conflict in the evidence, or a lack of evidence. If you have a reasonable doubt, you should find Defendant not guilty. If you have no reasonable doubt, you should find Defendant guilty.

You must decide this case on the evidence and the law. It is up to you to decide what evidence is reliable. You should use your common sense in deciding what evidence is reliable and what evidence should not be relied upon in considering your verdict.

A witness is a person who has knowledge related to this case. You will have to decide whether you believe each witness and how important each witness's testimony is to the case. You may believe all, part, or none of a witness's testimony. In deciding whether to believe a witness's testimony, you may consider, among other factors, the following:

1. The extent of the witness's opportunity to see, hear, or otherwise become familiar with any matter about which the witness testified.

2. The ability of the witness to accurately recall or communicate any matter about which the witness testified and the character and quality of that testimony.

3. The witness's manner and demeanor while on the stand.

4. Whether or not the witness has bias, an improper motive, or an interest in the outcome of the case.

5. The witness's attitude toward this trial or toward testifying.

6. Whether the witness's testimony was consistent or inconsistent with other testimony or evidence presented in this case.

7. Any previous statements made by the witness that are consistent or inconsistent with the witness's testimony.

8. The witness's character for honesty or veracity, or their opposites.

9. Whether the witness was offered money, preferred treatment, or any other benefit to testify or whether the witness received any threats or was under any pressure that might

have affected the truth of the witness's testimony.

10. The witness's previous conviction of a felony or past criminal conduct amounting to a misdemeanor.

You may rely upon your own conclusions about each witness. A juror may believe or disbelieve all or any part of the evidence or the testimony of any witness.

There are some general rules that apply to your deliberations. You must abide by these rules in order to return a verdict that is consistent with the law:

1. You must follow the law as it is explained to you in these instructions. If you fail to follow the law or if you disregard the law, any verdict you reach will be a miscarriage of justice.

2. You must decide the case only upon the evidence that you have heard from either the testimony of witnesses or exhibits that you have seen.

3. You must not decide the case for or against anyone because you feel sympathy for that person, or because you are angry at that person.

4. You must not decide the case based on your feelings about the lawyers in this case. The lawyers are not on trial.

5. You must not consider any potential sentence Defendant might receive. It is not your duty to consider punishment. Your only duty is to determine guilt or innocence. It is the judge's job to determine the proper sentence if you find Defendant guilty.

6. Whatever verdict you render must be unanimous; that is, each juror must commit to the same verdict. The verdict must be the verdict of each juror as well as that of the jury as a whole.

7. It is entirely proper for a lawyer to talk to a witness about what testimony the witness would give if called into the courtroom. The witness should not be discredited for talking to a lawyer about his or her testimony.

8. You must not decide this case based on feelings of prejudice, bias, or sympathy. Any

verdict you may reach should be based on the evidence and the law contained in these instructions.

Deciding a proper verdict is exclusively your job. I cannot participate in that decision in any way. Please disregard anything I might have said or done that made you think I preferred one verdict over another.

Only one verdict may be returned for the crime charged. The verdict must be in writing and the verdict form has been prepared for you. It is as follows:

(READ JURY VERDICT FORM)

In just a few moments, the Bailiff will escort you to the jury room. Once inside the jury room, the first thing you should do is elect a foreperson, who will preside over your deliberations. It is the foreperson's job to sign and date the verdict form when all of you have agreed on a verdict in this case and to bring the verdict back to the courtroom when you return.

In conclusion, let me remind you that it is imperative that you follow the law as I have explained it to you in these instructions. Regardless of how you feel about the laws, you must apply them.

SUPERIOR COURT OF THE STATE OF OCEANA

FOR THE COUNTY OF MALIWOOD

STATE OF OCEANA, Plaintiff,	Case No. MW924739
v.	**CHARGE(S):** 646.9(a) Stalking 1 count
ELIN SVENNSON, Defendant.	166 Violating a Restraining Order 1 count
	422 Making a Criminal Threat 1 count

VERDICT

As to the charge of stalking, in violation of Oceana Penal Code section 646.9(a), we, the jury,

find the Defendant, Elin Svennson:

_____ GUILTY

_____ NOT GUILTY

As to the charge of violating a restraining order, in violation of Oceana Penal Code section 166,

we, the jury, find the Defendant, Elin Svennson:

_____ GUILTY

_____ NOT GUILTY

As to the charge of making a criminal threat, in violation of Oceana Penal Code section 422, we, the jury, find the Defendant, Elin Svennson:

____   GUILTY

____   NOT GUILTY

So say we all.

_____
Foreperson of the Jury

_____
Date

CASE FILE No. 6

STATE OF OCEANA

V.

PAUL SLATER

(Spousal Battery)

SUPERIOR COURT OF THE STATE OF OCEANA

COUNTY OF MALIWOOD

STATE OF OCEANA,		Case No. MW957100
	Plaintiff,	
v.		**FELONY COMPLAINT**
PAUL SLATER,		
	Defendant.	

COUNT 1

On or about April 2, CY-1, in the City of Maliwood, Maliwood County, State of Oceana, a felony, in violation of section 273.5 of the Oceana Penal Code, commonly referred to as SPOUSAL ABUSE, was committed by the above named defendant, who at the time and place last aforesaid, did willfully and unlawfully inflict physical injury causing a traumatic condition upon Rebecca Slater.

COUNT 2

On or about April 2, CY-1, in the City of Maliwood, Maliwood County, State of Oceana, a felony, in violation of section 422 of the Oceana Penal Code, commonly referred to as MAKING A CRIMINAL THREAT, was committed by the above named defendant, who at the time and place last aforesaid, did willfully and unlawfully threaten Rebecca Slater.

IT IS SO ORDERED.

Simon Luna

Simon Luna
District Attorney, County of Maliwood

Witness List

Witnesses for the State:

1. Kelly Davey***

2. Rebecca Slater**

Witnesses for the Defense:

1. Paul Slater*

2. Merritt Shane***

Each side must call both witnesses listed for their respective party, and both parties stipulate that each party's expert witness would testify consistently with his or her provided statement.

*This witness must be played by a male.

**This witness must be played by a female.

***This witness may be either gender.

Stipulations

1. Both the Federal Rules of Criminal Procedure and Federal Rules of Evidence apply.

2. Assume each witness who gave an interview reviewed the officer's report of his or her interview and signed the interview to verify for accuracy.

3. All exhibits included in the file are authentic and, unless otherwise stated, are the original of that document.

4. Other than what appears in the officer's report of the interviews, there is nothing exceptional or unusual about the background of any of the witnesses that would bolster or detract from their credibility.

5. All dates are denoted by CY (current year) or CY-*n* (current year minus *n* years).

6. All pretrial motions shall be oral.

7. No party may invent witnesses or evidence that is not specifically mentioned in this case file.

8. "Beyond the record" is not a proper objection. Rather, the attorneys shall use cross-examination as the means of challenging a witness whose testimony strays beyond the facts contained in the case file.

9. The physical description of a witness, e.g., clothing, should be tailored to that of the student playing the witness, except for height, weight, and age.

10. The parties stipulate to the admittance of the physician's report of Rebecca Slater. This exhibit can be used by either side. The parties have waived hearsay objections for only this exhibit.

11. All witness statements were given under oath.

12. All witnesses called to testify who have identified Defendant Slater or any tangible evidence can, if asked, identify the same at trial.

13. The prosecution and defense may only call the two witnesses listed on their respective witness list.

14. The prosecution and defense have stipulated that the proper foundation has been laid for the medical report and they have stipulated that the medical expert would testify pursuant to his report. However, either side is free to dispute the contents of the report.

15. The witness Paul Slater must be male. The witness Rebecca Slater must be female. All other witnesses may be of either gender. The witnesses may be called in any order.

16. Oceana Penal Code section 273.5(a) reads as follows: "Any person who willfully inflicts upon a person who is his or her spouse, former spouse, cohabitant, former cohabitant, or the mother or father of his or her child, corporal injury resulting in a traumatic condition, is guilty of a felony."

17. Oceana Penal Code section 422 reads as follows: "Any person who willfully threatens to commit a crime which will result in death or great bodily injury to another person, with the specific intent that the statement, made verbally, in writing, or by means of an electronic communication device, is to be

taken as a threat, even if there is no intent of actually carrying it out, which, on its face and under the circumstances in which it is made, is so unequivocal, unconditional, immediate, and specific as to convey to the person threatened, a gravity of purpose and an immediate prospect of execution of the threat, and thereby causes that person reasonably to be in sustained fear for his or her own safety or for his or her immediate family's safety, shall be punished."

18. Dr. Ryan Sheppard is a licensed physician in the State of Oceana and was qualified to treat Rebecca Slater, and treated her in this case consistent with the training and practice he had received in compliance with all applicable standards.

COUNTY OF MALIWOOD SHERIFF'S DEPARTMENT
INVESTIGATION REPORT

RECORDS & STATISTICS BUREAU'S USE ONLY   DATE: **4/2/CY-1**   PAGE: **1** OF **5**

ACTION	ACTIVE (X) INACTIVE ( ) PENDING ( )	INDEX Yes (X) INFO No ( )	N of Adult Arrests: 1	No of Subject Detentions: 1	URN (File No.) MW957100		

CLASSIFICATION
DOMESTIC VIOLENCE

DATE, TIME OF OCCURRENCE
4/2/CY-1, 14:30 HOURS

LOCATION OF OCCURRENCE 3671 SANDSHELL LANE, MALIWOOD, OC	TYPE OF LOCATION RESIDENCE	TRACT

CODE: V - VICTIM, W - WITNESS, I - INFORMANT, R - REPORTING PARTY, P - PARTY

CODE V	NO. 1 OF 1	LAST NAME SLATER, REBECCA	FIRST	MIDDLE	SEX F	AGE 35	RACE WHITE

RESIDENCE ADDRESS 3671 Sandshell Lane,, Maliwood, OC	RES. PHONE (AREA CODE) (310) 555-3113

BUSINESS ADDRESS	RES. PHONE (AREA CODE)

CODE W	NO. 1 OF 1	LAST NAME SHANE, MERRITT	FIRST	MIDDLE	SEX M	AGE 40	RACE WHITE

RESIDENCE ADDRESS 3673 Sandshell Lane, Maliwood, OC	RES. PHONE (AREA CODE)

BUSINESS ADDRESS	RES. PHONE (AREA CODE)

CODE: S - SUSPECT,   SJ - SUBJECT,   M - PATIENT,   S / V - SUSPECT/VICTIM,   SJ / V - SUBJECT / VICTIM

CODE S	No 1 OF 1	LAST NAME SLATER, PAUL	FIRST	MIDDLE	DRIVER'S LICENSE (STATE & No) OC X5088797

RESIDENCE ADDRESS 3671 Sandshell Lane, Maliwood, OC	RES. PHONE (AREA CODE)

BUSINESS ADDRESS	BUS. PHONE (AREA CODE)

SEX M	RACE WHITE	HAIR BROWN	EYES BLUE	HEIGHT 6'0"	WEIGHT 180 LBS	DOB	AGE 37	WHERE DETAINED MALIWOOD

OBSERVABLE PHYSICAL ODDITIES/TATTOOS/SCARS	AKA / NICKNAME	BOOKING No. MW957100

CLOTHING WORN BLUE DENIM PANTS, PLAID SHIRT BUTTON-DOWN, BROWN LOAFERS	MAIN

CHARGE DOMESTIC VIOLENCE	WEAPON USED HAND

CODE	No OF	LAST NAME	FIRST	MIDDLE	DRIVER'S LICENSE (STATE & No)

RESIDENCE ADDRESS	RES. PHONE (AREA CODE)

BUSINESS ADDRESS	BUS. PHONE (AREA CODE)

SEX	RACE	HAIR	EYES	HEIGHT	WEIGHT	D.O.B.	AGE	WHERE DETAINED OR CITE No.

OBSERVABLE PHYSICAL ODDITIES	AKA / NICKNAME	BOOKING No.

CLOTHING WORN	MAIN

CHARGE	WEAPON USED

VEHICLE USED IN CRIME YES ( ) NO (X) UNKNOWN ( ) STORED ( ) IMPOUNDED ( )	YR	MAKE	BODY TYPE	COLOR	BY DEPUTY	BADGE No.
LICENSE (STATE & No.)		V.I.N./ FRAME No.			BY DEPUTY	BADGE No.
REGISTERED OWNER					STATION	UNIT / CAR No.	SHIFT
IDENTIFYING CHARACTERISTICS					APPROVED	BADGE No.	TIME
O.H.P. 180 SUBMITTED YES ( ) NO ( )	GARAGE NAME & PHONE				ASSIGNMENT	

Narrative Report – URN MW957100

At 14:00 hours on April 2, CY-1, I was on routine patrol with Deputy Marie Kathleen Stanford when we received a code three domestic violence (DV) call emanating from 3671 Sandshell Lane, Maliwood. The dispatch reported that the victim was bleeding from a head wound. The destination was only one mile from our location, and we arrived at said residence within two minutes. Upon arrival, I confirmed that an ambulance was on its way.

I rang the doorbell, and within seconds, a man answered the door and identified himself as Paul Slater. He was clearly agitated. Paul Slater led me over to where Rebecca Slater was sitting on a chair in the kitchen with a white towel pressed up against the right side of her head. The towel was soaked with what appeared to be blood. Mrs. Slater had her head down in her hands, and she was crying. Deputy Stanford went over to console her while I began questioning Mr. Slater.

Paul Slater told me that they had gotten in a verbal argument and his wife had held a kitchen butcher knife up to him. He claimed that he grabbed her right wrist to get her to drop the knife and she did in fact drop the knife, but in the process, he stated that she fell and hit the side of her head against the kitchen island counter. Hearing this, Mrs. Slater interrupted, "That's a lie! He pushed me! I never had a knife or any other weapon." Since it was only the two of them in the house, and Rebecca Slater had just identified her husband, Paul Slater, as the one who battered her, I decided to *Mirandize* Mr. Slater. I explained his constitutional rights, which he waived, and he began telling me his version of what happened. Then, the paramedics arrived and began treating Mrs. Slater's head wound. Mrs. Slater pointed to her husband and yelled, "Take him to jail! He's a wife beater. He threatened me, he grabbed my wrists, and then he pushed me into the counter. I have it all on tape."

"What tape? What the hell are you talking about?" Mr. Slater said to her. He appeared stunned and confused.

Mrs. Slater handed me her smart phone, which she said contained the violent incident on audio tape. She smiled as she handed me the smart phone and stated, "Thank God I taped the attack!" I took custody of the phone.

Prior to the paramedics applying a sterile butterfly bandage to Mrs. Slater's head wound, Deputy Stanford took photographs of the injury (see attached Exhibits I–K). It was a two inch long, deep gash. Deputy Stanford also took photos of the red marks on the victim's wrists. Each of her wrists had clearly visible red marks that went all the way around the wrists. Once the paramedics made sure that Mrs. Slater was stable, they escorted her out to the ambulance. I informed Mrs. Slater that Deputy Stanford and I would meet her at the ER and obtain a full statement from her as soon as we had preserved evidence and interviewed her husband.

As soon as Mrs. Slater was out the door, Mr. Slater's demeanor changed. He had appeared concerned for his wife and remorseful at first, but once she left, his anger flared. He exclaimed, "She's crazy; she's a liar! She was drunk and she fell back on her head. I was just trying to protect myself." He was shouting, and Deputy Stanford had to tell him to calm down.

Slater walked over to the island countertop and pointed excitedly to a large kitchen knife (see attached Exhibit F). He heatedly stated, "That's the knife! That's the knife she threatened me with. It was on the floor. I didn't want to leave it lying where someone could step on it, so I put it back on the counter. But you can see it's not in the block with the other knives."

I noticed that the knife was next to a cutting board on the kitchen counter. There was an orange on the cutting board next to the knife (see attached Exhibit D). There was also an empty metal water bottle about a foot away from the knife (see attached Exhibit E). I also noticed a cup that appeared to contain orange juice. I inspected the kitchen and found a set of knives in a wooden block with several empty slots (see attached Exhibit H). I put the knife that was on the counter into one of the slots and it fit. I then removed the knife from the block and put it back where it was on the cutting board, so that we could take photographs of the scene the way it looked when we found it. I inspected the counter where Mrs. Slater had indicated she had injured her head, and I did not see blood on it.

I did not call in a fingerprint forensic expert to lift and compare prints because obviously both of the Slater's prints would likely be on the objects in their own home. At my request, Deputy Stanford took photos of the scene including the island countertop showing the orange, the knife, the cutting board, and the metal water bottle (see attached Exhibits D–H).

I examined Mr. Slater's hands and arms and did not note any scratches, bruises, red marks, or any other indications of injury. Deputy Stanford took a photograph of Slater to verify that he had not sustained any injuries in the altercation (see attached Exhibit B).

Based on the fact that Rebecca Slater had identified her husband, Paul Slater, as the person who had pushed her, causing her head injury, coupled with the fact that he was much bigger and taller than her, as well as the fact that he had no injuries, I placed him under arrest. He was cooperative, although he was exhibiting mood swings. He once again appeared to be concerned for his wife's safety. He kept saying, "I'm so sorry this happened. I just want Bec to be fine." I asked, "Are you sorry you did this to your wife?" He responded, "I'm just sorry about everything. Poor Katie!" Suddenly, he buried his face in his hands and shouted, "Oh my God, I can't believe this is happening! What about my sweet Katie?"

When the suspect composed himself, he requested to call his neighbor, Merritt Shane, to have Shane pick up his six-year-old daughter, Katie, from school and watch her until Rebecca was released from the ER. I allowed him to make this phone call in my presence, then I cuffed him and transported him in my patrol vehicle to the Maliwood Sheriff's Station. At the sheriff's station, I attempted to complete the interview of suspect Slater, but he invoked his right to counsel. I booked him on spousal battery pursuant to section 273.5 of the Oceana Penal Code. I then went to the ER to check on Rebecca Slater and get a full statement from her (see attached Statement of Rebecca Slater, and see attached transcript of audio tape recording).

Three days later, Paul Slater agreed to an interview on the condition that he could hear the tape recording before speaking to me. I re-advised him of his *Miranda* rights and he again waived them. He claimed that he was innocent, and that this was a case of self-defense. He told me that he hired a private investigator who found a book belonging to the victim that supports Slater's claim that his wife set him up and trumped up these charges in an attempt to get custody of their daughter. The suspect provided me with a photo of this book (see attached Exhibit C). The title is, *Don't Get Mad, Get Custody!* I played the tape for the suspect. After hearing the tape, he gave a full statement (see attached Statement of Paul Slater).

I certify that the above is true to the best of my knowledge under the penalty of perjury.

Signed,

Deputy Kelly Davey

Deputy Kelly Davey

Maliwood County Sheriff's Department
Supplemental Police Report

Report Type: Interrogation of Paul Slater
*Recorded per Maliwood County Sheriff's Department Interrogation Procedures
Interviewer: Deputy Davey
Date and Time of Interview: April 5, CY-1, 15:45 hours

This interview occurred at the Maliwood County Sheriff's Station interview room. Paul Slater was bailed out and voluntarily came into the station to give an interview.

Deputy Davey (DD): Good afternoon, Mr. Slater. I want to make a few things clear before we begin. You understand you have the right to remain silent, correct?

Paul Slater (PS): Yes.

DD: That anything you say can and will be used against you in a court of law?

PS: Yes.

DD: You have the right to an attorney. If you cannot afford an attorney, one will be provided for you. Do you understand?

PS: Yes.

DD: Great. Well, Paul, I think you know why we're here.

PS: I do.

DD: Good, so let's start with the basics. Tell me your name and your address.

PS: My name is Paul Slater, and I reside at 3671 Sandshell Lane in Maliwood, Oceana.

DD: Okay, Paul, let's talk about the incident that took place between you and your wife.

PS: I'd be glad to! This whole thing was a setup. Bec wants to divorce me because I don't make enough money for her extravagant lifestyle. She totally set me up.

DD: Care to expand on that?

PS: She purposely pushed my buttons and then after she got me upset, she started tape recording our fight. I never threatened her and I didn't push her—it's all a lie. She's simply trying to make a case for custody; she's a lawyer and she knows how to work the system. It's complete bullshit that I threatened to kill her!

DD: Well, it doesn't look like complete bullshit, Paul. How do you explain her getting hurt? On the tape, she sounds like she was afraid of you.

PS: It's pretty funny, don't you think, that the one statement where I supposedly threatened her life didn't make the tape. That's because I never said that. Sure, I was pissed, and I was yelling, and I did call her a "bitch." Since when is that a crime? Now I see that she got me mad on purpose because she wanted to have a tape recording of me yelling and being angry.

DD: Paul you sound very upset on the tape recording; how can you deny that?

PS: Of course I was ticked off; Rebecca threatened to take my daughter away from me and move to Virginia. Her parents raised a spoiled brat and now she wants to go running home to mom and dad with all their money, and that's fine, but she's not taking Katie with her. It's not legal to take a kid and move out of state without permission of a court, and Rebecca knows that. She's a cunning lawyer and she manipulated me to make me irate.

DD: Did you think maybe you should have taken a step back? Sounds to me like you lost control, Paul.

PS: I was so upset by the idea of my daughter being taken away from me that I went to the garage to get in the car and go for a drive to calm down. When I got in the garage, I realized I was too upset to get behind the wheel.

DD: She thought you were going for a gun . . .

PS: I was not going for a gun. It is not even my gun. It's Rebecca's! Her dad gave it to her shortly after we moved in, for home protection. She's the one that goes target shooting. I barely even know how to use the thing and she knows that. She knows there's no way I was going for a gun. She's just manipulating everything to make me look violent so that she can take my daughter away from me. Katie is the only great thing in my life, and I just can't even believe this is happening!

DD: Pull yourself together, Paul; stay with me. You know what's on the tape so . . .

PS: Yeah, let's talk about what's on the tape. If you listen to it carefully, two things are crystal clear: first, I never threatened Bec; and second, you can see how she tried to provoke me—like when she accused me of going to get the gun. And then she said, "You were threatening me." I didn't know what she meant by that at the time she said it, but now I see the whole thing was just a setup. Who goes and gets a tape recorder when they're scared of someone, anyway? Give me a break. If she really thought that I was going to get a gun, do you really think that she'd go get a tape recorder? Why didn't she run out of the house or call for help if she was so scared?

DD: Have you ever gotten physical before Paul? Have you ever hit your wife? Someone else? You're a lot bigger than Rebecca.

PS: I've never been physically abusive to a woman and I never would. Sure I got into a few fistfights in high school, but those were with guys. And I got arrested once in college after a bar brawl, but that guy deserved it, and he got arrested too. The craziest thing about these charges is the claim that I pushed Bec. That is such bull. I didn't even get physical with Bec the time she got so drunk she got us thrown out of the Maliwood Beach Café. I have never hit or pushed her, no matter how angry she has made me—and believe me, she has made me furious.

DD: Let's go back to what happened at your house on the day of your arrest.

PS: Let's. If you listen to the tape, you can tell that she's taunting me. Do you remember where she says, "What are you gonna do, hit me?" If you listen carefully on the tape you can hear her laughing.

She wasn't scared; she was taunting me. Now I see why she was laughing—because she thought she was going to get me to say something threatening or violent to help her custody hearing. There's no threat. She claims that when I said, "I'll do anything to keep my daughter," that I was threatening her.

DD: Weren't you?

PS: That's insane—any good dad would do anything for his kid. I just meant that I would hire the best lawyer that I could and do whatever I could—within the bounds of the law—not to lose my only child.

DD: Can't you see how that can easily be seen as a threat? You're a smart guy, Paul.

PS: All I did was grab her wrists in self-defense. She pulled a butcher knife on me. She had been drinking that day and she pulled a knife on me when we were in the kitchen. I guess she did it to get a reaction on the tape. She was pulling the strings, and she knew that the audiotape would not show her actions. All I was doing was trying to get the knife away from her or get her to drop it. That's why I grabbed her wrists. I know she had red marks on her wrists. I don't deny grabbing them, but that was self-defense.

DD: Are you sure about that?

PS: How else do you explain the part of the tape where I yell, "Oh my God, what are you doing?" That's 'cause she was pointing a butcher knife at me. She wanted me to push her so she could claim that I am too violent to share custody of our daughter. We struggled over the knife and the knife fell to the ground. You can hear it clatter on the tape. She fell against the counter in the struggle over the knife, but I did not push her.

DD: If you didn't push her, then how did she fall?

PS: She probably lost her balance partly because she was drinking vodka and orange juice that day. Sometimes she would sneak alcohol in a juice drink like that, to make it look like she wasn't having alcohol. She wasn't fooling me—I could always smell it on her breath. She was drinking that day, but you guys didn't even test her blood alcohol level. I held both of her wrists when she came at me with the knife, and in the struggle she fell over.

DD: Paul, she's really hurt—and you don't seem too upset about that. It will go better for you if you tell us what really happened.

PS: Well I guess Bec thinks she's pretty clever, now that she has a tape with me yelling. She even has her medical records that she had to get stitches. She can take those with her to family court when she divorces me. It's just a good thing my private detective found that book in her home office desk drawer. I mean, come on, she has a book on how to win your child custody and divorce case. Right in the book is a chapter on getting proof that your spouse has a temper. It even suggests tape recording an argument. What a coincidence! The book is called, *Don't Get Mad, Get Custody!* My private investigator has a photo of it.

DD: Well, Paul, I'll tell you what—I'm about to walk out of here. Do you have anything else to add?

PS: I guess you just made up your minds that I was the bad guy because she was bleeding. Then the next thing I knew the cuffs were on me. I'm gonna hire a lawyer and fight these false charges. The sad truth is that even knowing that Bec set me up for criminal charges, I'd still take her back if that meant keeping my kid. And you know, we have been married for ten years. That's a long time, and even though I think that her parents spoiled her and she is really demanding, I still care about her.

INTERROGATION TERMINATED.

Statement of Rebecca Slater

My name is Rebecca Slater. I have been married to my husband, Paul Slater, for ten years. We are currently separated. Our marriage started falling apart about two years ago, but we tried everything to make it work because we have a young daughter, Katie, who we both love immensely. Katie is now six years old and in first grade. Paul has always had a temper, and his anger increased towards the end of our marriage. We were having significant financial problems, which caused a great deal of frustration for Paul. Paul made a decent amount of money as a general contractor prior to the recession, but once that hit, our finances plummeted.

I come from a well-off family, and my parents offered to help us out financially many times, but Paul always refused. Instead, he insisted that the two of us should be able to pay our own bills, and he was adamant that I resume my law practice. We had agreed that I would be a full-time mom until Katie started kindergarten. However, when we made this agreement, Katie was only a baby and I had no idea how much she would still need me around when she was in school. I'm not the kind of mom who can put her work before her kids. Paul was supposed to finish architecture school, but he never did, so we had to rely instead on contractor jobs. Now that so few people are building homes, these jobs are very few and far between—it's been over a year since he's had a big project.

On the day Paul attacked me, April 2, CY-1, Katie was at school, so Paul and I were the only ones home. We have had verbal arguments before, but this was the first time one had escalated into a physical altercation. Well, Paul did grab my wrists really hard once, when we were at a café and we had been drinking a little too much, but April 2 was the first time he was really violent. What ignited the fight was a notice that, because we were so far behind in our mortgage payments, the bank was going to begin foreclosure proceedings. Paul went ballistic and started screaming at me. He said that I was spoiled, materialistic, and a frivolous spender. I admit that I am used to a high standard of living, coming from an affluent family in Virginia, but I had made significant efforts to decrease my spending over the last year or so. I was really disappointed in Paul for not being a better provider so that I could stay home and raise

Katie. Anyway, he was belittling me and getting really heated, and I was really angry that he had fallen

so behind in the mortgage payments that we were going to lose our house. What kind of a man can't even

make house payments? I had been thinking of leaving Paul for months, and the foreclosure notice was

the final straw. We began yelling at each other, but Paul was the one who was really heated. I was just

fed up. I wanted out.

Paul started cussing at me and I decided, then and there, that I'd had it with the marriage. I told

Paul that I was going to leave him, and he completely lost it and went berserk. He told me that he would

never let me leave. I said, "I know the law and I know my rights, and Katie and I are out of here!" He

said, "You're worthless!" He used the "F-word" and started screaming louder, and he shouted, "Katie is

not going anywhere!" I told him he couldn't even afford to take care of Katie and he didn't know the first

thing about parenting. I told him that he couldn't stop me from leaving and that I would seek primary

custody of Katie.

Then, he totally threatened me. I'll never forget it. He came towards me with an irate look on his

face. His face was red from anger, and his fists were clenched at his sides. He yelled, "I'll see you dead

before you take Katie away from me!" Those were his exact words. He threatened my life. I was so

scared I started to cry. I told him that he was scaring me. He turned in a huff and stormed away to the

garage. Then I started panicking because we keep a loaded gun in the garage. It is a home security gun

and is kept loaded in a gun safe. Paul was in a rage; I had never seen him so angry. He had just

threatened to kill me and I didn't know what he might do.

I panicked, and I was not thinking clearly. I wanted to get out of the house but my car was in the

garage, and that's where Paul was, so I could not go there. In retrospect, I realize I should have called

911 right away, but I was so shocked that Paul had just threatened my life, and I felt like I needed proof

of how crazy he was being. He does not lose his temper in front of other people, and I wanted to

document how verbally violent he was being so people would believe me. So, I turned on the recording

application of my smart phone and put it in my pants pocket. I don't think he knew about this function on

my cell phone. After I made sure that my smart phone was recording, I ran over to the portable phone to call for help. Just as I grabbed the phone, I could hear that Paul was back in the house running towards me. It was like a nightmare, when you try to dial the phone but can't. I fumbled with the phone, and I was so nervous, I was having trouble even dialing. I was trying to call 911, but I only got as far as the 9 when Paul yanked the phone away and threw it on the ground.

I was really frightened and upset, but when I saw that Paul did not have the gun, I felt some sense of relief. You can hear our exact argument from this point because it is all on the tape recorder. I can briefly summarize the argument that is on the tape. You can hear Paul scream at me to put the phone down. I accused him of threatening me and he did not deny it. We argued more about me leaving him and taking Katie. I told him he was a bad parent, and he cussed at me and screamed. He threatened me again. It was not as clear of a threat as the one that was not on tape, but he did tell me that he would do anything to keep Katie, and then he repeated, "and I mean anything." This was clearly a threat on my life, especially in the context of him just threatening to kill me minutes before he came back into the house.

He was screaming, and so I ran to the kitchen to try to get away from him. He chased me and as he went to grab my wrists, he knocked a metal water bottle off our kitchen island counter. You can hear it bang onto the ground on the tape. Then he got physically violent. He had never done that before April 2. He grabbed my wrists hard. I had bright red marks afterward and both wrists had bruises. I tried to pull away from Paul, but he was too strong. He is much bigger than me. He pushed me hard and I fell and slammed my head into the corner of the island counter. It hurt so much. My head was pouring blood and I ended up needing twelve stitches. I am still stunned that Paul physically attacked me. My dad never would have laid a hand on my mom. I should have listened to my dad. He warned me that Paul would not make a good husband.

After pushing me into the counter, Paul realized he had gone too far. He said he was so sorry. He got a towel and pressed it to my head and then he called 911.

I heard from one of the responding officers that Paul said I held a knife up to him, but that is a lie. I never had a knife and I did not threaten Paul in any way. He is 6'2" and I'm 5'6", so that is just ridiculous. Why would I pull a knife on someone so much bigger and stronger than me? Obviously, he could just grab it away from me. Also, I'm a lawyer; I wouldn't do anything as stupid as pulling a knife on someone. Paul also exaggerates about my drinking. I do like to drink, but I did not have any alcoholic drinks on April 2. I was going to pick Katie up from school that afternoon, and I would never drink before that.

It is also untrue that I threatened to take Katie and move back to Virginia. I would love to do that, but I know that Paul is entitled to a court hearing, and on April 2, I never mentioned anything about taking Katie out of state. Paul is just trying to justify his rage. He is making this up, but even if I had said something to that effect, it would not excuse his threats or violence.

I did have a book titled, *Don't Get Mad, Get Custody!* A friend gave it to me, but I never read it. Paul is still the father of my child, and I feel sorry for him that he is having such a tough time financially, but I will not stay in an abusive marriage. I have already filed for divorce. Paul needs to learn a lesson, and he should end up with this on his record so he does not abuse someone else in the future. I don't trust him to control his temper, and I don't want him spending time with Katie unless he is with a court-monitored supervisor.

I have read the above statement. It is complete, accurate, and true.

Signed: *Rebecca Slater*

Rebecca Slater

Witness: *Deputy Kelly Davey*

Deputy Kelly Davey

Statement of Merritt Shane

My name is Merritt Shane. I have been married for fifteen years. I own and manage a hardware store, Maliwood Merritt's Hardware. My spouse, Sam, and I are neighbors and friends of the Slaters. We first met them when they moved in eight years ago. We occasionally have dinner with the Slaters, so I have had ample opportunities to observe their demeanors over the years. Sometimes they would argue, especially after Rebecca had been drinking, but it never got physical. I was shocked when I heard the charges. Paul does not have a violent temper, and I can't imagine him hurting a woman.

From what I heard, it sounds like they just had a bad verbal argument, and Rebecca slipped and fell. Paul wouldn't push her or hurt her on purpose; he's not that way, even when she is being really mean. Rebecca does have a mean streak, especially when she's drinking. Sam and I have seen her drunk at lots of dinner parties, and she even stumbles and slurs her words sometimes. I have been embarrassed for Paul to have to deal with her when she gets like that. One time, the four of us were having dinner together at the Maliwood Beach Café, and Rebecca was yelling and making such a scene that she and Paul were asked to leave. He was so embarrassed; he was furious with her. He grabbed her arm and led her out of the restaurant. We all go to Maliwood Beach Café a lot, so it was especially embarrassing for Paul to have his wife make a scene.

The day after they were asked to leave the café, I went over to their house to borrow a vacuum cleaner because ours was broken. Rebecca didn't remember being drunk or being thrown out of the café, but she complained that her arm hurt and there was a red mark around the area where Paul grabbed her arm to lead her out of the café. I saw Paul firmly grip her arm and lead her out of the café, but Paul never hit or pushed her. He wouldn't do that. He was just trying to get her to leave with him so that she wouldn't continue to make a scene.

Sam and I have known the Slaters for eight years, and we have never seen either of them become physically violent. They argued more than most couples, so I'm not surprised they split up, but Paul is definitely not the violent type. He's actually a really nice guy. You should see how sweet he is with

Katie. He adores that kid! I talked to Paul the day after his arrest. He came over because he was distraught and needed a friend. Paul told me that on the day of his arrest, April 2, Rebecca threatened to take Katie and move back to Virginia with her folks. When Paul told me this, he was so sad he even had tears in his eyes. He said he would never let Rebecca take Katie so far away. He is a really devoted dad. I think it was really cold of her to threaten to take their child all the way across the nation like that. I could see how that comment would have really upset him, seeing as he is so close to his kid, but still he would not beat his wife. I know Rebecca cut her head and got stitches, but I think she just fell because she was drunk, or maybe he grabbed her arms to try to calm her down. I have never seen her act physically violent, but when she is drinking, she can get a little out of hand.

Obviously, Sam and I were not there when Rebecca hurt her head and Paul got arrested. I haven't seen Rebecca since the day of Paul's arrest. After she got out of the hospital, she moved out of the house and took Katie with her. Paul has been a wreck. He misses Katie so much. He even seems to miss Rebecca, even though she caused him all these problems. I saw photos of Rebecca's injuries from the police report. I know her head injury looked bad, and I'm sure she really was hurt, but I think she just hit her head by falling. I've seen her stumble so many times after having lots of drinks, and on more than one occasion, I've even seen Paul catch her to keep her from falling down. Granted, some of these times, I'd been drinking myself; we all four enjoyed going out to dinner, but Rebecca was the only one who would be stumbling and practically falling down. She is a beautiful looking woman, and I think that's part of the reason Paul stuck by her all these years, but beauty on the outside only counts for so much. I know Paul also stayed in the marriage because he adores Katie so much and he worried about the damage that would be done to her if he and Rebecca split up. And of course, he was really concerned about the possibility of not being able to raise his daughter. And now look what has happened!

Anyway, the point is that Paul is just despondent, and he told me that he wishes the whole incident had never happened. I remember the exact words he used when I saw him the day after his arrest. He came over in tears and said, "I'm so sorry Bec got hurt. I'd do anything to undo the fight."

It seems like this was just an argument between a husband and a wife and should be dealt with by marriage counseling or by a family court in divorce proceedings, but this kind of case does not belong in criminal court. I know Paul and he is not a batterer. He would never threaten to kill his wife. Despite her sometimes cold, even cruel, attitude, he still loves her.

The cops in Maliwood are too quick to make arrests. I got a DUI once and that was such a B.S. arrest. I wasn't even drunk, but I had to spend the night in a downtown cell. That was a nightmare. I ended up getting off the hook because the deputies lost the blood sample that was used to test my blood alcohol level, but I was innocent anyway. That was a humiliating experience. I heard that the cops don't even have a sample of Rebecca's blood alcohol from the day Paul was arrested for battering her. I'm not surprised. I mean they arrest me when I'm not drunk, but they don't even test her alcohol level when she falls and gets a bunch of stitches in her head. Instead, they just arrest Paul. Go figure. No wonder dads lose custody of their kids so easily. The system is biased against dads in custody cases and against husbands in domestic violence cases. That's just a fact. But just because a guy is a lot bigger than his wife does not mean he battered her. I know Paul would not beat his wife. He's just not the type.

I have read the above statement. It is complete, accurate and true.

Signed: *Merritt Shane*

      Merritt Shane

Witness: *Deputy Kelly Davey*

      Deputy Kelly Davey

The Tape Recording

PAUL: Put that down!

REBECCA: What are you doing? What are you doing? Get away from me!

PAUL: Calm down.

REBECCA: You're scaring the hell out of me—I thought you went to get the gun.

PAUL: The gun? Are you crazy?

REBECCA: You were threatening me.

PAUL: I wasn't going for the gun. You're such a drama queen.

REBECCA: I've had it, Paul. I can't take any more of this marriage. You're a lousy dad, and now we're gonna lose our home because of you.

PAUL: Let's make one thing clear, Rebecca: the lousy parent is you. You can go anytime and anywhere, but you're not taking Katie away from me.

REBECCA: You don't even provide for us. My parents were right about you—you never amounted to anything. You couldn't even get through architect school, and now I'm stuck with an unemployed construction worker for a husband.

PAUL: I'm a building contractor, Rebecca. You love to belittle me just because you used to be a hotshot lawyer—but now your nothin' but a lousy mom who drinks too much.

REBECCA: You're a loser, Paul. You've always been a loser. It just took me awhile to figure that out.

PAUL: Shut the hell up!

REBECCA: Truth hurts, Paul.

PAUL: That's enough, you bitch!

REBECCA: Katie and I are leaving you and there's nothing you can do about it.

PAUL: If you think there's a chance that you can take Katie out of state, you better go back to the law books, Bec.

REBECCA: We're leaving you and there's nothing you can do about it.

PAUL: You've gone too far this time. I can't believe I picked such a tyrant to be the mother of my child, but Katie's the only good thing in my life and you're not taking her from me.

REBECCA: How are you gonna stop me?

PAUL: I'm a lot stronger than you, Bec, and I will do anything it takes to keep my daughter—and I mean anything.

REBECCA: What are you gonna do, hit me? (Laughs)

(Pause)

REBECCA: I'm gonna go pack some things for Katie and me. Then I'm gonna pick her up from school—so don't plan on seeing either of us for awhile.

PAUL: No way; that's not happening.

REBECCA: Oh yeah?

PAUL: You've crossed the line; that's it, Rebecca.

REBECCA (in a screaming voice): Get away from me!

(Sound of running feet)

PAUL: We're not done talking—get back in here.

(Pause)

PAUL: Oh my God, what are you doing? Don't!

REBECCA: Leave me alone. You're hurting me! Let go!

(Sound of a clatter, like something fell or was thrown to the ground)

(Pause and then a thump-like sound)

REBECCA: Oh my God, now look what you've done! I can't believe it—I'm bleeding, you bastard.

PAUL: Calm down, calm down . . . I'll call 911.

(Running sound)

EXHIBIT A

St. Andrews Hospital✝

EMERGENCY UNIT & TRAUMA CENTER

15261 Victoria Circle
Maliwood, OC, 90120

```
Patient Name: Slater,
Rebecca
Address: 3671 Sandshell Ln,
Maliwood, OC
Phone Number: (310)555-3113
DOB: 11/28/CY-35 (Age 35)
SSN: 987-65-4321
Height: 5'6''
Weight: 130
Blood Type: B-
Insurance: CO-PAY
```

Emergency Room Physician's Report

Date: April 2, CY-1
Time: 2:30 p.m.

Summary: Patient transported to ER on April 2, CY-1. Paramedics' verbal report noted that a butterfly bandage had been applied to patient's wound on the right front side of her head to control bleeding. Butterfly saturated with blood. Patient was given and signed written consent to receive treatment at St. Andrews; bandage removed, wound sterilized, and 12 sutures placed to head wound measuring 1.75 inches in diameter. Patient tolerated well with a pain scale level of 4 reported and no signs or symptoms of distress noted. Breathing unlabored and lung sounds clear bilaterally; all vitals taken and within normal limits. Patient awake and alert with a GCS of 15. Patient was asked how the incident occurred. Patient stated: "My husband did this to me. He pushed me into our kitchen counter after grabbing my wrists and threatening me. I have had it with him." Upon further physical assessment, distinct red marks circling both wrists were noted. The injury appeared to be consistent with the right side of the head striking a hard object. In my opinion, the head injury could have resulted from either being pushed or falling. In addition, I saw no evidence to support the use of intoxicants. No toxicology screen ordered. Patient was given post-operative teaching. Patient advised to keep wound clean and dry and to return to St. Andrews in 14 days or to see her primary care giver in that time frame for suture removal and further assessment. Patient appears to have understood teaching and agreed to comply. Patient discharged.

EXHIBIT B

EXHIBIT C

EXHIBIT D

EXHIBIT E

EXHIBIT F

EXHIBIT G

EXHIBIT H

EXHIBIT I

EXHIBIT J

EXHIBIT K

Jury Instructions

Members of the jury, I thank you for your attention during this trial. Please pay close attention to the instructions I am about to give you.

In this case, Paul Slater, Defendant, is charged in two counts. The first count charges Defendant with inflicting an injury on his spouse that resulted in a traumatic condition in violation of Oceana Penal Code section 273.5. To prove that Defendant is guilty of this crime, the People must prove that:

1. Defendant willfully and unlawfully inflicted a physical injury on his spouse; AND

2. The injury inflicted by Defendant resulted in a traumatic condition; AND

3. Defendant did not act in self-defense.

Someone commits an act *willfully* when he or she does it willingly or on purpose.

A *traumatic condition* is a wound or other bodily injury, whether minor or serious, caused by the direct application of physical force. A traumatic condition is the result of an injury if: the traumatic condition was the natural and probable consequence of the injury; the injury was a direct and substantial factor in causing the condition; AND the condition would not have happened without the injury.

The second count that Defendant is charged with is having made a criminal threat in violation of Oceana Penal Code section 422. In order to prove that Defendant is guilty of this crime, the People must prove that:

1. Defendant willfully threatened to unlawfully kill or unlawfully cause great bodily injury to Rebecca Slater;

2. Defendant made the threat orally, in writing, or by electronic communication device;

3. Defendant intended that his statement be understood as a threat and intended it to be communicated to Rebecca Slater;

4. The threat was so clear, immediate, unconditional, and specific that it communicated to Rebecca Slater a serious intention and the immediate prospect that the threat would be carried out;

5. The threat actually caused Rebecca Slater to be in sustained fear for her own safety; AND

6. Rebecca Slater's fear was reasonable under the circumstances.

Someone commits an act *willfully* when he or she does it willingly or on purpose.

Someone who intends that a statement be understood as a threat does not have to actually intend to carry out the threatened act. An immediate ability to carry out the threat is not required.

Great bodily injury means significant or substantial physical injury. It is an injury that is greater than minor or moderate harm.

Sustained fear means fear for a period of time that is more than momentary, fleeting, or transitory.

Defendant has pleaded not guilty to the charges. The fact that a criminal charge has been filed against Defendant is not evidence that the charge is true. You must not be biased against Defendant just because he has been arrested, charged with a crime, or brought to trial.

A defendant in a criminal case is presumed to be innocent. This presumption requires that the People prove Defendant guilty beyond a reasonable doubt.

Proof beyond a reasonable doubt is proof that leaves you with an abiding conviction that the charge is true. The evidence need not eliminate all possible doubt because everything in life is open to some possible or imaginary doubt.

In deciding whether the People have proved their case beyond a reasonable doubt, you must impartially compare and consider all the evidence that was received throughout the entire trial. Unless the evidence proves Defendant guilty beyond a reasonable doubt, he is entitled to an acquittal and you must find him not guilty.

You must decide what the facts are in this case. You must use only the evidence that is presented in the courtroom. *Evidence* is the sworn testimony of witnesses, the exhibits admitted into evidence, and anything else I tell you to consider as evidence. The fact that Defendant was arrested, charged with a crime, or brought to trial is not evidence of guilt.

Nothing that the attorneys say is evidence. In their opening statements and closing arguments, the attorneys will discuss the case, but their remarks are not evidence. Their questions are not evidence. Only the witnesses' answers are evidence. The attorneys' questions are significant only if they help you understand the witnesses' answers. Do not assume that something is true just because one of the attorneys asks a question that suggests it is true.

You must disregard anything you see or hear when the court is not in session, even if it is done or said by one of the parties or witnesses.

You alone must judge the credibility or believability of the witnesses. In deciding whether testimony is true and accurate, use your common sense and experience. You must judge the testimony of each witness by the same standards, setting aside any bias or prejudice you may have. You may believe all, part, or none of any witness's testimony. Consider the testimony of each witness and decide how much of it you believe.

In evaluating a witness's testimony, you may consider anything that reasonably tends to prove or disprove the truth or accuracy of that testimony. Among the factors that you may consider are:

1. How well could the witness see, hear, or otherwise perceive the things about which the witness testified?

2. How well was the witness able to remember and describe what happened?

3. What was the witness's behavior while testifying?

4. Did the witness understand the questions and answer them directly?

5. Was the witness's testimony influenced by a factor such as bias or prejudice, a personal relationship with someone involved in the case, or a personal interest in how the case is decided?

6. What was the witness's attitude about the case or about testifying?

7. Did the witness make a statement in the past that is consistent or inconsistent with his or her testimony?

8. How reasonable is the testimony when you consider all the other evidence in the case?

9. Did other evidence prove or disprove any fact about which the witness testified?

10. Did the witness admit to being untruthful?

11. What is the witness's character for truthfulness?

12. Has the witness been convicted of a felony?

13. Has the witness engaged in other conduct that reflects on his or her believability?

14. Was the witness promised immunity or leniency in exchange for his or her testimony?

Do not automatically reject testimony just because of inconsistencies or conflicts. Consider whether the differences are important or not. People sometimes honestly forget things or make mistakes about what they remember. Also, two people may witness the same event, yet see or hear it differently.

If you do not believe a witness's testimony that he or she no longer remembers something, that testimony is inconsistent with the witness's earlier statement on that subject.

If you decide that a witness deliberately lied about something significant in this case, you should consider not believing anything that witness says. Or, if you think the witness lied about some things, but told the truth about others, you may simply accept the part that you think is true and ignore the rest.

Facts may be proved by direct or circumstantial evidence or by a combination of both. Direct evidence can prove a fact by itself. For example, if a witness testifies he saw it raining outside before he came into the courthouse, that testimony is direct evidence that it was raining. Circumstantial evidence also may be called indirect evidence. Circumstantial evidence does not directly prove the fact to be decided, but is evidence of another fact or group of facts from which you may logically and reasonably conclude the truth of the fact in question. For example, if a witness testifies that he saw someone come inside wearing a raincoat covered with drops of water, then that testimony is circumstantial evidence because it may support a conclusion that it was raining outside.

Both direct and circumstantial evidence are acceptable types of evidence to prove or disprove the elements of a charge, including intent and mental state and acts necessary to a conviction, and neither is necessarily more reliable than the other. Neither is entitled to any greater weight than the other. You must decide whether a fact in issue has been proved based on all the evidence.

Before you may rely on circumstantial evidence to conclude that a fact necessary to find the defendant guilty has been proved, you must be convinced that the People have proved each fact essential to that conclusion beyond a reasonable doubt.

Also, before you may rely on circumstantial evidence to find the defendant guilty, you must be convinced that the only reasonable conclusion supported by the circumstantial evidence is that the defendant is guilty. If you can infer two or more reasonable conclusions from the circumstantial evidence, and one of those reasonable conclusions points to innocence and another to guilt, you must accept the one that points to innocence. However, when considering circumstantial evidence, you must accept only reasonable conclusions and reject any that are unreasonable.

You have heard evidence that Defendant made [an] oral or written statement[s] (before the trial/while the court was not in session). You must decide whether Defendant made any (such/of these) statement[s], in whole or in part. If you decide that Defendant made such [a] statement[s], consider the statement[s], along with all the other evidence, in reaching your verdict. It is up to you to decide how much importance to give to the statement[s].

Consider with caution any statement made by Defendant tending to show his guilt unless the statement was written or otherwise recorded.

Deciding a proper verdict is exclusively your job. I cannot participate in that decision in any way. Please disregard anything I might have said or done that made you think I preferred one verdict over another. Only one verdict may be returned for each of the crimes charged. The verdict must be in writing and the verdict form has been prepared for you. It is as follows:

(READ JURY VERDICT FORM)

In just a few moments, you will be taken to the jury room by the bailiff. The first thing you should do is elect a foreperson who will preside over your deliberations like the chairperson of a meeting. It is the foreperson's job to sign and date the verdict form when all of you have agreed on a verdict in this case and to bring the verdict back to the courtroom when you return.

In closing, let me remind you that it is important that you follow the law spelled out in these instructions in deciding your verdicts. Even if you do not like the laws, you must apply them. There are no other laws that apply to this case.

SUPERIOR COURT OF THE STATE OF OCEANA

FOR THE COUNTY OF MALIWOOD

STATE OF OCEANA,	Plaintiff,	Case No. MW957100
v.		**CHARGE(S):** 273.5 Spousal Battery 1 count
PAUL SLATER,	Defendant.	
		422 Making a Criminal Threat 1 count

VERDICT

As to the charge of inflicting an injury on a spouse that resulted in a traumatic condition, in violation of Oceana Penal Code section 273.5, we, the jury, find the Defendant, Paul Slater:

_____   GUILTY

_____   NOT GUILTY

As to the charge of making a criminal threat, in violation of Oceana Penal Code section 422, we, the jury, find the Defendant, Paul Slater:

_____   GUILTY

_____   NOT GUILTY

So say we all.

_____
Foreperson of the Jury

_____
Date

CASE FILE No. 7

STATE OF OCEANA

V.

SKYLAR SPENCE

(Murder)

SUPERIOR COURT OF THE STATE OF OCEANA

COUNTY OF MALIWOOD

STATE OF OCEANA,		Case No. MW111799
	Plaintiff,	
v.		**FELONY COMPLAINT**
SKYLAR SPENCE,		
	Defendant.	

COUNT 1

On or about September 27, CY-1, in the City of Maliwood, Maliwood County, State of Oceana, a felony, in violation of section 187 of the Oceana Penal Code, commonly referred to as MURDER, was committed by the above named defendant, who at the time and place last aforesaid, did willfully and with malice aforethought murder Cameron Brown.

IT IS SO ORDERED.

Simon Luna

Simon Luna
District Attorney, County of Maliwood

Witness List

Witnesses for the State:

1.   Casey Haley**

2.   Morgan Evans**

Witnesses for the Defense:

1.   Skylar Spence*

2.   Bobby Hathaway**

Each side must call both witnesses listed for their respective party, and both parties stipulate that each party's expert witness would testify consistently with his or her provided statement.

*This witness must be played by a male.

**This witness may be either gender.

Stipulations

1. Both the Federal Rules of Criminal Procedure and Federal Rules of Evidence apply.

2. Assume each witness who gave an interview reviewed the officer's report of his or her interview and signed the interview to verify for accuracy.

3. All exhibits included in the file are authentic and, unless otherwise stated, are the original of that document.

4. Other than what appears in the officer's report of the interviews, there is nothing exceptional or unusual about the background of any of the witnesses that would bolster or detract from their credibility.

5. All dates are denoted by CY (current year) or CY-*n* (current year minus *n* years).

6. All pretrial motions shall be oral.

7. No party may invent witnesses or evidence that is not specifically mentioned in this case file.

8. "Beyond the record" is not a proper objection. Rather, the attorneys shall use cross-examination as the means of challenging a witness whose testimony strays beyond the facts contained in the case file.

9. The physical description of a witness, e.g., clothing, should be tailored to that of the student playing the witness, except for height, weight, and age.

10. All witness statements were given under oath.

11. All witnesses called to testify who have identified Defendant Spence or any tangible evidence can, if asked, identify the same at trial.

12. The text messages are authenticated under the Federal Rules of Evidence 902(11) and are admissible as certified business records under Federal Rules of Evidence 803(6).

13. The expert witnesses' reports of Emily Laetz and Andy Jones are stipulated to as being an accurate reflection of what each expert would testify to if called as a witness. Either side may constructively read into the record the expert witnesses' testimony in whole or in part or move the testimony into the record. Any such testimony by the stipulated experts is subject to objections pursuant to the Federal Rules of Evidence. The parties do not stipulate to the correctness of the experts' opinions, but they waive hearsay objections to these experts' statements.

14. The prosecution and defense may only call the two witnesses listed on their respective witness list.

15. The prosecution and defense have stipulated that the proper foundation has been laid for the medical report, and they have stipulated that the medical expert would testify pursuant to his report. However, either side is free to dispute the contents of the report.

16. Both sides stipulate to the authenticity of Bradley James's memo and waive hearsay and foundation objections to its admission.

17. Section 187 of the Oceana Penal Code provides: "Murder is the unlawful killing of a human being with malice aforethought."

18. Skylar Spence must be played by a male. All other witnesses can be either gender. The witnesses may be called in any order.

COUNTY OF MALIWOOD SHERIFF'S DEPARTMENT
INVESTIGATION REPORT

RECORDS & STATISTICS BUREAU'S USE ONLY

DATE: **9/27/CY-1** PAGE: **1** OF **4**

ACTION	ACTIVE (X) INACTIVE ( ) PENDING ( )	INDEX Yes (X) INFO No ( )	N of Adult Arrests: 1	No of Subject Detentions: 1	URN (File No.) MW111799

CLASSIFICATION
MURDER INVESTIGATION

DATE, TIME OF OCCURRENCE
09/27/CY-1, 15:20 HOURS

LOCATION OF OCCURRENCE 1984 HYDE WHARF DRIVE, MALIWOOD, OC	TYPE OF LOCATION MARINA	TRACT

CODE: V - VICTIM, W - WITNESS, I - INFORMANT, R - REPORTING PARTY, P - PARTY

CODE V No. 1 OF 1	LAST NAME BROWN, CAMERON	FIRST	MIDDLE	SEX M	AGE 50	RACE WHITE

RESIDENCE ADDRESS 2011 MAGPIE ROAD, MALIWOOD, OC	RES. PHONE (AREA CODE)

BUSINESS ADDRESS	RES. PHONE (AREA CODE)

CODE W No. 1 OF 1	LAST NAME EVANS, MORGAN	FIRST	MIDDLE	SEX M	AGE 64	RACE WHITE

RESIDENCE ADDRESS 2003 GLOAMING WAY, MALIWOOD, OC	RES. PHONE (AREA CODE) 555-555-7892

BUSINESS ADDRESS	RES. PHONE (AREA CODE)

CODE: S - SUSPECT, SJ - SUBJECT, M - PATIENT, S / V - SUSPECT/VICTIM, SJ / V - SUBJECT / VICTIM

CODE S No. 1 OF 1	LAST NAME SPENCE, SKYLAR	FIRST	MIDDLE	DRIVER'S LICENSE (STATE & No) OC HTTT03

RESIDENCE ADDRESS 1985 GREENWOOD HILLS, MALIWOOD, OC	RES. PHONE (AREA CODE)

BUSINESS ADDRESS	BUS. PHONE (AREA CODE)

SEX M	RACE WHITE	HAIR GRAY	EYES HAZEL	HEIGHT 6'0''	WEIGHT 185 LBS	DOB 07/04/CY-50	AGE 50	WHERE DETAINED MALIWOOD

OBSERVABLE PHYSICAL ODDITIES/TATTOOS/SCARS	AKA / NICKNAME	BOOKING No. MA111799

CLOTHING WORN BLACK TROUSERS, WHITE DRESS SHIRT, BLACK LOAFERS	MAIN

CHARGE MURDER	WEAPON USED SCUBA GEAR

CODE No. OF	LAST NAME	FIRST	MIDDLE	DRIVER'S LICENSE (STATE & No)

RESIDENCE ADDRESS	RES. PHONE (AREA CODE)

BUSINESS ADDRESS	BUS. PHONE (AREA CODE)

SEX	RACE	HAIR	EYES	HEIGHT	WEIGHT	D.O.B.	AGE	WHERE DETAINED OR CITE No.

OBSERVABLE PHYSICAL ODDITIES	AKA / NICKNAME	BOOKING No.

CLOTHING WORN	MAIN

CHARGE	WEAPON USED

VEHICLE USED IN CRIME YES ( ) NO (X) UNKNOWN ( ) STORED ( ) IMPOUNDED (X)	YR	MAKE	BODY TYPE	COLOR	BY DEPUTY HALEY	BADGE No. 1007

LICENSE (STATE & No.)	V.I.N./ FRAME No.	BY DEPUTY	BADGE No.

REGISTERED OWNER	STATION MWD	UNIT / CAR No.	SHIFT DAY

IDENTIFYING CHARACTERISTICS	APPROVED	BADGE No.	TIME

O.H.P. 180 SUBMITTED YES ( ) NO ( )	GARAGE NAME & PHONE	ASSIGNMENT

Narrative Report – URN MW111799

At 15:20 hours on September 27, CY-1, emergency operators received a call from Morgan Evans, a boat captain, reporting that there was an accident during a SCUBA dive he facilitated. He reported that a diver had died. Evans stated that he was still at sea but on his way in to the Maliwood Marina.

My partner, Detective Hastings, and I responded to the call and arrived at the marina at approximately 15:38 hours, just as the boat was docking. Evans and a person who identified himself as Skylar Spence were on the boat when it docked. Detective Hastings called a special task force of three deputy sheriff divers to go back to the location of the dive to find and recover the body. The divers were also instructed to recover any dive equipment for inspection while I interviewed Evans and Spence (see attached statements).

I initially learned that the man reported dead was Cameron Brown. I spoke to Spence first. Spence was distraught over the incident and kept saying that he couldn't believe his best friend was gone. He had trouble focusing and kept looking off in other directions when I was speaking to him. He calmed down enough to answer some questions and said that Brown was an inexperienced diver, but had wanted to become better. Sometime during the dive, Brown ran out of air, panicked, and took in water while attempting to buddy breathe with Spence. Spence was instructed not to leave the marina so that the deputy sheriff divers could look at his diving equipment. When questioned about the equipment, Spence related that he rented Brown's dive gear from Starfish Divers.

Next, I spoke with Evans (see attached Statement of Morgan Evans). He was very shook up by Brown's death and said that he had never had anyone die on any of his dive trips. I smelled alcohol on his breath, and he admitted that he drank one beer over the duration of the boat trip. Evans said that Spence was in charge of the dive equipment. Evans also stated that he thought this might be a homicide rather than an accident, and he suspected Spence of foul play. When I asked why, Evans related that prior to the dive, he asked Spence why he and Brown were not using secondary regulators (see attached Exhibits F, I, and J, which show that only a primary regulator was attached to the buoyancy control device, commonly referred to as a BCD). Evans related that Spence told him to do his job and just drive the boat. Evans was concerned about the divers not having the safety precaution of a back up stage of the regulator known as an octopus. , Evans then said he found it odd that the bubbles coming from the divers were in separate locations for an extended period during the dive. Evans explained that if the two divers were buddy breathing, then the bubbles on the surface of the water should have been closer in proximity.

I walked around the boat and noticed two empty beer bottles (see attached Exhibit H). I saw Spence's cell phone sitting on the deck near his gear. I looked at his recent text messages. The most recent was from Carl Glitz and said, "What's going on? We're concerned. I thought you said this was a done deal." The response from Spence read, "I almost have him convinced, just give me a little more time. One way or the other, you'll have your deal by October." There were a couple texts between Spence and Brown about where to meet for the dive and it appeared that all other messages had been deleted.

The department's divers arrived at approximately 16:22 hours and suited up. Evans escorted the three divers and me on his boat to the location of the dive. The divers began their search dive at 17:05 hours. At 17:18 hours, the divers surfaced with the body, later confirmed to be Brown. The divers related to me that according to their dive computers (which are devices that measure the depth and time of a dive, thus allowing the diver to make safety calculations), the body was recovered at 112 feet. I verified this by looking at their dive computers, and each showed a maximum dive depth of 112 feet. Brown was brought on deck with all of his dive gear intact, including his tank, BCD with integrated weights, and regulator. His bluish complexion and lack of visible injury pointed to drowning, heart attack, or embolism as the cause of death. Brown wore a two-piece wetsuit, amounting to 6mm of material on his arms and legs and 12mm around his core. The amount of weight found in the integrated weight pocket of Brown's BCD weighed a total of 27 pounds. Brown's dive computer did not work, so the depth of his dive was unknown. Upon inspecting his equipment, one of the department's divers noticed a small slit in the regulator. I took photographs of the dive equipment, BCD, and regulator (see attached Exhibits F–G, I–J). Brown's tank, computer, and BCD were sent to dive equipment experts for further inspection.

Next, Spence's gear was inspected. His dive computer was in working order and able to inform us of his maximum depth, dive time, temperature and the amount of air in his tank (see attached Exhibit G). The water temperature was 62°F. Spence's dive had lasted for forty-one minutes and his maximum depth had been 110 feet. His tank had 550 pounds of air remaining. All of Spence's equipment appeared normal upon a visual inspection.

After Spence consented to a search of his vehicle, I found one secondary regulator in the trunk. This secondary regulator, also known as an "octopus," was not attached to any other equipment. I also found a wrench next to the secondary regulator. I removed the secondary regulator, photographed it, and took it as evidence (see attached Exhibits K and L, which show the secondary regulator. Exhibit L shows a close-up of the mouthpiece of the secondary regulator).

The testing results from the dive equipment experts, which were received three days after the accident, established that Brown's tank was completely out of air, the computer battery was dead, and the regulator leaked air. Neither diver used a secondary regulator.

Signed,

Casey Haley

Detective Casey Haley

Maliwood County Sheriff's Department
Supplemental Police Report

Brown's damaged equipment, as well as other dive irregularities, called for a greater investigation into the relationship between Brown and Spence.

Spence related to me that he became close friends with Brown in college (see attached Spence Interview). The relationship continued, and they co-owned the Maliwood Beach Hotel. There was interest from Glitz Hotels to buy the hotel as part of its recent venture to expand its presence along the California coast. Spence and Brown had a contractual agreement that required both to consent to a sale of the hotel (see attached Spence Interview).

I contacted Carl Glitz, President and Owner of Glitz Hotels, and confirmed his interest in buying the hotel. He provided a contract proposal (see attached Exhibit A) that was presented to Spence and Brown, in which he proposed to buy the Maliwood Beach Hotel for $200 million. He noted that he never received a reply from Brown, but he did begin correspondence with Spence, who he believed to be in charge of the hotel's operation and finances.

Further investigation of Spence's bank accounts revealed that he is heavily in debt. His savings accounts are depleted. His checking account reveals regular weekend visits to Las Vegas (see attached Exhibit B). Spence's Maliwood home is valued at $2.2 million, but it is mortgaged at $2 million. He leases cars, including his Ferrari and vintage Alpha Romeo. His second home in the Hamptons, which is also heavily mortgaged, is for sale. Spence also owns a condo in Las Vegas near the Strip, which he frequents about twice per month (see attached Spence Interview).

An investigation into Brown's finances revealed no financial problems. His family and employees at the Maliwood Beach Hotel uniformly report that he enjoyed his job and had never expressed any desire to sell the hotel.

I interviewed several employees at the Maliwood Beach Hotel on September 30, CY-1. The office manager told me that she overheard Brown and Spence arguing over the sale of the Maliwood Hotel a week prior to Brown's death. She said that Spence sounded agitated, even angry, and he told

Brown that this would be the best offer they could ever get. Brown said that it wasn't about the money and reminded Spence that they didn't choose to co-own a hotel just for the money. Spence asked Brown to look over the contract, but Brown refused the request.

I also spoke to Spence's secretary. I asked her if she knew of any financial problems he was having. She said she suspected he was a gambler, but did not know anything for sure. She did say that she once saw something odd. About a week prior to Brown's death, Spence received a letter with no return address. He opened it up in front of her. He read it, crumpled it up, threw it in the trash, and quickly walked out of the room. Curious, she opened it up and read it. She kept the letter and provided it to me. The letter read: "Pay by October 31st or find Black Beauty's HEAD in Your Bed!!" (see attached Exhibit C). We asked her what it meant, and she said that Black Beauty was one of Spence's prized racehorses.

On October 1, CY-1, I went to Spence's home at 12:00 hours. I rang the intercom, but no one answered. I noticed that the gate that leads up to his driveway was left open. Trash bins were moved to the edge of the property, but had not been taken to the curb. The lid to the black bin was open, and on top of the trash pile was a crumpled ball of paper. The paper was in plain view, so I grabbed it to see if it was of interest. I found a note similar to the one the secretary showed me. It was a small note that appeared to have been read and discarded. The following statement was written on the note: "TIME IS RUNNING OUT! PAY OR PRAY!" I seized the note (see attached Exhibit D) because I thought it establishes that Spence was being threatened, perhaps by someone linked to his gambling debts.

Two hours later, I returned to the Spence residence. This time when I rang the intercom, a housekeeper answered and let me in. She informed me that Spence was not in. I asked if she could show me to Spence's study. She led me to the study and left. I turned on the computer and opened the web browser. I then clicked on "history" and saw that there was a search for "dive fatalities" on September 15, CY-1. I immediately took a screenshot to prove this suspicious search (see attached Exhibit E). I then seized the computer so that an expert could examine it and determine what searches Spence had done in the weeks leading up to Brown's death (see attached report).

I swear under penalty of perjury that the foregoing is true and accurate.

Signed,

Casey Haley

Detective Casey Haley

Maliwood County Sheriff's Department
Supplemental Police Report-Interoffice Memo

Date: October 2, CY-1

To: Detective Casey Haley

From: Forensic Scientist Bradley James, Ph.D.

Subject: Data retrieved from Spence's computer

Mr. Spence's desktop computer was delivered to my office yesterday, October 1, CY-1. This morning at 09:17 hours, I installed a software program on the computer. I created the program, named CacheReport, which scans the hard drive of the computer and computes the specific number of times a given term or phrase was entered in any internet search engine.

The program is 100% accurate and has been tested by this office extensively.

The report generated by the software is conclusive and provides that the particular phrase "dive fatalities" was searched 48 times between August 30, CY-1 and September 19, CY-1 on the computer seized from the home office of Mr. Spence.

I swear under penalty of perjury that the foregoing is true and accurate.

Signed,

Bradley James

Bradley James

Skylar Spence Interview

Detective Casey Haley (CH): This is Detective Haley. Today's date is Oct. 1, CY-1. I'm here with Skylar Spence who I've asked to come in for an interview pursuant to the investigation into the death of Cameron Brown. He has agreed to come in and talk with me. Mr. Spence, although you have not been charged with a crime at this point, you are a suspect in the death of Cameron Brown. Mr. Spence, please state your name for the record.

Skylar Spence (SS): My name is Skylar Spence.

CH: Mr. Spence, you understand that you have the right to remain silent, anything you say can and will be used against you. You have the right to have a lawyer present. If you cannot afford a lawyer, one will be appointed for you at no cost to you. Do you understand and waive these rights?

SS: Yes, Sir.

CH: Mr. Spence, please tell me the nature of your relationship to the deceased, Mr. Brown.

SS: Cameron Brown was my best friend. We were in the same fraternity at USC. We co-owned the Maliwood Beach Hotel for five years.

CH: Were you and Brown getting along at the time of his death?

SS: Brown and I were getting along just fine, as we always have.

CH: Who planned the diving trip?

SS: The dive was his idea. He had been begging me for months to go on a dive with him. He was a novice and wanted more dive experience with a Divemaster, which I am. Listen, he and I have always been close. Even our families are close! I am married with two children, and my wife Sandy and I are college sweethearts from USC and have been happily married for twenty-five years. In fact, Sandy and I were best friends with Cameron and his wife Katherine. Sandy and I are both devastated over this loss.

CH: Is it true that you're in serious debt?

SS: No.

CH: Did Brown know about your gambling habits?

SS: I don't know. It is true that I have some gambling debts, but this is not anything unusual for me. I go to Vegas almost every weekend. I'm a high roller—I've won and lost huge amounts of money over the years. This is not anything that would make me desperate. I own two houses, a condo, and I have an exotic car collection and own prized racehorses. Granted, recently, I haven't had a big win.

CH: Were you in any serious trouble though? Anything that you couldn't handle? Any bookies coming after you? That sort of thing. I mean, it's understandable for you to be desperate if you can't pay debts to people willing to retaliate.

SS: I'm not sure what you mean. I wasn't in any serious trouble.

CH: But your accounts are pretty depleted, aren't they?

SS: Listen, I'd need just one more big win, and I could pay off all my debts.

CH: So is it true that Glitz made you an offer? That must have been some kind of a Godsend, right? Everyone knows about Glitz. Never fails to make a profit. Didn't you need to convince Brown to sell the hotel? Wouldn't that have solved all your problems?

SS: I admit that the partnership agreement we had regarding the Maliwood Beach Hotel provided that neither Cameron nor I could sell the hotel without the other's approval; however, I was not desperate to sell. There's no reason for me to kill anyone for money, especially not my best friend. I did want to sell the hotel, but that was just because owning it was becoming a hassle, and we got a great offer. Carl Glitz wanted to buy it, and we would have made millions. I was making progress in talking Cameron into selling the hotel—but I was also fine with not selling. Besides, if my debts were *that* bad, I could have told Cameron that we had no choice but to sell. He'd have come around.

CH: So tell me what happened on the day of September 27.

SS: On September 27, Cameron and I went for a day dive I had arranged two weeks prior with Captain Evans. This was a way for us to create a local getaway. What do they call it . . . a "staycation." Cameron wanted me to help him improve his dive skills, and he also didn't want anyone else to accompany us on the dive trip. Since I'm a Divemaster, I was in charge of the equipment for the dive. I own my own gear and rented Cameron's from Bobby at Starfish Divers. You can check with Starfish Divers that the equipment appeared to be in working order. Both tanks were full; I checked prior to the dive. Evans saw me checking the air in the tanks and questioned me suspiciously. But this was ridiculous because the only way to check the air is to let some air out of the tank. When Cameron and I got to a depth of ten feet, he pointed to his dive computer and showed me that the screen was blank. Typically a dive computer goes into dive mode by about seven feet and the screen displays information, such as depth and time left on the dive without a decompression stop. Apparently, the battery had run out on his dive computer, which is nothing to be panicked about. I pointed to him, pointed to myself, and then pointed at my functioning dive computer, suggesting that we both dive on my profile and both use my computer. He put his thumb and forefinger together to sign "okay" to me. I did the same in return.

CH: So what happened next?

SS: We continued descending and proceeded with the dive. I've done this before when I've either forgotten my computer or had a friend's computer malfunction. It is not difficult or risky because you normally dive next to your buddy anyway, so you and your buddy will have very similar dive profiles. Therefore, diving on the same profile is not dangerous. There is no way I could have known that Cameron's regulator would malfunction or that it would run out of air. Unfortunately, I didn't know until it was too late. It is not cause for alarm when there is a leak in a regulator. I had no idea that Cameron would panic. He was usually a very levelheaded person.

CH: So get back to what happened.

SS: Evans insinuated that Cameron was over-weighted, and that is just absurd. He weighed 175 pounds and was provided with 27 pounds of weight, which is the typical amount of weight for a dive with a two-piece 6mm wetsuit for a person of his weight. Maybe 25 pounds would be more typical, but most divers would rather be a little over weighted so they don't have trouble descending.

CH: I understand, so go on.

SS: Everything was going fine on the dive. It's true that Cameron's dive computer was apparently malfunctioning, but that would not have been unsafe in any way as long as he stayed with me, since I was diving in a safe profile. We were planning on doing a 70-foot dive, but I was forced to go to 100 feet or so because one of Cameron's pocket weights fell down to the sea floor. I had Cameron stay at the 70-foot level while I retrieved the weights. This might have been what Evans was referring to when he saw the two sets of bubbles move apart—as I left Cameron for this period of time. Cameron must have panicked when his weight fell out, and I could see him breathing quickly. He must have used too much air. After I retrieved the weight, he gave me the sign for no air. I could not tell if he actually had run out of air or if there was a leak in his regulator. Either way, the appropriate maneuver was to buddy breathe, and this is what I attempted to do.

CH: What do you mean by buddy breathing?

SS: This means that the two partners take turns taking two breaths from the working regulator and slowly come up to the surface together. This is a last resort, but it is taught and practiced during diving certification, or at least it was when I got certified. When buddy breathing, it is crucial to purge the regulator by blowing out air from your mouth or by pushing the purge button prior to breathing in, so that you do not breathe in water and choke.

CH: So what happened?

SS: I put my regulator into Cameron's mouth, so that we could buddy breathe. I am quite positive that Cameron panicked and forgot to purge my regulator. He must have panicked and inhaled water because he began coughing and choking—eventually suffocating. It was the most traumatic moment of my life; I was desperately trying to communicate to Cameron to cough and breathe out into the regulator before breathing in. He ran out of air and was drowning. I tried to bring him up to the surface, but it was impossible. I keep having nightmares about seeing Cameron gagging and turning blue—watching a good friend die right in front of me.

CH: Is that it?

SS: That's it.

CH: This is the end of the interview.

[END OF TAPE]

Statement of Morgan Evans

My name is Morgan Evans, and I own a thirty-six foot Tiara cabin cruiser, which I principally use as a SCUBA boat. I am sixty-four years old and have been leading diving expeditions as a boat captain for twenty-three years. I am divorced. My passion is being a boat captain, and I take my job seriously. I served in the U.S. Navy, and I am a Vietnam veteran and received a Purple Heart for my service. Prior to my service in the navy, I was an avid and experienced diver. However, a shrapnel injury during Vietnam caused damage to my inner ear resulting in my inability to equalize in the water. Since the shrapnel injury, I have been unable to continue diving. Luckily, conducting diving expeditions on my boat allows me to continue sharing my love for diving with others.

On or about September 27, CY-1, I took Skylar Spence and Cameron Brown on a one day SCUBA expedition. Spence hired me two weeks before that date, and specified that he wanted to dive in a remote location off Maliwood with a depth of at least 100 feet. Spence was insistent that he be the only one to handle the equipment for himself and Brown. He also made a big deal about the fact that he wanted the dive to be private with no other divers around. He said that this would make the dive special and not so commercial. Typically, I have a helper on board who assists with all equipment, but Spence insisted that no one be on the boat except Brown, him, and me. At the time of the dive, his insistence to handle all the equipment without assistance seemed slightly odd, but I did not question him because he is a dive master.

Just prior to embarking, I realized I had forgotten my prescription sunglasses in my car and went out to retrieve them. I use prescription sunglasses when I am onboard the boat. I lost the prescription sunglasses with my most up to date prescription, so the ones I was wearing the day Brown died are about four years old, but I could still see well enough. In the parking lot, I saw Spence at the back of his pickup truck fiddling with one of the air tanks. I heard the sound of air escaping out of one of the tanks, so I went up to question him about it. I casually asked him what he was doing, and he got very defensive. He told me, something like, "I was just checking the air. I already told you I want to take care of all the equipment myself. Mind your own business! Your job is just to skipper the boat!" I also noticed that the regulators each had only one second stage, instead of the more common set up of two second stages, also known as a primary stage and a backup stage, or octopus. That was unusual, and I asked Spence why the BCDs did not have secondary regulators. He responded, "I'm old school. That type of extra equipment is just another thing to get in the way."

I kept my opinions to myself for the moment, but when we were all back on the boat I started to feel uneasy about them diving without secondary regulators. It especially didn't make sense to me that a novice diver would dive without the most current and safe dive recommendations. In the presence of Spence and Brown, I again asked why they didn't have an octopus on each of their BCDs. I thought that Spence might explode at me, considering his reaction the first time I asked, but surprisingly he didn't. He casually explained that he uses the same gear he bought in the 1980s, which did not have an octopus because they were not common practice back then. He then said that he didn't think the whole octopus craze was a good idea anyway and that he knew several new divers who had gotten their octopus tangled badly in kelp, which then had to be cut out. He told Brown that he didn't recommend using an octopus. Brown laughed and said it was fine; Brown clearly wanted to be the same kind of diver as Spence. I could tell Brown was deferring to Spence, who was more experienced and clearly leading the dive. Spence reiterated that he knew what he was doing and that I only needed to worry about the boat. Now, I wish I wouldn't have listened to him, but he was the dive master and he was the one who hired me. I should mention that he was paying me twice my normal rate, but I don't think this influenced my judgment.

I checked both their dive cards. Both were certified divers. Spence was a Divemaster and Brown was an Open Water diver, which is a basic diver.. Spence planned the dive, and Brown accompanied him. I asked Spence how deep of a dive he was planning, and he told me seventy feet. Spence set up the tanks and all of the equipment used by the two men. He explained the dive profile to Brown. I distinctly remember Brown saying that he had never gone past fifty feet and that he felt apprehensive about diving deeper than that. Spence said they could keep the dive to about sixty feet, and to just stay with him, that he knew what he was doing. He said he would make sure Brown was fine. Spence provided the weights, and I saw him putting weights into Brown's BCD pockets. It looked like Spence was putting a lot of weights into Brown's pockets. I asked how much weight Spence was giving Brown, and Spence just said, "I know what I'm doing. I'm the Divemaster here."

Spence helped outfit Brown and then he outfitted himself. He helped Brown walk over to the deck at the stern of the boat. Brown took a giant stride to enter the water and Spence followed him. I watched their bubbles as they descended. Their bubbles were close together, which is normal. It is my responsibility as Captain to keep an eye on where the divers are, and I can tell this by the location of the air bubbles. I noticed that the two sets of bubbles were close together for about twenty minutes. During the course of the dive, I grabbed a cold beer from the ice chest at the stern of the boat. I knew I wouldn't have to drive the boat back for at least an hour. Upon returning to the bow of the boat, I noticed something unusual; there were two sets of bubbles approximately seventy-five feet apart from each other. There were no other bubbles or divers in the area. This concerned me because during dive expeditions, divers need to stay within close proximity of each other. This is a crucial rule, so that if one diver experiences a problem, such as equipment failure or low air, his dive buddy can assist him. I kept a close eye on the two sets of bubbles using my binoculars, and after five or ten minutes there was only one set of bubbles to be seen. That worried me.

Within five minutes of there only being one set of bubbles, Spence came to the surface without Brown. He was very distraught. He yelled up to me that Brown had panicked and drowned. Spence was breathing heavily and was freaked out. I asked Spence why he had abandoned his buddy, but he simply denied doing so. I told him that I saw that the two sets of bubbles were far apart, but he completely denied this. He pointed to my empty bottle of beer and called me an "old drunk." I felt like decking him, but because I now had a really serious situation on my hands, I kept my temper in check. I immediately got on my radio and called for help.

I demanded that Spence tell me what happened. He said that Brown must have run out of air because he gave the sign for running out of air, which is to move the index finger across the throat in a slashing motion. Then Spence said he took the regulator out of his own mouth and put it in Brown's mouth. This technique is known as "buddy breathing." Spence claimed that Brown panicked and started choking and taking on water; he wasn't breathing and quickly began turning blue. Spence related that he was taking breaths from the regulator and kept attempting to give it back to Brown, but Brown was panicking and was unable to get air. Spence claimed he tried to bring Brown up to the surface but failed.

I checked Spence's dive computer, and it showed a maximum depth of 110 feet. I checked Spence's regulator and it functioned fine. I was told that when Brown's regulator was tested it had a leak. It could not be determined if this leak was from wear or if it was sabotaged. It is not that unusual for a regulator to leak, but this is why it is necessary for a diver and his dive buddy to each carry a back up regulator.

I have never before taken out a dive boat when anyone died. This was a horrible and shocking experience. In the future, I am going to check all dive equipment before letting divers on my boat go into the water. I will also require them to wear secondary regulators.

I swear under penalty of perjury that the foregoing is true and accurate.

Signed,

Morgan Evans

Morgan Evans

Statement of Emily Laetz

My name is Emily Laetz, and I am thirty-five years old. I completed my undergraduate degree at University of Virginia with a major in biology and a minor in environmental sciences. I worked for the National Oceanic and Atmospheric Administration (NOAA) for two years on its Coral Reef Conservation Program. Around this time, I got my scientific diver certification because I was diving regularly to conduct research for NOAA. Before my scientific certification, I was certified as a diver under PADI, which is the Professional Association of Diving Instructors, when I was sixteen years old. I went back to school and got my masters in marine biology at Duke University. I continued studying the impacts of climate change and anthropogenic activities on coral reefs. For the last five years, I traveled around the world on dive boats and research expeditions. On the research cruises, I collect data on ocean acidification and ecosystem responses to climate change with a number of other scientists. I do a lot of the dive work and data crunching. In between these cruises, I make some extra money by working on dive boats—mostly certifying new divers.

About six months ago, I was appointed by the governor of Oceana to be a member of the working group on Global Climate Change and Ocean Acidification as part of the National Ocean Policy Initiative. In addition to this position, I frequently testify for plaintiffs on SCUBA-related cases, usually SCUBA accidents and equipment failure. I am paid $500 per hour. I am willing to testify for either side, but because I work for the government, I end up testifying for the plaintiff 80% of the time.

I studied all documents, statements, and the police report related to the Spence case. Additionally, I inspected the SCUBA gear pertinent to the case. I did not find it necessary to interview any witnesses myself in order to form my opinion. It is clear to me that Brown's death was not an accident. The two most convincing pieces of evidence are that Brown's primary regulator was sabotaged and that neither diver dove with a secondary regulator. Most incriminating is the fact that the secondary regulator on Brown's rented equipment must have been physically removed with a wrench prior to the dive.

Spence picked up Brown's rented gear from Bobby Hathaway at Starfish Divers the morning of the dive. Hathaway inspected the rented equipment and found that everything was in working order, including the regulator. Every dive shop will always inspect the regulator before renting it out because this is such a crucial piece of equipment, and they don't want the liability of renting out bad gear. Brown's recovered regulator clearly had a leak, which was coming from a small, slit-shaped hole in the regulator. While leaky regulators are not unheard of, they do not happen over the duration of a car ride. There is no reason for the regulator to have acquired a hole; this is not typical wear and tear for this type of equipment, which is extremely durable. Usually if there is a leak in a regulator, it is from the purge button getting stuck and leaking air or the incorrect assembly of the tubes connecting the air to the regulator and BCD, not from a physical hole in the regulator. I believe the regulator was intentionally punctured and sabotaged for the dive.

The removal of Brown's secondary regulator and Spence's failure to use a secondary is absolutely reckless to the point of being criminal. This is a standard piece of equipment used as a precaution for unpredicted mishaps. Since the introduction of secondary regulators in diving, air-related accidents have dropped significantly. Out of air problems account for approximately 43% of all fatal dive accidents, which is a much lower percent then before the invent of the octopus.. A dive shop would never rent gear without a secondary regulator, and it does not make sense for Spence to go out of his way to remove the secondary regulator, especially when diving with a novice. I carefully reviewed Spence's statement to the detective, and his reasons for not using secondary regulators simply do not add up; the secondary regulators hook into a clip on the BCD, so they do not inconvenience the diver, and the likelihood of a secondary malfunctioning is slim. It is dangerous to whomever you are diving with to refuse to use a secondary regulator, and it is even stranger to go to the extra effort to remove a secondary that is already attached to the rest of the dive gear.

In addition to these two main points, Brown may have been over-weighted, and it is suspicious that the victim ran out of air while Spence had enough time to surface with 550 pounds of air remaining in his tank. The compressed mixture of air is referred to as a measurement in pounds. Generally, divers begin the dive with 2500 to 3000 pounds of air and are advised to surface with at least 500 pounds of air. Starfish Divers confirmed that Hathaway filled two tanks with air for Spence and Brown. It is odd that Evans saw Spence releasing air from one of the tanks. This is not a standard procedure. Some divers may let a touch of air out to make sure that they grabbed a tank with air, but letting air out continuously for more than 1–2 seconds is not typical. If the tanks were just picked up from the dive shop and this was the first dive of the day, there is really no reason to let air out of the tanks. In fact, Spence and Brown planned for only one dive and brought one tank of air each; there was no possibility that empty tanks were mixed in with their equipment.

Being an experienced diver, Spence knew that even letting a small amount of air out of the tank could make a big difference at depth. Due to increased pressure at greater depths, the air in a diver's tank compresses, meaning the volume of air decreases, as he goes deeper. As a result, a diver will have less air to breathe at sixty feet than at ten feet because the air molecules compress and you need to breathe in more air molecules per breath to get the same volume of air to fill your lungs. Spence's dive computer showed a depth of over one hundred feet. A diver consumes more air at deeper depths due to increased density of the air. In other words, the air is consumed faster the deeper the dive. In fact, divers use up the air four times faster at 100 feet than at the surface. This is the equivalent of taking four breaths at 100 feet for every one breath taken at the surface. Consequently, a diver uses air more quickly on a deep dive and this limits the dive time.

As a dive master, Spence should also know that novice divers routinely intake more air than experienced divers. More experienced divers use less air because they are calm, have better control over their buoyancy, are often in better shape, can swim efficiently, and are accustomed to taking slow, long breaths. It is not uncommon for a new diver to use air twice as quickly as an experienced diver. With this information, Spence knew that letting out a small amount of air from Brown's tank would have a big impact on the novice diver during their deep dive. Furthermore, the actual depth of the dive was too deep for a novice diver.

Another unusual occurrence was the separation of the divers' bubbles as witnessed by Evans. Dive buddies are always supposed to dive together. In this case, this standard precaution was crucial because the two men were diving on one computer and one of the divers was a novice. The two men needed to stay on the same dive profile in order to share the computer. Spence claims he was retrieving weights for Brown, but in that case the bubbles should have stayed in approximately the same area because Spence was diving to a greater depth and not moving laterally. If weights fell out of Brown's BCD, they would fall to the seafloor because they are heavy. The weights would not drift seventy-five feet away. It is even more disturbing that one set of bubbles ceased, signaling the stoppage of breathing, while the two sets of bubbles were separated. The separation of the bubbles is highly indicative of foul play and inconsistent with a dive accident.

While it is tragic that Brown suffocated and died while SCUBA diving, there are too many coincidences in this case for Brown's death to be the result of equipment malfunction and panic. Evans saw Spence letting air out of the tank, Spence did not use a secondary regulator and removed Brown's secondary regulator, Brown's computer failed to turn on, Brown's primary regulator leaked after clearing an inspection at Starfish Divers the morning of the dive, Brown may have been over-weighted, Spence's computer showed a depth of 110 feet, and Evans saw the air bubbles of the two divers separate by about seventy-five feet. By ignoring standard safe dive practices, providing Brown with sabotaged equipment, and allowing himself to be separated from his dive buddy, Spence not only failed to act as a responsible dive master, he is actually responsible for killing Brown.

I swear under penalty of perjury that the foregoing is true and accurate.

Signed,

Emily Laetz

Emily Laetz

Statement of Bobby Hathaway

My name is Bobby Hathaway. I am twenty-eight years old and single. My family moved to

Maliwood after my dad retired from the Marines, so I've lived here since I was a teenager. I am the

manager of Starfish Divers. I am fortunate to be paid to do what I enjoy. SCUBA diving is my passion.

I sell SCUBA gear, do the purchasing for the store, and organize SCUBA trips. I have been diving since I

was twelve, and I take customers out on dive trips several times a year. We mostly go to the outer islands

because the water clarity is not very good for diving in Maliwood. Very few people actually dive off of

the Maliwood coast because the water is cold and the visibility is not nearly as good as it is in the islands.

Skylar Spence came in the store on August 27, CY-1, to rent dive equipment for his friend. I was

somewhat surprised that they were diving off the Maliwood coast because it is not a popular dive area.

Spence commented that he and his friend were looking for a remote place to dive so they could have a

more special and less commercial dive experience. He kept talking about some of the old dives he did in

his twenties and thirties when so few people dove and it was unusual to see anyone else in the water; it

was just you and the fish. This made sense to me because the islands do get really crowded, which can

scare the fish away and detract from the enjoyment of the dive. Spence also commented that he and his

best friend needed a break from work and wanted to have some guy time, like adventurers in the

wilderness, so they did not want to dive where there would be other people bothering them. I remember

thinking that this sounded like a great chance for best friends to enjoy the day together. I do similar dives

with my dive buddies all the time. We have an ongoing bet on who can find the best new and publicly

unknown dive spot.

Spence showed me his PADI certification, which proved that he was a dive master. This means

he is trained and qualified to guide other divers. I have a copy of Spence and Brown's dive cards, as this

is standard when someone rents dive equipment. I had recognized Spence as soon as he came in the store

because he is a frequent customer. Spence has hundreds of dives under his belt, and I respect his

capabilities. In fact, Spence participated in some of my island group dives, and I can tell you he is a highly competent and considerate diver. I specifically remember instances when he helped out novice divers and put them at ease if they were nervous. Some of the other employees at Starfish Divers think Spence is a 'cowboy' because he insists on doing things the old fashioned way, but I have always respected him.

I rented Spence one standard SCUBA tank filled with air, one buoyancy control device (BCD) with a primary stage and a secondary stage (known as an octopus) attached to the regulator.. I understood that this equipment was for Brown. I filled one tank that Spence already owned with air. I do recall suggesting that Spence rent a secondary regulator for his own BCD, but he just shook his head, and explained that fancy modern equipment is just "more junk to get in the way." He related that he has been using his regulator for thirty years and didn't see any reason to get rid of something that wasn't broken. SCUBA gear is very expensive, so I don't blame him. He said that he and his friend already had masks, snorkels, fins, and wetsuits.

I filled up the tanks myself, so I know that the nitrogen/oxygen levels were accurate and that the tanks were full. I checked the equipment before renting it, and both the regulator and the octopus looked fine and passed inspection. There were no visible holes or tears in either the primary or secondary regulator. I have since learned that there was an accident and that Brown's regulator may have had a leak. It is not uncommon for a regulator to leak, and it should not be a serious problem. Unanticipated problems are why it's important for even experienced divers to use an octopus. I tried to convince Spence to use an octopus, but I could not force him to rent one for himself. I also could not ensure that the octopus rented for his friend would be used. It is not illegal to dive without a secondary regulator. Some people, particularly older divers who were certified before the alternate air source existed, choose to dive with just one regulator, and this is their choice. In the past, every diver who got certified had to prove that he or she can buddy breathe in order to obtain SCUBA certification. Some certification courses (such as PADI) no longer teach buddy breathing, because most divers dive with an octopus. Even so, old school divers consider the octopus to be a backup precaution, not a necessary piece of equipment. Divers dove for decades before secondary regulators became standard equipment. My understanding is that my store is being sued for filling an air tank for a diver that I knew was not planning to use an octopus, but this is ridiculous. We only rent out BCDs with secondary regulators attached, and even if we insisted that divers refilling their own tanks rent secondary regulators, we could not force them to use them. Besides, like I said, people dove for decades without secondary regulators, and some divers just feel more comfortable doing it the old-fashioned way. This is unwise, but not against dive regulations.

If there is a leak in the regulator, it is not really dangerous, unless the diver neglected to pay attention to his air supply, dove too deep for a controlled emergency swimming ascent, or failed to buddy breathe and panicked, which is apparently what Mr. Brown did. It is imperative that a diver purges his regulator before breathing under water. This means that the diver either presses the purge button or simply breathes out before breathing in, otherwise water will come into the regulator and into the diver's mouth, causing him to choke on the water and possibly suffocate. All divers are taught this purging technique, and it is reinforced throughout dive training. I know that Brown was a certified PADI diver. I have a copy of his dive card. We are a reputable dive outfit and only rent to certified divers. Unfortunately, some divers (and I later found out that Brown was one of these) dive so seldom that they don't keep their skills up. Obviously, dive outfitters need to trust that certified divers know what they are doing. It would be impossible for my store employees to test the skills of every diver before renting out our equipment.

Since the accident, I have examined both the regulator and the octopus that I rented Spence. It is obvious that the octopus was detached from the BCD, which, as I stated, is not against dive regulations. I am confident that the primary regulator was not sabotaged in any way. If a regulator were punctured, this would leave obvious marks. I inspected the regulator after the dive accident, and it did not look sabotaged. I am not entirely surprised that the octopus was removed. Like I said, Spence is an old school diver and may not believe that secondary regulators are beneficial. I have had several other customers who rent BCDs and remove the secondary regulator; it's not unheard of.

I understand that Brown was given twenty-seven pounds of weight in his BCD, which is an appropriate amount of weight for a 175-pound man, given the thickness of his wetsuit. Wetsuits make people more buoyant, and these wetsuits were thick because the water was chilly. Brown needed that amount of weight or he would have risen to the surface too quickly, which is dangerous.

Our dive computers are designed so that the screen displays information at a depth of between five to seven feet. This is known as the computer's dive mode. Once the computer senses atmospheric pressure, it displays the depth and the dive time remaining before a diver needs to surface or make a decompression stop. Thus, Brown may not have known that his computer was not working until he was seven feet underwater. This is generally not a problem because divers should always dive with a buddy, and if one diver's computer is not working, he can simply rely on the profile of his dive buddy's computer. Brown also had the option of coming up. He would have seen at ten feet that the computer was not working, so if he chose to continue the dive, that is not Spence's fault.

Diving is a great sport, but every SCUBA diver assumes the risk of the sport. I have a copy of the waiver that Brown signed acknowledging that there are serious potential risks to diving. When Brown and Spence came into my store, Brown seemed excited about the dive. Spence was the one who checked out and rented the equipment. Brown let Spence make all the decisions regarding the dive, but this was appropriate because Spence was a dive master and Brown was a novice. Brown provided his dive card and signed the waiver. They both seemed happy about the dive and relaxed. Spence did not seem nervous in any way. Brown seemed the most eager about the dive, and I got the impression that the excursion was his idea. I also specifically recall Brown saying that he was really glad that they were going to dive in a remote area because he did not like dives that were too commercial and crowded.

Spence rented the top of the line equipment and said that he wanted to be sure that his best friend would be "safe and comfortable." I remember these words because I thought it was considerate. Spence also paid for the equipment.

Everyone in the store feels so badly about what happened to Brown, but it seems pretty clear that he panicked and forgot his dive training about how to buddy breathe. I saw Spence in the dive shop a few days after the dive accident, and he was grief stricken. He said he had lost his best friend, and he would give anything for Brown not to have panicked and drowned.

I swear under penalty of perjury that the foregoing is true and accurate.

Signed,

Bobby Hathaway

Bobby Hathaway

Statement of Andy Jones

My name is Andy Jones. I am a commercial diver. I am married with four grown kids. I got my start diving in my twenties, while serving in the Navy from 1974-1980. I was in the SEAL program, but I didn't make it through. Over 75% of people don't make it through the program, but it's an honor to be accepted into the program in the first place, and I learned a lot from that training.

Most people go diving for recreation, but I've made it my career. I've been a HAZMAT diver for over 30 years now and I've seen it all. HAZMAT diving is arguably the most dangerous type of commercial diving out there. My areas of expertise are pollution and nuclear waste control. If there's a disaster, my team assists for safety and cleanup.

I was hired by the defense to render an opinion as to whether the death of Cameron Brown appeared to be an accident. I was paid $500 an hour for my work to come up with my conclusions. My conclusions are in no way influenced by the fact that I was hired by the defense. Regardless of whether I'm hired by the prosecution or the defense, I always render an objective, neutral finding. I have testified for both sides as an expert witness over the past five years. Typically, I testify for the defense because the government has its own go-to experts, such as current military divers.

After a thorough investigation of the evidence and several witness interviews, my conclusion is that Brown's death was a tragic accident. I conducted this investigation by first examining the SCUBA equipment worn by Brown and Spence. Next, I read the police report, including all witness statements. Finally, I interviewed Skylar Spence, Bobby Hathaway, and Morgan Evans. My conclusion is that this was an accident for the following reasons:

1. The equipment was not sabotaged. Any malfunction was due to normal wear and tear.

2. There is nothing compelling from the witness interviews to conclude that there was foul play.

3. While unfortunate, based on my entire investigation, nothing that happened stands out as malicious intent.

4. Diving can be a risky sport. Total equipment failure is rare, but minor issues such as leaks or

    tears are not uncommon. It is not unique for a novice diver to panic while buddy breathing

    and drown.

I carefully inspected the regulator from Brown's BCD. I did find a small tear, however, it

appeared to be consistent with normal wear. The tear did not appear to be jagged, as I would expect it to

be if it was intentionally slit with a knife or other blunt instrument. It appears to be a small opening that

is consistent with rubber breaking down over continual use. Rental equipment, in particular, is more

susceptible to this type of malfunction because it is used frequently by many divers. It's just common

sense that people treat their own equipment far more carefully than rental equipment.

I do not believe that it was reckless for Spence to remove the secondary regulator from the BCD.

Many of my colleagues who are long time divers choose not to use a secondary regulator. This piece of

equipment, also known as an octopus, does provide an extra safety net, especially for beginning divers.

However, many of us old time divers prefer not to have an extra hose. When I interviewed Spence, his

explanation about being concerned that a secondary would get caught on seaweed made perfect sense. As

a HAZMAT diver, I usually dive in a drysuit with a helmet, which has a direct air supply. Given that I

don't use a secondary on my professional dives, I usually opt out of using one on my recreational dives as

well. Like Spence, I prefer diving the old fashioned way, so the octopus feels unnecessary.

Regarding the bubbles being separated, of course that sounds suspicious, but there appears to be a

reasonable explanation. Spence stated that he had gone down to the ocean floor to retrieve Brown's

dropped weights. This would account for the bubbles appearing to be separated. Also, Evans admitted to

drinking beer, which could clearly have affected his perception. Who's ever heard of a dive captain

drinking beer on the job? It's just not professional.

When I talked to Spence, he sounded distraught and I found it hard to believe that he would have

murdered his best friend. Evans did not seem to have a detailed memory of the events. I assume his

judgment was clouded by beer. My interview of Bobby Hathaway confirmed my opinion that this was just an accident. While Hathaway did not notice a tear in the regulator, the small tear could have been easily overlooked when the equipment was rented.

My conclusion is that Brown panicked when his regulator was leaking and he was low on air. Spence told me that when he tried to buddy breathe, his friend panicked and did not breathe out before breathing in from the regulator, which caused him to suffocate and drown. Although sad, this is an inherent risk of buddy breathing. Divers should not get themselves in a situation where they are so low on air that they have to resort to sharing an air supply; however, buddy breathing is a technique that is taught in every dive class and no diver can obtain SCUBA certification without demonstrating an ability to perform this task. The reality of the situation is that divers who are almost out of air do not always comply with the rules.

Along with cardiac arrest, running out of air and equipment failure are the most common causes of diver accidents and deaths. Diving is a relatively safe sport; there is approximately one death out of every 200,000 dives. Brown was a novice diver, and it appears that he got nervous and used up his air supply too quickly. Coupled with the leaky regulator, this caused him to run out of air. In retrospect, of course it would have been better for both divers to have had an octopus, given that one diver ended up having a leaky regulator and running out of air; however, there was no reason to predict that outcome.

My expert opinion is that Brown's death was the result of a tragic accident.

I swear under penalty of perjury that the foregoing is true and accurate.

Signed,

Andy Jones

Andy Jones

Exhibit A

❖ GLITZ HOTELS ❖

1600 Boardwalk Ave.
Atlantic, NX
Phone: (572) 555-1789
E-Mail: moneybags@glitz.com

September 1, CY-1

Skylar Spence & Cameron Brown
Co-Owners, Maliwood Beach Hotel

Dear Mr. Spence & Mr. Brown:

As you know, my company has been expanding and on the rise since I established it years ago. We've conquered the east coast, and now we plan to conquer the west coast.

Your hotel shows promise. I'd be interested in buying the hotel and turning it into one of my own.

I don't like to beat around the bush, so to speak. I'm going to be short and to the point. I'm a businessman. Let's arrange a meeting. Bring your attorneys, and let's get together and write up an official contract for sale of the hotel. This will be a sweet deal for you.

I'm going to offer you $200 million dollars for the Maliwood Beach Hotel. Trust me, you won't regret this. Nobody ever regrets selling to me. I've developed half of this country!

But as you know, time is money. Let me know by October 1, CY-1 if you will agree to sell.

Sincerely,

Carl Glitz

Carl Glitz,
Founder and President of Glitz Hotels

Exhibit B

BANK OCEANA

CUSTOMER: SKYLAR SPENCE

CHECKING ACCT# 00112233445566

DATE	DESCRIPTION	TYPE	STATUS	AMOUNT	BALANCE
08/05	CHECKCARD GASOLINE, OC	—	C	$45	$15,000.79
08/05	ATM WITHDRAWAL THE VENETIAN HOTEL, LAS VEGAS	-	C	$200	$14,800.79
08/05	WITHDRAWAL BANK OCEANA, LAS VEGAS BRANCH	-	C	$1,500	$13, 300.79
08/06	ATM WITHDRAWAL MGM GRAND HOTEL AND CASINO, LAS VEGAS	-	C	$100	$13, 200.79
08/06	ATM WITHDRAWAL WYNN, LAS VEGAS	-	C	$100	$13, 100.79
08/06	CHECKCARD BELLAGIO BUFFET, LAS VEGAS	-	C	$20	$13,080.79
08/06	WITHDRAWAL BANK OCEANA, LAS VEGAS BRANCH	-	C	$5,000	$8, 080.79
08/12	WITHDRAWAL BANK OCEANA, LAS VEGAS BRANCH	-	C	$1,500	$6, 580.79
08/12	ATM WITHDRAWAL, HOOTERS CASINO, LAS VEGAS	-	C	$200	$6, 380.79
08/12	CHECKCARD LV STEAKHOUSE	-	C	$236.45	$6, 344.34
08/13	CHECKCARD, TICKETS, CELINE DION IN CONCERT AT CAESARS	-	C	$313.99	$6, 030.35
08/13	ATM WITHDRAWAL, CAESARS PALACE, LAS VEGAS	-	C	$200	$5, 830.35
08/19	WITHDRAWAL BANK OCEANA, LAS VEGAS BRANCH	-	C	$5,000	$830.35
08/19	CHECKCARD GASOLINE, LAS VEGAS	-	C	$30	$800.35
08/19	ATM WITHDRAWAL, MANDALAY BAY HOTEL AND CASINO	-	C	$200	$600.35
08/19	WITHDRAWAL BANK OCEANA, LAS VEGAS BRANCH	-	C	$500	$100.35
08/20	CHECKCARD FORUM SHOPS BURBERRY	-	C	$185.99	-$85.64
08/20	FEE	-	C	$35	-$120.64

Exhibit C

Exhibit D

Exhibit E

Exhibit F

Exhibit G

Exhibit H

Exhibit I

Exhibit J

Exhibit K

Exhibit L

Exhibit M

Jury Instructions

Members of the jury, I thank you for your attentiveness during this trial. Please pay close attention to the instructions I am about to give you.

In this case, Defendant, Skylar Spence, is charged with murder in the first degree. A person who unlawfully kills another person with malice aforethought is guilty of the crime of murder in violation of Oceana Penal Code section 187. To prove the crime of murder, the State must prove the following elements beyond a reasonable doubt:

1. A human being was killed;

2. The killing was unlawful; and

3. The killing was done with malice aforethought.

Unlawful means that a killing is neither justifiable nor excusable.

Malice may be either express or implied. Malice is express when there is a manifested intent to unlawfully kill a person. Malice is implied when:

1. The killing is the result of an intentional act;

2. The natural consequences of the act are dangerous to human life; and

3. The act was deliberately performed with knowledge of the danger to, and with conscious disregard for, human life.

When it is shown that a killing resulted from the intentional doing of an act with express or implied malice, no other mental state need be shown to establish the mental state of malice aforethought. The mental state constituting malice aforethought does not necessarily require any ill will or hatred of the person killed. The word *aforethought* does not imply deliberation or the lapse of substantial time. Rather, it only means the required mental state must precede rather than follow the act.

Defendant has entered a plea of not guilty. This means that you must presume or believe that Defendant is not guilty unless and until the evidence convinces you otherwise. This presumption stays with Defendant as to each material allegation in the indictment through each stage of the trial until it has been overcome by the evidence to the exclusion of and beyond a reasonable doubt.

To overcome Defendant's presumption of innocence, it is the State's burden to prove the following:

1. The crime with which Defendant is charged was committed.

2. Defendant is the person who committed the crime.

Defendant is not required to prove anything.

The State has the burden to prove the elements beyond a reasonable doubt. Whenever the words *reasonable doubt* are used, you must consider the following: A reasonable doubt is not a mere possible doubt, because everything relating to human affairs is open to some possible or imaginary doubt. Reasonable doubt is the state of the case that, after hearing and considering all the evidence, leaves the minds of the jurors in the condition that they cannot say they feel an abiding conviction of the truth of the charge.

It is to the evidence introduced during this trial, and to it alone, that you are to look for that proof. A reasonable doubt as to the guilt of Defendant may arise from evidence, a conflict in the evidence, or a lack of evidence. If you have a reasonable doubt, you should find Defendant not guilty. If you have no reasonable doubt, you should find Defendant guilty.

You must decide this case on the evidence and the law. It is up to you to decide what evidence is reliable. You should use your common sense in deciding what evidence is reliable and what evidence should not be relied upon in considering your verdict.

A witness is a person who has knowledge related to this case. You will have to decide whether you believe each witness and how important each witness's testimony is to the case. You may believe all, part, or none of a witness's testimony. In deciding whether to believe a witness's testimony, you may consider, among other factors, the following:

1. The extent of the witness's opportunity to see, hear, or otherwise become familiar with any matter about which the witness testified.

2. The ability of the witness to accurately recall or communicate any matter about which the witness testified and the character and quality of that testimony.

3. The witness's manner and demeanor while on the stand.

4. Whether or not the witness has bias, an improper motive, or an interest in the outcome of the case.

5. The witness's attitude toward this trial or toward testifying.

6. Whether the witness's testimony was consistent or inconsistent with other testimony or evidence presented in this case.

7. Any previous statements made by the witness that are consistent or inconsistent with the witness's testimony.

8. The witness's character for honesty or veracity, or their opposites.

9. Whether the witness was offered money, preferred treatment, or any other benefit to testify or whether the witness received any threats or was under any pressure that might have affected the truth of the witness's testimony.

10. The witness's previous conviction of a felony or past criminal conduct amounting to a misdemeanor.

You may rely upon your own conclusions about each witness. A juror may believe or disbelieve all or any part of the evidence or the testimony of any witness.

There are some general rules that apply to your deliberations. You must abide by these rules in order to return a verdict that is consistent with the law:

1. You must follow the law as it is explained to you in these instructions. If you fail to follow the law or disregard the law, any verdict you reach will be a miscarriage of justice.

2. You must decide the case only upon the evidence that you have heard from either the testimony of witnesses or exhibits that you have seen.

3. You must not decide the case for or against anyone because you feel sympathy for that person, or because you are angry at that person.

4. You must not decide the case based on your feelings about the lawyers in this case. The lawyers are not on trial.

5. You must not consider any potential sentence Defendant might receive. It is not your duty to consider punishment. Your only duty is to determine guilt or innocence. It is the judge's job to determine the proper sentence if you find Defendant guilty.

6. Whatever verdict you render must be unanimous; that is, each juror must commit to the same verdict. The verdict must be the verdict of each juror as well as that of the jury as a whole.

7. It is entirely proper for a lawyer to talk to a witness about what testimony the witness would give if called into the courtroom. The witness should not be discredited for talking to a lawyer about his or her testimony.

8. You must not decide this case based on feelings of prejudice, bias, or sympathy. Any verdict you may reach should be based on the evidence and the law contained in these instructions.

Deciding a proper verdict is exclusively your job. I cannot participate in that decision in any way. Please disregard anything I might have said or done that made you think I preferred one verdict over another.

Only one verdict may be returned for the crime charged. The verdict must be in writing and the verdict form has been prepared for you. It is as follows:

(READ JURY VERDICT FORM)

In just a few moments, the Bailiff will escort you to the jury room. Once inside the jury room, the first thing you should do is elect a foreperson, who will preside over your deliberations. It is the foreperson's job to sign and date the verdict form when all of you have agreed on a verdict in this case and to bring the verdict back to the courtroom when you return.

In conclusion, let me remind you that it is imperative that you follow the law as I have explained it to you in these instructions. Regardless of how you feel about the laws, you must apply them.

SUPERIOR COURT OF THE STATE OF OCEANA

FOR THE COUNTY OF MALIWOOD

STATE OF OCEANA, Plaintiff, v. **SKYLAR SPENCE,** Defendant.	Case No. MW111799 **CHARGE(S):** 187 Murder in the first degree 1 count

VERDICT

As to the charge of murder in the first degree, in violation of Oceana Penal Code section 187, we, the jury, find the Defendant, Skylar Spence:

____ GUILTY

____ NOT GUILTY

So say we all.

_____
Foreperson of the Jury

_____
Date

CASE FILE No. 8

STATE OF OCEANA

V.

ERIK CLARK

(Rape)

SUPERIOR COURT OF THE STATE OF OCEANA

COUNTY OF ROCKPORT

STATE OF OCEANA, v. **ERIK CLARK,**	Case No. RP101711 **FELONY COMPLAINT**

STATE OF OCEANA,

Plaintiff,

v.

ERIK CLARK,

Defendant.

Case No. RP101711

FELONY COMPLAINT

COUNT 1

On or about February 18, CY-1, in the City of Rockport, Rockport County, State of Oceana, a felony, in violation of section 261 of the Oceana Penal Code, commonly referred to as RAPE, was committed by the above defendant, who at the time and place last aforesaid, forcibly raped Grace O'Malley.

IT IS SO ORDERED.

Oliver Y. Felix

Oliver Y. Felix
District Attorney, County of Rockport

Witness List

Witnesses for the State:

1.   Grace O'Malley**

2.   Lee Donne***

Witnesses for the Defense:

1.   Erik Clark*

2.   River Coleridge***

Each side must call both witnesses listed for their respective party, and both parties stipulate that each party's expert witness would testify consistently with his or her provided statement.

*This witness must be played by a male.

**This witness must be played by a female.

***This witness may be either gender.

Stipulations

1. Federal Rules of Criminal Procedure and Federal Rules of Evidence apply.

2. Each witness who gave a statement agreed under oath at the outset of the statement to give a full and complete description of what occurred and to correct the statement for inaccuracies and completeness before signing it.

3. All witnesses called to testify who have identified the Defendant or identified tangible evidence can, if asked, identify the same at trial.

4. All exhibits in the file are authentic and, unless otherwise noted, are the original of that document.

5. Other than what appears in the officer's reports of the interviews, there is nothing exceptional or unusual about the background of any of the witnesses that would bolster or detract from their credibility.

6. All dates are denoted by CY (current year) or CY-*n* (current year minus *n* years).

7. All pretrial motions shall be oral.

8. No party may "invent" witnesses or evidence not specifically mentioned in this problem.

9. "Beyond the record" is not a proper objection. Rather, attorneys shall use cross-examination as a means of challenging a witness whose testimony strays beyond the facts contained in the officer's reports of the interviews.

10. The physical description of a witness, e.g., clothing, shall be tailored to that of the student playing the witness, except for height, weight, and age.

11. The expert witnesses' reports are stipulated to as being an accurate reflection of what each expert would testify to if called as a witness; it is therefore unnecessary to call either expert as a witness.

12. Erik Clark has entered a plea of not guilty and has requested a trial by jury.

13. Oceana Penal Code section 261(a)(2) reads as follows: "Rape is an act of sexual intercourse accomplished with a person not the spouse of the perpetrator where it is accomplished against a person's will by means of force, violence, duress, menace, or fear of immediate and willful bodily injury on the person or another."

14. The Medical Examiner's report is authentic. The parties have agreed to its admissibility, but not to the accuracy of its conclusions.

15. The prosecution and defense may only call the two witnesses listed on their respective witness list.

16. The witnesses may be called in any order.

17. February 17, CY-1, was a Monday.

18. Erik Clark must be played by a male, and Grace O'Malley must be played by a female. All other witnesses may be either gender.

CITY OF ROCKPORT SHERIFF'S DEPARTMENT
INVESTIGATION REPORT

RECORDS & STATISTICS BUREAU'S USE ONLY			DATE: **2/18/CY-1**	PAGE: 1 OF 3

ACTION	ACTIVE (X) INACTIVE ( ) PENDING ( )	INDEX Yes (X) INFO No ( )	N of Adult Arrests 1	No of Subject Detentions 1	URN (File No.) RP101711

CLASSIFICATION
RAPE INVESTIGATION

DATE, TIME OF OCCURRENCE
02/18/CY-1, 0050 HOURS

LOCATION OF OCCURRENCE 3976 OLYMPIA BLVD, ROCKPORT, OC, ROCKPORT MEDICAL PLAZA	TYPE OF LOCATION PARKING STRUCTURE	TRACT

CODE: V - VICTIM, W - WITNESS, I - INFORMANT, R - REPORTING PARTY, P - PARTY

CODE V NO. 1 OF 1	LAST NAME O'MALLEY, GRACE	FIRST	MIDDLE	SEX F	AGE 25	RACE WHITE

RESIDENCE ADDRESS 550 MAPLE DRIVE, ROCKPORT, OC	RES. PHONE (AREA CODE) N/A

BUSINESS ADDRESS 3976 OLYMPIA BLVD, ROCKPORT, OC, ROCKPORT MEDICAL PLAZA	RES. PHONE (AREA CODE)

CODE NO. OF	LAST NAME	FIRST	MIDDLE	SEX	AGE	RACE

RESIDENCE ADDRESS	RES. PHONE (AREA CODE)

BUSINESS ADDRESS	RES. PHONE (AREA CODE)

CODE: S - SUSPECT, SJ - SUBJECT, M - PATIENT, S / V - SUSPECT/VICTIM, SJ / V - SUBJECT / VICTIM

CODE S No 1 OF 1	LAST NAME CLARK, ERIK	FIRST	MIDDLE	DRIVER'S LICENSE (STATE & No) OC12070411

RESIDENCE ADDRESS 746 W. 38TH STREET, ROCKPORT, OC	RES. PHONE (AREA CODE)

BUSINESS ADDRESS	BUS. PHONE (AREA CODE)

SEX M	RACE WHITE	HAIR BR	EYES BR	HEIGHT 5'11''	WEIGHT 175 LBS	DOB 09/30/CY-28	AGE 28	WHERE DETAINED ROCKPORT

OBSERVABLE PHYSICAL ODDITIES/TATTOOS/SCARS RED DRAGON TATTOO, RIGHT SHOULDER	AKA / NICKNAME	BOOKING No. OC

CLOTHING WORN WHITE TSHIRT, BLUE JEANS, BLACK BOOTS	MAIN

CHARGE RAPE	WEAPON USED

CODE Nc OF	LAST NAME	FIRST	MIDDLE	DRIVER'S LICENSE (STATE & No)

RESIDENCE ADDRESS	RES. PHONE (AREA CODE)

BUSINESS ADDRESS	BUS. PHONE (AREA CODE)

SEX	RACE	HAIR	EYES	HEIGHT	WEIGHT	D.O.B.	AGE	WHERE DETAINED OR CITE No.

OBSERVABLE PHYSICAL ODDITIES	AKA / NICKNAME	BOOKING No.

CLOTHING WORN	MAIN

CHARGE	WEAPON USED

VEHICLE USED IN CRIME YES ( ) NO (X) UNKNOWN ( ) STORED ( ) IMPOUNDED (X)	YR 2000	MAKE YAMAHA	BODY TYPE MTRCYL	COLOR BLACK	BY DEPUTY DONNE	BADGE No. 1026

LICENSE (STATE & No.) OC 55VVS51	V.I.N./ FRAME No.	DEPUTY	BADGE No.

REGISTERED OWNER ERIK CLARK	STATION AMZ	UNIT / CAR No. 0331	SHIFT NIGHT

IDENTIFYING CHARACTERISTICS	APPROVED	BADGE No.	TIME

O.H.P. 180 YES ( ) SUBMITTED NO ( )	GARAGE NAME & PHONE	ASSIGNMENT

Narrative Report – URN RP101711

At 00:50 hours on February 18, CY-1, emergency operators received a call from Grace O'Malley, who reported that she had been raped by an unknown attacker in the parking structure of the Rockport Medical Plaza at 3976 Olympia Blvd.

At approximately 01:00 hours, I arrived on the scene and O'Malley, a nurse at the Medical Plaza, was sitting at the stairwell of level P2 of the subterranean parking structure of the plaza. She appeared to be crying. I approached and asked her if she needed immediate medical attention. She declined, so I then asked what had happened (see attached Statement of Grace O'Malley). In her statement, O'Malley indicated that an unknown attacker approached her from behind just as she reached the bottom of the stairwell. He forced her to the ground, choked her, pulled down the pants of her scrubs, and forcibly raped her. She related that the attack was over in about five minutes because O'Malley had pushed the panic button on the remote key to her vehicle, which she had in her hands at the time she was assaulted. After the alarm was set off, the attacker ran to and drove off on a black motorcycle, located approximately fifteen feet from where the attack took place. O'Malley was not able to determine the make and model of the motorcycle, nor could she observe the license plate number. She did remember that the attacker smelled of cigarettes and alcohol. O'Malley believed she saw her attacker flick a cigarette away as he was choking her. O'Malley could not make out any discernable facial features of her attacker because he was wearing a full-face black helmet with a tinted shield. She remembered, however, that he had a red, snake-like tattoo on his left shoulder, and was a white man of average height and weight.

On level P2 of the structure where O'Malley identified the attack took place, I had the stairwell cordoned off. A cigarette butt was found next to the stairwell, and forensics was called in to collect it (see attached Exhibit Q). I put on gloves and examined the butt, which was labeled "Marlboro" (see attached Exhibit R). Based on a visual analysis of the butt, this particular cigarette was a Marlboro Red. Forensics undertook a fingerprint analysis, but could only recover partial prints that were smudged. Thus, the prints could not be analyzed to identify the attacker. No other evidence was collected from the scene. The parking structure has surveillance cameras, and one camera captured an image of what appears to be a man fleeing on a black motorcycle. The man was wearing a motorcycle helmet, and his face was obscured. The camera near the stairwell, was malfunctioning and recorded no images.

At 01:05 hours, paramedics transported O'Malley to the ER at Rockport Medical Plaza. They had a rape trauma expert examine her and obtain a rape kit. Upon examination, it was reported that O'Malley had vaginal tears consistent with forcible rape (see attached Exhibit B). There was also bruising visible on her neck and evidence of choking (see attached Exhibit O). Her knees and shoulders were also bruised, consistent with being thrown down to the ground (see attached Exhibit N). The results of the rape kit confirmed that no semen was recovered (see attached Exhibit B). There were no scrapings under O'Malley's fingernails. Forensics did not recover any hair evidence, blood, or fibers that might lead to the identity of the attacker.

The cigarette butt was tested for DNA by the sheriff's criminologist. On February 21, CY-1, the results were run with high priority through the FBI felony databank, which returned a hit. The DNA was a match for Erik Clark, and the sample was from his second-degree felony burglary from CY-5. It was later determined that in CY-3, Clark was also convicted of misdemeanor sexual battery, for which he remains on probation.

Signed,

Deputy Lee Donne

Deputy Lee Donne

Rockport County Sheriff's Department
Supplemental Police Report

At 11:00 hours on February 21, CY-1, my partner and I went to the apartment of suspect Clark. His roommate, River Coleridge, answered the door and agreed to let us enter and search the apartment. During the search, we found two types of cigarettes: Marlboro Reds and Parliaments (see attached Exhibit J). We seized both packs as well as a cigarette butt in an ashtray on the coffee table, which was noticeably a Marlboro cigarette based on a visual inspection of the filter (see attached Exhibit K). During the search, Clark arrived at the apartment. He confirmed that he owned a black full-face motorcycle helmet with a tinted shield (see attached Exhibit E). Clark also confirmed that the black motorcycle downstairs belonged to him. Forensics photographed the motorcycle (see attached Exhibit F). There was also an almost empty bottle of tequila on the kitchen counter and a trash bin filled with beer bottles near the counter (see attached Exhibits L & M). Upon questioning, Clark confirmed that he had a red dragon tattoo on his right shoulder (see attached Exhibit I). It appeared similar to the description given by O'Malley. She described a red, snake-like tattoo, which would have a similar appearance to a red dragon tattoo since the witness was only able to observe part of the tattoo. Based on the foregoing, Clark was arrested for the rape of O'Malley. Clark was cooperative and taken to the station without incident.

At the station, Clark waived his *Miranda* rights and agreed to talk to us without the assistance of counsel (see attached Erik Clark Interrogation). He told us that he had been at the Rockport Medical Plaza on the afternoon of February 17, CY-1, because of a doctor's appointment (see attached Exhibit C). He stated that he did not rape the victim and that he was at home when the rape occurred. He also stated that Coleridge, his roommate, would be able to confirm his alibi. At 14:00 hours, Coleridge came down to the Sheriff's Office and provided us with a statement (see attached Statement of River Coleridge).

Signed,

Deputy Lee Donne
Deputy Lee Donne

Statement of Grace O'Malley

My name is Grace O'Malley, and I'm a nurse at the Rockport Medical Plaza. I am twenty-five years old, single, and only recently started working as a nurse. Three years ago, I graduated with my Bachelor's degree in biology from the University of Rockport and then went to nursing school to get my R.N. About six months ago I started as an R.N. at the Plaza. I work long hours and they are often irregular, but it never worried me until I was attacked. I've always thought that Rockport was a safe city.

Last Monday, February 17, I went to work as usual. I got in at noon. I had a twelve-hour shift that day. I was already tired when I went into work because the night before was my parents' wedding anniversary. They live in Maliwood, so I had to drive there for dinner. By the time I got to my apartment, I had only six hours until my next shift. I went to bed, slept five hours, threw on my scrubs, and went to work.

It was a normal workday. I didn't notice anything out of the ordinary. A lot of people come in and out of the Plaza. When I finished work at midnight, I just wanted to get home and sleep. I was exhausted. I had some paperwork I needed to straighten out before I left, and then I had to wash up. By the time I started walking to the parking structure, it was already forty minutes past midnight. I had checked my phone to see if I had any missed calls throughout the day, which I did. My mom had called earlier in the evening and left me a message wishing me a good night and thanking me for the bottle of champagne I'd given them for their anniversary. I cleared the message, checked the time, and headed into the structure. I remember being irritated when I saw the time. I had to be at the Plaza at 6 a.m. the next day, so I was worried about having another night with little sleep.

The parking structure at the Plaza is subterranean. You enter on P1, and then you have to descend the staircases to get to the lower levels. I think there are eight levels, but I never have to park down below that far. I wanted to take the elevator that night, but it was out of order. Just my luck. I was already so damn tired, but at least I didn't have to climb up the stairs. As I was going down the stairs, I took my keys out of my purse. I just wanted to get in my car right away, get home, and go to bed.

When I got to the bottom of the stairwell on P2, I was attacked from behind. I didn't see him coming, and I didn't even hear the guy come up behind me. I got to the bottom of the stairs and that was it. Out of nowhere some guy grabbed me from behind. He was so strong. I just remember how tightly he grabbed me. He pinned my arms at my sides, so I couldn't move at all. I just remember thinking: "Please God, don't let me die here like this." I really thought I was going to be killed. I remember that I started crying right away, and I tried to scream but nothing would come out. I also remember that a second after he grabbed me something flew by my face. When I looked at the ground I saw a lit cigarette butt. He must have flicked it just before grabbing me, but when I turned to see his face he had a black helmet on. I was confused, but he must have been smoking. He reeked. I used to be a smoker, but quit years ago. Now, I can't stand the smell. On top of that, he also smelled of alcohol. I just wanted to throw up. I started gagging too. And then I tried to scream again, but this just made it worse.

When I tried to scream a second time, he grabbed my throat with one of his hands and started choking me. He never let go of my waist though. He kept his other arm wrapped tightly around me. He then forced me down to the ground. My knees hit the concrete. It hurt really bad; I thought I'd broken something. Then he pulled down my scrubs, let go of my throat, and turned me around forcing me on my back. When he turned me around, I noticed that his pants weren't zipped up and that he was exposing himself. Then he started to rape me. It was so scary and shocking.

He was a white guy. His build wasn't very big or muscular. He just seemed really average. I was shocked he was so strong when I saw his body frame. I do remember that he had a tattoo. When he was on top of me, I noticed one on his left shoulder. It was a red snake or some kind of serpent like that. I think it was on his left shoulder, but it's such a blur now that I'm not exactly sure. I just remember lying on my back with tears streaming down my face. I remember feeling like I was being torn from the inside and a tugging burning sensation. Unfortunately, I did not get a good enough look to identify him.

I then remembered feeling a sharp pain in my hands. I was squeezing my keys and my car key was jabbing my palm. Then it occurred to me that I had the remote key in my hand, so I felt for the panic button with my thumb and pressed it. Until then it was like I was deaf; I just couldn't hear anything happening around me. It was as if time stood still. I kept hoping that someone would walk by and stop this, but no one did. But when I hit that button, the alarm started blaring. It must have been the echo caused by the structure, but whatever it was, it worked. The man who attacked me was startled. He got off me, zipped up, and ran over to a black motorcycle parked in the corner. He jumped on and sped off. I tried to see a license plate, but it happened so fast and I just wanted to pull my scrubs back on. I was relieved to be alive, but in pain and scared. It then occurred to me that I could still be in serious danger. He could turn around and come at me a second time, or even try to kill me. I grabbed my cell phone and immediately called 911.

I didn't want to go to my car because I was too scared to move. I wasn't sure how badly injured I was. I just felt so sore. And I was shaking. I felt cold, and then I started to panic. I thought: "What if he had AIDS? What if I got pregnant? But at least I'm alive. At least it was over." So I just sat at the stairs and waited.

The police got there right away. They told me that my call came in at 12:50 a.m. I hadn't realized how long just a few minutes could last. I've lived through some strong earthquakes that seemed to last forever, but this was worse. This felt like hours, and it felt like it was never going to end. I just wish I'd seen his face. I just hope that the police get the guy who did this to me; I don't want to have to treat any of his victims at the Plaza. He can't get away with this. He just can't.

Signed,

Grace O'Malley

Grace O'Malley

Erik Clark Interrogation

Deputy Lee Donne (LD): This is Deputy Donne. I am sitting here with Erik Clark at the Rockport City Police Department interview room. I read Mr. Clark his *Miranda* rights verbatim per my *Miranda* card. He waived his *Miranda* rights, including his right to have an attorney present. This interview is being audio recorded and today's date is February 21, CY-1, and it's about 14:00 hours. Mr. Clark, please state your name for the record.

Erik Clark (EC): My name is Erik Clark.

LD: So Mr. Clark, you like to ride motorcycles, yeah?

EC: Yeah, I've been riding 'em for a long time.

LD: Do you have a car, or do you always ride your motorcycle?

EC: I always ride my motorcycle.

LD: And is this your helmet?

EC: Yeah, you took it from my apartment. It's obviously my helmet.

LD: So tell me what you did last Monday.

EC: That was five days ago. I don't remember every second of the day. But I can tell you that I didn't rape anyone.

LD: Anything special happen? Did you have some drinks that night with your roommate? Did you have a few too many? It's okay if you did. It's not a crime. We all get a little carried away now and then.

EC: I was wasted that night. In fact, I was too wasted to go out and do anything! What I can tell you is this: I had a doctor's appointment earlier in the day, ran some errands, some guy almost hit me on the way home from the grocery store. Idiot drivers all over this city. Then I made a burger and had some drinks with River and watched some *Leno*. It was a quiet, nothing kind of a day.

LD: And you didn't go anywhere else that night?

EC: No, I didn't do anything else that night. I went to sleep.

LD: Any problems recently with your girlfriend?

EC: No, we're cool.

LD: Does she know about you?

EC: I don't know what you mean.

LD: You know, that you've been to jail. You were convicted of burglary five years ago, right?

EC: She's no fool. I did my time. I'm a good man, I work hard.

LD: Oh really? I hear you're unemployed.

EC: That's just temporary. And anyways, it gives me more time to volunteer at the local homeless shelter. Like I said, I'm a good guy. I work hard. I only broke into that store as a favor to River. No one was at the store, it's not like it was a violent crime. We both served time. Man, I don't want to talk about that.

LD: What about that misdemeanor sexual battery conviction? Does she know about that?

EC: I don't got to own up to anything. It came down to he said she said. And besides, she was wearing a sweater, and I just put my arm on her shoulder. She claims I grabbed her breasts. The whole thing was totally stupid.

LD: You're still on probation for that though.

EC: Yeah, no shit!

LD: Guess that's a touchy subject. Let's talk about the tattoo on your shoulder. What is that exactly?

EC: It's a red dragon. My girlfriend drew it, so I had it done.

LD: Your current girl?

EC: Nope, this girl I used to mess around with in high school.

LD: So you've always been a ladies' man?

EC: To hell with you, man! I told you it was he said she said.

LD: All right, you don't want to talk about that. So tell me who was on *Leno* that night?

EC: Some old actress. I don't remember. River and I were talking through most of it.

LD: Drinking and smoking, having a good time, that kind of thing?

EC: Yeah, we were chillin'.

LD: So you smoke?

EC: Yeah, is that a crime too now?

LD: No, but are these your cigarettes?

EC: Yeah, what are you getting at?

LD: One of these cigarette butts was found in the parking structure at the Rockport Medical Plaza. The guy who smoked it raped a nurse there last Monday night.

EC: Lots of people smoke those cigarettes. You should be out looking for the real rapist, not wasting your time talking to me, man! Besides, lots of people smoke Marlboros.

LD: Yeah, but this one was smoked by you. We ran a DNA test on it. That's how we found you. And let's face it, you've got a record.

EC: Okay, so that was one of my cigarettes, but I can explain.

LD: Try me.

EC: I already told you I had a doctor's appointment earlier that day. That's where it was at. I came out of my appointment. They had me waiting forever, so I was stressed. Then, I lit up. I went to the structure to get my bike, and I must've put out my smoke in the structure. You don't got anything on me unless you want to charge me for littering! Man, I want a lawyer. You fools got the wrong guy. I'm through talking to you!

INTERROGATION TERMINATED.

Statement of River Coleridge

Deputy Lee Donne (LD): This is Deputy Lee Donne. The date is February 21, CY-1, and it's about 14:00 hours. River Coleridge has voluntarily come in to the Rockport City Police Department for an interview. Please state your name for the record.

River Coleridge (RC): My name is River Coleridge.

LD: How do you know Clark?

RC: I've been Erik's friend for a long time. We went to high school together and have been good friends ever since. He is a really easygoing and trustworthy guy. That's why he's my roommate. That and we have a lot in common. We listen to the same bands and both play guitar. He actually taught me how to play. He's cool. Lots of people like him because he is so friendly. His girlfriend even comes over sometimes and cooks us dinner. They have a good relationship.

LD: You and Clark have gotten into some trouble together. Tell me about that.

RC: It's true we did get into some trouble together. It was a long time ago. About five years ago, I was working at this electronics store in downtown Rockport. It's near the train station. Erik and I were really strapped for cash, so I came up with this idea. Next to my work there was a jewelry store. They got a lot of business, and one of the delivery guys told me that they had a lot of cash on hand. My old shift ended after they closed, so I suggested to Erik that we break in after my shift and take the cash. We were both arrested, but we did our time. And that was five years ago, and ever since, Erik and I have really gotten back on track.

LD: What are things like now? How is work for you two? Are you having trouble making ends meet still?

RC: Erik was laid off recently, but he's been trying really hard to get a new job. He used to work at the auto parts factory in San Andreas. Getting laid off wasn't the end of the world though because he had a tough commute. He rides a motorcycle, so that helped. He gets unemployment now, but still pays his share of the rent.

LD: That's good to hear, but how do you know he didn't rape anyone? Were you with him every second of the night last Monday?

RC: Listen, Erik's just not that kind of guy. He didn't have it easy growing up. He never knew his dad, and his mom worked two jobs to support the family. He's made an effort to give back to the community too. He wants to help people who don't have much. Once a month he even volunteers at Oceana Mission. On top of that, every Thanksgiving he's at that soup kitchen serving turkey dinners.

LD: But were you with him the entire night? What do you remember from that night?

RC: Yes, I was! Erik didn't do it! He doesn't have a temper and everyone knows that rape is a crime of anger. Besides, he has a nice, pretty girlfriend. And you know what else? He was wasted that night. There is no way he raped anyone, and I know for a fact that he didn't. I was with him all night on Monday, February 17. I remember clearly because we always watch *The Tonight Show with Jay Leno* on Monday nights together. Monday is the best night to watch Jay because that's when he does headlines. We get a kick out of headlines. Every Monday, we eat some dinner and have a few beers while watching

Jay. It's a good way to unwind. I remember having dinner late that night because Erik was out all day running errands. I know he had a doctor's appointment earlier that day and was complaining that they kept him waiting a long time. He was also mad that there was a long line at the grocery store. He didn't get back to the apartment until around 8:00 p.m. We then made some burgers and talked about the old days. At 11:30 p.m., we started watching *Leno*. We watched the whole show. I even remember hearing the opening credits for Jimmy Fallon. That night, I ended up passing out on the sofa for a little bit, but I know it was after *Leno* had ended. Erik brought some tequila home from the store because he said he needed something a little stronger to unwind that day. I had one too many shots though and passed out on the couch. I wasn't out long though, and Erik was asleep in his bedroom when I woke up. I'm sure Erik was too drunk to go anywhere that night. Besides, why would he have left?

LD: Is it possible that he left the apartment while you were passed out? The Plaza isn't too far from your place. He could have gone and come back before you knew it.

RC: No way! Look, we live in a small two-bedroom apartment together. Our place is on the second floor, and we have a small sofa in the living room. The front door is to the left of the T.V., and his bedroom door is on the right. When I got up to go to bed, it was a little past 2:00 a.m. I know for sure because I had to plug my cell phone in the charger and saw the time. Erik was fast asleep in bed. There's no way he could have left and come back without waking me up. He would have had to walk through the living room, and I'm a light sleeper. Plus, Erik was drunk that night, so there is no way he'd have gotten up and driven his motorcycle somewhere. Why would he have done this anyway when he has a sweet girlfriend he gets along with real well? He's just not the type of person to go out and rape someone.

LD: That's touching, but how do you explain all the evidence we found at your apartment?

RC: What evidence? That wasn't evidence. They even took *my* Parliaments! The cops didn't show up to our place until the next Friday morning. At 11:00 a.m. or so, they knocked at the door, so I let them in. They told me that they had a match on some DNA and wanted to speak to Erik. He wasn't there just then. They then started looking around the place. I don't know what they were looking for, but then Erik came home and asked if they had a warrant. They told us they didn't need one. They saw his helmet on the floor next to the sofa and took it. There was an ashtray on the coffee table and our cigarette packs were next to it. The cops asked if I smoked, and I told them that I did. They then took the cigarettes too. Then they asked if the bike downstairs belonged to Erik. Erik told them that it did, and the cop called someone to go take a picture of it. The next thing I know this detective was reading Erik his rights. It was unreal! They actually arrested him! I was so shaken I had to call in sick for work that day. Erik's mom and his girlfriend keep calling me trying to figure out what happened that night. I was with him the whole time. Your theory is impossible. He didn't do it. There is no way. You got the wrong guy!

I have reviewed this transcript. It is a complete and accurate account.

Signed: *River Coleridge*

                River Coleridge

Witnessed: *Deputy Lee Donne*

                Deputy Lee Donne

EXHIBIT A

ROCKPORT MEDICAL PLAZA ❋

EMERGENCY UNIT & TRAUMA CENTER
3976 Olympia Blvd.
Rockport, OC 90122

Patient Name: O'Malley, Grace
Address: 550 Maple Drive,
Rockport, OC
Phone Number: (555) 555-6904
DOB: 04/11/CY-25 (Age 25)
SSN: 123-99-1768
Height: 5'2"
Weight: 125
Blood Type: O+
Insurance: INSURED

Emergency Room Physician's Report

Date: Feb. 18th, CY-1
Time: 1:10 a.m.

Summary: Grace O'Malley ("Patient") was brought into the emergency room by paramedics after being found in the Rockport Medical Plaza's parking structure. The patient called emergency after being attacked in the parking structure. Patient reports being forced to engage in intercourse against her will by an unknown attacker. Patient is a white female of short stature and small build.

Assessment and baseline vitals taken upon arrival—all within normal limits. Breathing was unlabored and lungs sounded clear bilaterally. Patient, however, seemed anxious. Patient was awake and alert with GCS 15. Bruising noted on patient's neck measuring 3 in. x 1 in. and 2 in. x .75 in. Bruising also noted on patients right and left knees, both measuring 1 in. x 2 in. At 01:40 hours, a rape kit was completed with assistance from RN. Samples taken. Patient has vaginal tearing consistent with forcible rape. At 02:30 hours, patient discharged with literature for support groups and advised to follow up with primary care giver within 7 days.

Diagnosis: The patient suffered from vaginal tears and bruising consistent with forcible rape.

EXHIBIT B

STATE OF OCEANA, COUNTY OF ROCKPORT

SEXUAL ASSAULT EVIDENCE

Patient	Date
Grace O'Malley	February 18, CY-1
Hospital	Examiner
Rockport Medical Plaza	Adele Warner

1. Collect dried and moist secretions, stains, and foreign materials. Scan the area with a Wood's Lamp.

    __ Findings X No Findings

2. Collect pubic hair through combing or brushing.

3. Examine the vagina and cervix. Check the boxes if there are assault-related findings.

    __ No findings X Vagina __ Cervix

4. Collect 4 swabs from the vaginal pool. Prepare one wet mount slide and one dry mount slide.

5. Collect 2 cervical swabs (if over 48 hours post assault).

6. Examine the buttocks, anus, and rectum (if indicated by history).

    Exam done: __ Yes   X Not applicable

EXHIBIT C

ROCKPORT MEDICAL PLAZA
3976 OLYMPIA BLVD, ROCKPORT, OC

DR. WATSON   PATIENT: ERIK CLARK
SUITE 100A   APPT: 9 A.M.
(555) 555-1776

ITEM	DESCRIPTION	QUANTITY	PRICE
1	Physical Exam	1	298.00
		Subtotal:	298.00

Total Due: $ 298.00

Total Paid: $ 298.00

Balance: $ 0.00

PAID

APPROVED BY *E.A.S* DATE: *Feb. 11 C.Y.-1*

EXHIBIT D

⬤ RPD

ROCKPORT POLICE DEPARTMENT
1066 Hastings Road
Rockport, OC 90122

RECORD OF ARRESTS AND PROSECUTIONS

NAME: Clark, Erik
SSN: 112-23-3445
DOB: 09/30/CY-28

HEIGHT: 5'11''
WEIGHT: 175 lbs
RACE: W

ADULT

Charge: PC 459 (Burglary in the second degree)
Date: 03/31/CY-5
Description: Subject and an accomplice broke into a jewelry store after business hours and stole $5,000 from the safe.
Disposition: Convicted; sentenced to 1 year in state prison.

Charge: PC 243.4(e) (Misdemeanor Sexual Battery)
Date: 11/05/CY-3
Description: Subject was in a bar when he began talking to a woman. He then put his arm around her and fondled her breasts.
Disposition: Convicted; sentenced to 3 years probation.

Charge: PC 314 (Indecent Exposure)
Date: 10/26/CY-2
Description: Subject was at an adult nightclub. He approached one of the dancers and offered to buy her a drink. When she refused, he then allegedly unzipped his pants and exposed himself to her.
Disposition: Charges dropped.

--ROCKPORT POLICE DEPARTMENT—

EXHIBIT E

EXHIBIT F

EXHIBIT G

EXHIBIT H

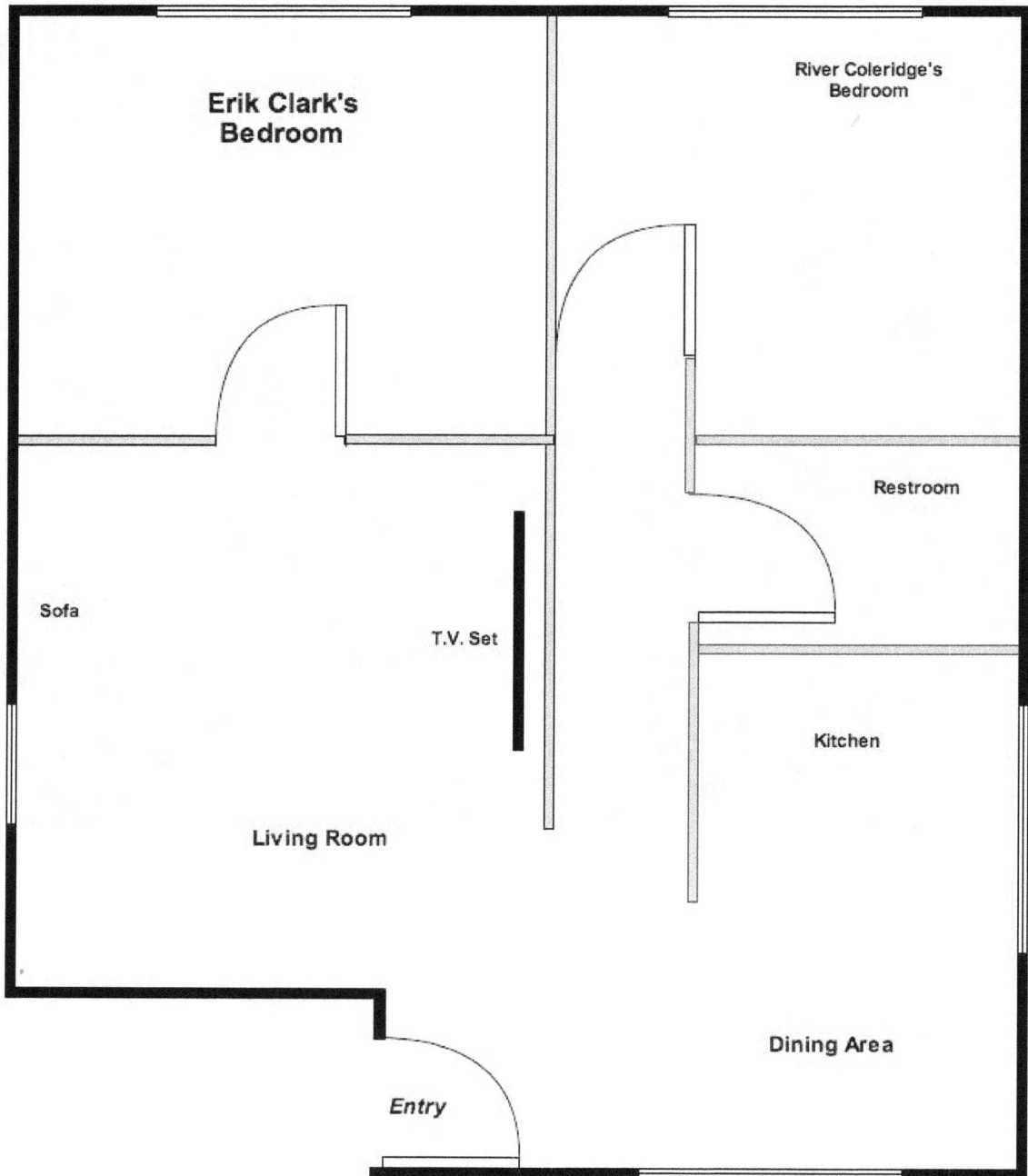

Erik Clark's Bedroom

River Coleridge's Bedroom

Restroom

Sofa

T.V. Set

Kitchen

Living Room

Dining Area

Entry

EXHIBIT I

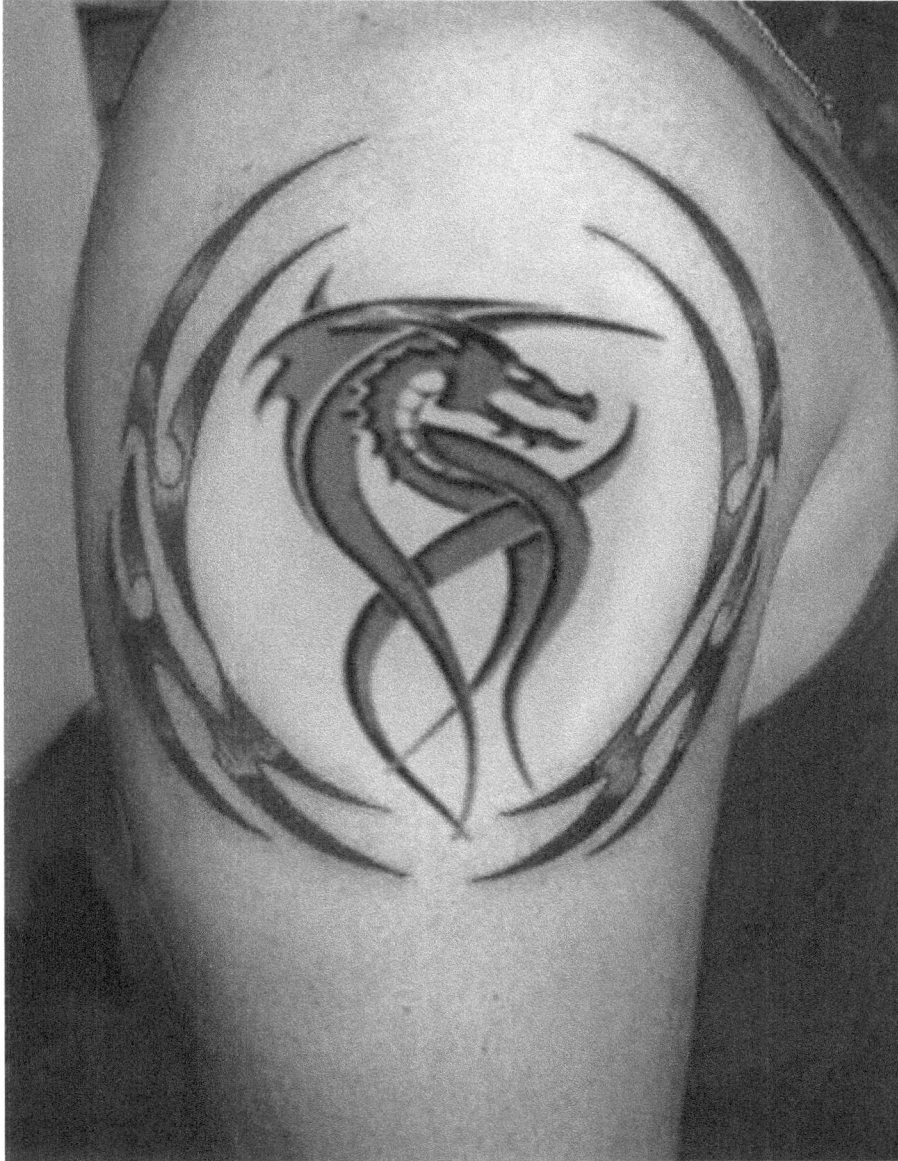

EXHIBIT J

EXHIBIT K

EXHIBIT L

EXHIBIT M

EXHIBIT N

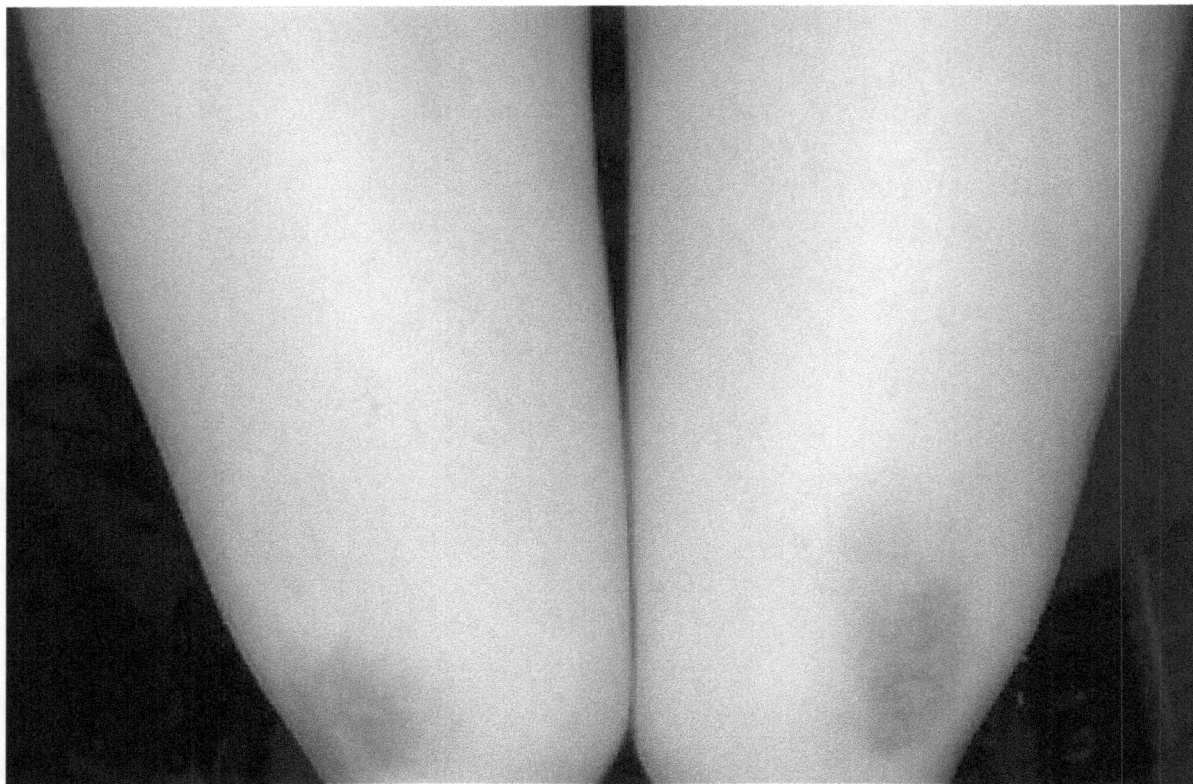

EXHIBIT O

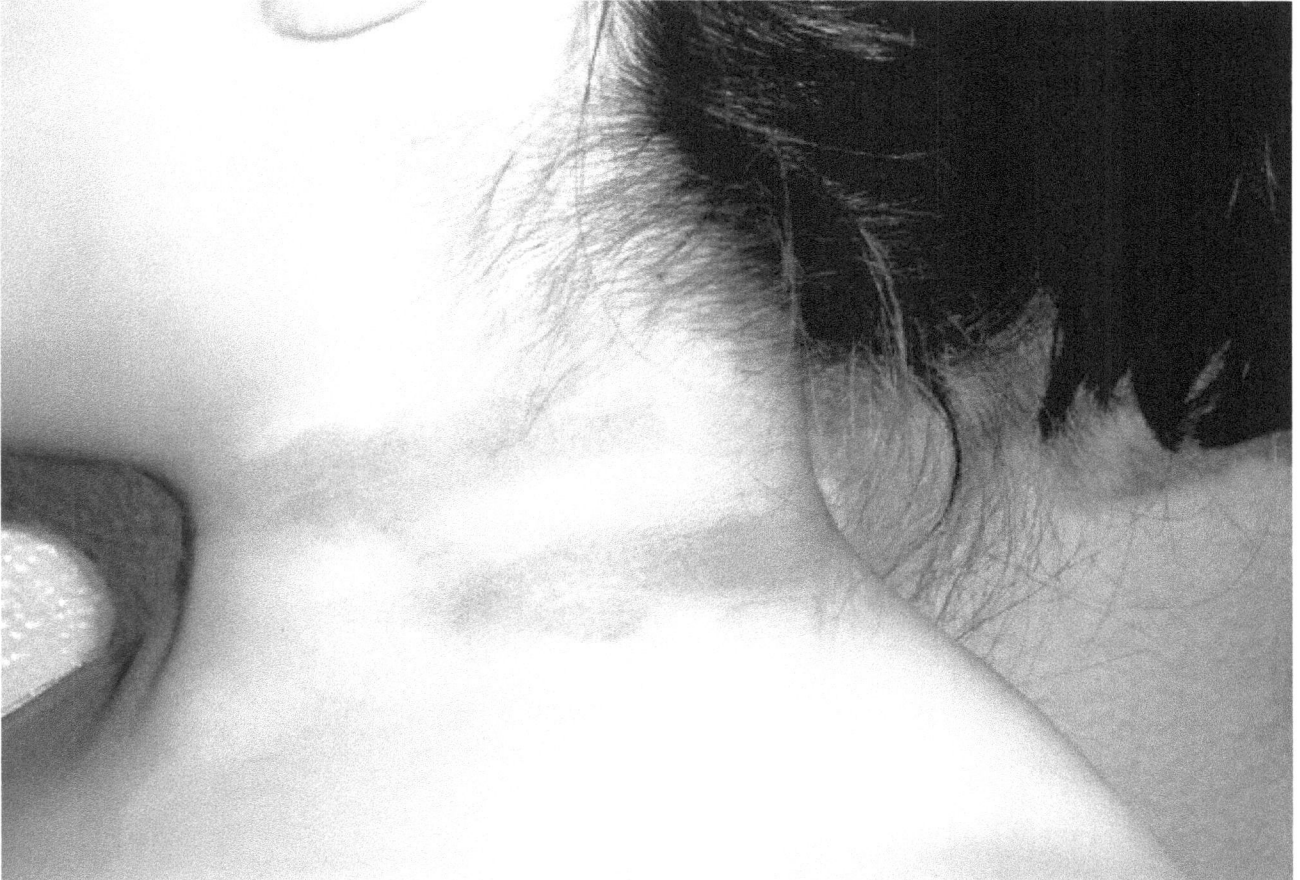

EXHIBIT P

EXHIBIT Q

EXHIBIT R

Jury Instructions

Members of the jury, I thank you for your attentiveness during this trial. Please pay close attention to the instructions I am about to give you.

In this case, Erik Clark is charged with the rape of Grace O'Malley by force in violation of Oceana Penal Code section 261. To prove this crime, the State must prove the following elements beyond a reasonable doubt:

1. Defendant, Erik Clark, had sexual intercourse with Grace O'Malley;

2. He and the woman were not married to each other at the time of the intercourse;

3. She did not consent to the intercourse; and

4. Defendant accomplished the intercourse by force, violence, duress, menace, or fear of immediate and unlawful bodily injury to the woman or to someone else.

Sexual intercourse means any penetration, no matter how slight, of the vagina or genitalia by the penis. Ejaculation is not required.

To *consent,* a woman must act freely and voluntarily and know the nature of the act. A woman who initially consents to an act of intercourse may change her mind during the act. If she does so, under the law, the act of intercourse is then committed without her consent if:

1. She communicated to Defendant that she objected to the act of intercourse and attempted to stop the act;

2. She communicated her objection through words or acts that a reasonable person would have understood as showing her lack of consent; and

3. Defendant forcibly continued the act of intercourse despite her objection.

Intercourse is *accomplished by force* if a person uses enough physical force to overcome the woman's will.

Duress means a direct or implied threat of force, violence, danger, or retribution that would cause a reasonable person to do or submit to something that she would not do or submit to otherwise. When deciding whether the act was accomplished by duress, consider all the circumstances, including the woman's age and her relationship to Defendant.

Menace means a threat, statement, or act showing an intent to injure someone.

Intercourse is *accomplished by fear* if the woman is actually and reasonably afraid or she is actually but unreasonably afraid and Defendant knows of her fear and takes advantage of it.

Erik Clark has entered a plea of not guilty. This means that you must presume or believe that Erik Clark is not guilty unless and until the evidence convinces you otherwise. This presumption stays with Erik Clark as to each material allegation in the indictment through each stage of the trial until it has been overcome by the evidence to the exclusion of and beyond a reasonable doubt.

To overcome Defendant's presumption of innocence, the State has the burden to prove the following:

1.   The crime with which Defendant is charged was committed.

2.   Defendant is the person who committed the crime.

The State has the burden to prove the elements beyond a reasonable doubt. Whenever the words *reasonable doubt* are used, you must consider the following: A reasonable doubt is not a mere possible doubt, because everything relating to human affairs is open to some possible or imaginary doubt. Reasonable doubt is the state of the case that, after hearing and considering all the evidence, leaves the minds of the jurors in the condition that they cannot say they feel an abiding conviction of the truth of the charge.

It is to the evidence introduced during this trial, and to it alone, that you are to look for that proof. A reasonable doubt as to the guilt of Defendant may arise from evidence, a conflict in the evidence, or a lack of evidence. If you have a reasonable doubt, you should find Defendant not guilty. If you have no reasonable doubt, you should find Defendant guilty.

You must decide this case on the evidence and the law. It is up to you to decide what evidence is reliable. You should use your common sense in deciding what evidence is reliable and what evidence should not be relied upon in considering your verdict.

A witness is a person who has knowledge related to this case. You will have to decide whether you believe each witness and how important each witness's testimony is to the case. You may believe all, part, or none of a witness's testimony. In deciding whether to believe a witness's testimony, you may consider, among other factors, the following:

1. The extent of the witness's opportunity to see, hear, or otherwise become familiar with any matter about which the witness testified.

2. The ability of the witness to accurately recall or communicate any matter about which the witness testified and the character and quality of that testimony.

3. The witness's manner and demeanor while on the stand.

4. Whether or not the witness has bias, an improper motive, or an interest in the outcome of the case.

5. The witness's attitude toward this trial or toward testifying.

6. Whether the witness's testimony was consistent or inconsistent with other testimony or evidence presented in this case.

7. Any previous statements made by the witness that are consistent or inconsistent with the witness's testimony.

8. The witness's character for honesty or veracity, or their opposites.

9. Whether the witness was offered money, preferred treatment, or any other benefit to testify or whether the witness received any threats or was under any pressure that might have affected the truth of the witness's testimony.

10. The witness's previous conviction of a felony or past criminal conduct amounting to a misdemeanor.

You may rely upon your own conclusions about each witness. A juror may believe or disbelieve all or any part of the evidence or the testimony of any witness.

There are some general rules that apply to your deliberations. You must abide by these rules in order to return a verdict that is consistent with the law:

1. You must follow the law as it is explained to you in these instructions. If you fail to follow the law or disregard the law, any verdict you reach will be a miscarriage of justice.

2. You must decide the case only upon the evidence that you have heard from either the testimony of witnesses or exhibits that you have seen.

3. You must not decide the case for or against anyone because you feel sympathy for that person, or because you are angry at that person.

4. You must not decide the case based on your feelings about the lawyers in this case. The lawyers are not on trial.

5. You must not consider any potential sentence the Defendant might receive. It is not your duty to consider punishment. Your only duty is to determine guilt or innocence. It is the judge's job to determine the proper sentence if you find the Defendant guilty.

6. Whatever verdict you render must be unanimous; that is, each juror must commit to the same verdict. The verdict must be the verdict of each juror as well as that of the jury as a whole.

7. It is entirely proper for a lawyer to talk to a witness about what testimony the witness would give if called into the courtroom. The witness should not be discredited for talking to a lawyer about his or her testimony.

8. You must not decide this case based on feelings of prejudice, bias, or sympathy. Any verdict you may reach should be based on the evidence and the law contained in these instructions.

Deciding a proper verdict is exclusively your job. I cannot participate in that decision in any way. Please disregard anything I might have said or done that made you think I preferred one verdict over another.

Only one verdict may be returned for the crime charged. The verdict must be in writing and the verdict form has been prepared for you. It is as follows:

(READ JURY VERDICT FORM)

In just a few moments, the Bailiff will escort you to the jury room. Once inside the jury room, the first thing you should do is elect a foreperson, who will preside over your deliberations. It is the foreperson's job to sign and date the verdict form when all of you have agreed on a verdict in this case and to bring the verdict back to the courtroom when you return.

In conclusion, let me remind you that it is imperative that you follow the law as I have explained it to you in these instructions. Regardless of how you feel about the laws, you must apply them.

SUPERIOR COURT OF THE STATE OF OCEANA

FOR THE COUNTY OF ROCKPORT

STATE OF OCEANA,	Case No. RP101711
Plaintiff,	
v.	**CHARGE(S):**
	261
ERIK CLARK	Rape
Defendant.	1 count

VERDICT

As to the charge of rape, in violation of Oceana Penal Code section 261, we, the jury, find the

Defendant, Erik Clark:

_____   GUILTY

_____   NOT GUILTY

So say we all.

_____

Foreperson of the Jury

_____

Date

www.ingramcontent.com/pod-product-compliance
Lightning Source LLC
Chambersburg PA
CBHW082136210326
41599CB00031B/6002